F60643

S0-BEZ-545

3.98

PSYCHOLOGY, RELATIVISM, AND POLITICS

PSYCHOLOGY, RELATIVISM, AND POLITICS

WILLIAM P. KREML

NEW YORK UNIVERSITY PRESS / NEW YORK & LONDON

Copyright © 1991 by New York University
All rights reserved
Manufactured in the United States of America

Library of Congress Cataloging-in-Publication Data
Kreml, William P.
  Psychology, relativism, and politics / William P. Kreml.
    p. cm.
  Includes bibliographical references and index.
  ISBN 0–8147–4610–1 (alk. paper)
  1. Political psychology. 2. Political science. 3. Relativity.
I. Title.
JA74.5.K72 1990
320'.01'9—dc20   90–6527
                          CIP

New York University Press books are printed on acid-free paper,
and their binding materials are chosen for strength and durability.

Book design by Ken Venezio

With thanks to Fred I. Greenstein

CONTENTS

FOREWORD

Robert Jervis has recently lamented that the "study of individual personalities and personality types has fallen out of favor in psychology and
political science." Though we have many studies "of the belief systems
of particular individuals," Jervis says, "these often remain separated
from the analysis of general cognitive processes."

In *Psychology, Relativism, and Politics,* William Kreml has created an
original political philosophy around the differences that exist in the
cognitive processes of different personalities. As cognitive differences are
fundamental to political philosophy, Kreml argues, so too cognitive
differences are central to the real world of politics as well as to the
dialectical processes of history.

In keeping with Richard Bernstein's requirements for commensurability, Kreml suggests that human cognitions are understandable along a
variety of spectrums, the principal spectrum being that which runs between Kant's and Hegel's idealistically based definitions of analytic and
synthetic knowledge. Kreml goes on to argue that to the degree that
political structures unduly favor one or the other cognition, as psychological adaptations to political systems vary to the degree that each
psychology "fits" into the system's prevailing political structures, that
system is similarly inequitable. In a postmaterial world, Kreml insists,
political structures must be held to a standard of equity that allocates
the price of relative psychological "fit" across the personalities that
work, or would work, within them. Further, Kreml demonstrates history's requirement that any political system contain a balance of cognitions
in order to transcend its historical crises.

From this philosophical vantage point, Kreml gives us fresh insight
into the epistemological similarities, and the inadequacies, of the mater-

ialistic Marxist and the empiricist liberal traditions. He also sheds new light on the cognitive preferences of America's Constitutional Framers as those preferences reflect themselves in the government's principle structures. Finally, Kreml explains the current paralysis and the current inequities of the American political order as resulting in great part from an imbalance in the cognitive capabilities of the American government. As dyadic, contractual and cognitively analytic relations have increasingly bound interest groups to the national bureaucracy and the Congress, the synthetic cognition, which as Hegel taught it is particularly necessary in times of political transition, has become increasingly unavailable to the government.

This original work of political philosophy, with its inventive application to the American political system, challenges all materialistically based political philosophies as well as all previous, materialistically based criticisms of America's government. It is a philosophical and political *tour de force.*

The University of South Carolina   BETTY GLAD

ACKNOWLEDGMENTS

I wish to express my gratitude to those who made enormous contributions to this book. At the University of South Carolina, these people included M. Glenn Abernathy, Jerel Rosati, Betty Glad, Earl Black, William Mishler, James Myers, Mark Tompkins, Charles W. Kegley, Jr., Daniel Sabia, and Peter Sederberg of the Government and International Studies Department and Martin Donougho of the Philosophy Department. Steven B. Smith at Yale University, Fred I. Greenstein at Princeton University, Leroy Rieselbach at Indiana University, Michael Maggiotto at Bowling Green University, and Nicholas A. Onuf at the American University all offered worthwhile suggestions. I thank the Department of Government and International Studies at the University of South Carolina, and particularly Lori Joye, for assistance with a variety of clerical chores. I also thank the Institute of International Studies, and particularly Arthur Vanden Houten, for assistance with the notes. Finally, I thank Nancy Posselt and Daniel Postel for their reading and correcting of the manuscript. For whatever errors remain, the responsibility is solely mine.

PSYCHOLOGY, RELATIVISM, AND POLITICS

INTRODUCTION

This book contains both a theory and an application of that theory. Its centerpiece is a relativistic perspective on human nature that is based on what I believe to be overwhelming evidence of the single most fundamental differentiation among human psychologies. The book is divided into two parts. The first explains the theory, and the second applies the theory to the United States and its government.

In chapter 1, part 1, I will begin with a discussion of why the classic "environment versus heredity" debate has thus far limited the development of a psychologically relativistic perspective. I will argue that this debate can and should be transcended and that an acceptance of reasonably static adult personalities can serve as the catalyst for a relativistic theory. Social statics have not been in favor with social scientists in the twentieth century for ideological reasons, but this disfavor is now counterproductive. An understanding of the essential, permanent, differences among human personalities permits a better theory of politics.

In chapter 2, I will place an understanding of analytic and synthetic cognitions as they are found in Kant's *Critique of Pure Reason* and Hegel's *Science of Logic* into a psychological context. I will suggest that the issue of meaning is best understood in the context of these writers' own epistemologically oriented work. The contrast between their work, and the failure of either Kant or Hegel to understand the relationship of cognition to psychology, can be overcome by a relativistic theory.

In chapter 3, I will describe the nature of psychological relativism. I will refer to representative research in both affective and cognitive psychology and argue that this research now describes the principal psychological range sufficiently to permit its use in a relativistic theory.

In chapters 4 and 5, I will discuss the nature of Marxist and liberal political thought respectively. I will argue that neither of these materialistically based political theories embrace, nor is capable of embracing, the relativistic perspective. Because they are based on rationalistic epistemological assumptions and on essentially prepsychological understandings of human nature and its differences, neither liberalism nor Marxism permits a relativistic perspective.

In chapter 6, I will describe the standard of equity for a relativistic theory. Utilizing the Weberian notions of rational, or monocratic, structures on the one hand and collegial structures on the other, I argue for a standard of equity that allocates what Fred I. Greenstein has called the psychological "price" of working within different structural arrangements. Greenstein's price was properly related to the cognitive nature of any institution's decisions. I suggest that the balance among any institution's cognitions foretells the allocation of that structure's psychological price.

In chapter 7, I will review the dynamic of institutional structures and describe the effect of that dynamic on the psychology of institutional decision making. As institutions are not psychologically neutral, so too they are not static. If institutions alter themselves in psychologically significant ways, then the burden of the psychological price over time will also be altered. I close part 1 with a prescription for the redress of the institutional and psychological imbalance.

Part 1 of this book is unabashedly prescriptive. Its design of a new psychological standard for political equity includes a psychological balance of postmaterial political structures and processes as a precondition for political equity. Though it does not deny the existence of, nor the political importance of, objective, real-world conditions such as class, race, nationality, and so forth for politics, it adds a wholly new form of concern to these objective considerations. It is the concern of the mediating mind and particularly of the relative subjectivities of different minds and their different ways of knowing political reality.

In part 2, the theory of psychological relativism is applied to the American political system. After a review of the cognitive nature of the Framers' original governmental design (chapter 8), I will review the cognitive nature of the American legal system (chapter 9), as well as the cognitive nature of the structural and procedural innovations of the unwritten Constitution that responded to (1) the National Period's economic dependency, (2) the Civil War, and (3) and the Great Depression (chapter 10). After reviewing the current gridlock of American political institutions and the cognitive imbalances that have contributed to that gridlock (chapter 11), I will prescribe remedies that respond to America's political inequities from the perspective of a psychologically relativistic theory of politics (chapter 12).

I

THE THEORY

Chapter One

HUMAN DIFFERENTIATION

In *The Decline of the West,* Oswald Spengler emphasized the importance of the "structure of the intellect." Spengler argued that such a structure was more than an "illusion" and suggested that "history spread out before us contains more than one style of knowing." He also suggested that understandings of the "deep and final things" were "not to be reached by predicating constants but by studying differentiae and developing the organic logic of differences." In the end, however, Spengler acknowledged that the "comparative morphology of knowledge forms" was a "domain which Western thought has still to attack."[1]

The discovery of a "comparative morphology of knowledge forms" is not an easy task. The placing of that comparative morphology into a political perspective is a more difficult task because knowledge forms imply a permanency of human perspective. A political theory based on knowledge forms imports some notion of human statics. It also imports the idea of a fundamental differentiation among ways of thinking as that differentiation grows from static personalities.

The creation of a political philosophy based on psychological differentiation has most likely not been attempted before now because prevailing social science orthodoxies have discouraged consideration of static psychologies. Such orthodoxies result from what is still a divisive debate within the social sciences. They have grown out of the tired and unproductive battle between the holders of the environmental view and genetic view of how human beings become who they are.

The "environment versus heredity," or nature-nurture, debate is the argument over whether the human essence is inherent or a product of

7

the environment it grows in, and it continues to burden social understanding. The entrenchments in this century-old battle have been dug so deeply that virtually all of the debates in the social sciences have stumbled into them at one time or another. Not surprisingly, the alliances within that battle have remained virtually unchanged. But these alliances are frequently reduced to their meanest political identifications.

The behavioralist, largely environmental, S-R (stimulus-response) view of human nature is still uncomfortable with the notion that psychological permanence exists. It thus denies the basis for Spengler's "comparative morphology of knowledge forms." The antibehavioralist, largely genetic, S-O-R (stimulus-organism-response) view generally supports at least a measure of psychological permanence. This position basically accepts consideration of differences in knowledge forms.

Historically, there was good cause for the alignment of political identifications within the debate over statics. In the early stages of the debate, the statics position was given a rightward thrust by the social Darwinists. These maladapters of the evolutionary theories of Charles Darwin extended Darwin's explanation for the origin of species to a justification for the nineteenth century's often ruthless competitiveness.

Conceptually, the statics that the social Darwinists propounded were "vertical." The survival and domination of certain human qualities over other human qualities, as these qualities played themselves out in an industrially dominated distribution of wealth, was what social statics came to be. The social Darwinists, with their favored superiorities of classes, nationalities, races, sexes, and so forth, thus captured the statics position. Their verticalities precluded any Spenglerian sense of a subjectively rooted difference among those who thought differently about things because of some quality of their mind. They precluded especially consideration of the cognitive form of thinking. The response to social Darwinism's statics, however, attempted to dispose of statics generally and not just Herbert Spencer's social statics.

The political left from the late nineteenth century through most of the twentieth century overwhelmingly championed the antistatics or environmental position on human nature, dispatching any sense of human statics or psychological permanency. The left believed that the only way to argue for social improvement was to ascribe the excessive social dominance that forestalled it to the conditions of man. This was their strategy to combat the injustice of the industrial age and those who rationalized that injustice by ascribing human misery to a supposedly objective world. As the position of statics seemed incapable of lending assistance to the reformers, those who argued for or against statics were enlisted in their appropriate entrenchments during each succeeding generation. Jensen and Shockley, Kamin and Gould, are no more than today's infantry in a very old war.[2] The alliances of political ideology with social statics, however, must now be very different from what they have been.

Among all the difficulties that statics suffered, its perceived alliance with verticalities, or its perceived support for economic-, racial-, nationality-, or other dominations—was the most critical. But the perspective of statics need not be one of verticalities. It can provide an insightful perspective into the differences among human psychologies. Each human personality, at least past the age of six according to Freud, has a permanence to it.[3] It is reasonable to suggest that differences across human personalities can underpin richer understandings of the human political condition within the context of a wholly new political philosophy.

A new, relativistically based political philosophy builds on the permanence of the human personality. Instead of permitting politically motivated perspectives on an issue like social statics to define a political philosophy, political philosophy can dispassionately describe the nature of human differentiation and construct itself on such a description. An understanding of the static differences among human personalities can permit a better understanding of the "comparative morphology of knowledge forms" in a political context. Coupled with an understanding of the relativity of human psychologies that underlies it, this permits the development of a psychologically relativistic philosophy of politics.

THE QUESTION OF RELATIVISM

In political theory relativism has endured its own controversial history. The relativistic position has been both opposed to and likened to absolutism. As a result, relativism has suffered from much the same kind of intellectual illegitimacy that absolutism has suffered. Richard Bernstein, among others, has found relativism most often to be nihilistic or random.[4] Such relativism has meant either a belief in a nothingness about the world or, at least, a belief in the inability of people to determine what does and what does not exist.

Relativism, however, can take a middle position between pure absolutism, or a belief in the validity of only one perspective, and pure relativism, a belief in a random or an infinite number of perspectives. This middle position embraces the perspective of a *bounded* relativism. Bounded relativism is a condition in which the nature of the differentiation is both limited and known. Relativism without randomness suggests a differentiation of perspective that is identifiable at the same time that it is restricted to a particular range, or a finite number of ranges, of differentiation.

In *Beyond Objectivism and Relativism,* Bernstein reviewed the debate between Paul Feyerabend (who at his most extreme wished to be known as a "flippant dadaist") and those who have argued for scientific orthodoxy.[5] Bernstein argued that these logically diametrical positions are not as different as they seem. Each position, in a psychologically sensitive manner, appealed for Bernstein to some fixed notion of reason. Any psychologically relativistic theory, and accordingly any psychologically relativistic theory of politics, must begin with a description of the causes of different perspectives on reason. A psychologically relativistic theory suggests that differentiated ways of thinking, or the "comparative morphology of knowledge forms" that make up thinking, are derived from different, but understandably different, psychologies. These forms are matters of a range of human minds that is both bounded and knowable.

Bernstein suggests that a nonnihilistic relativistic theory must begin with a search for different perspectives. But it must include a sense of how such perspectives are "commensurable."[6] A theory based on known or knowable differentiations can be made out of differences that are capable of comparison. True relativism requires known and bounded differentiations. It requires differentiations that are no more random or nihilistic at one end of the relativism-to-objectivism range than they are singular or objective. Like the spectrum of colors, it is relative along a commensurable or a comparative range. The knowing of the bounded relativism along the very styles of knowing, as Spengler would put it, permits the development of a psychologically relativistic theory of politics.

THE OBJECTIVIST TRADITION

The notion of any differentiated perspective on human nature is rare in political theory. The belief in a universal human nature, along with a belief in the universality of human reason, has been central to Western thought from the time of the Greeks. Even Plato, the most organic of the classical thinkers, gave only slight consideration to human differentiation. Concerned with different qualities of political leadership, Plato's definitions of the gold, silver, and bronze or iron man did not differentiate among human psychologies. Plato's discussion of what typically brought about political conflict identified the "just man" with the "just city" and argued that three psychological elements corresponded to three natural constituencies in the just society. But he did not argue that "the elements and traits that belong to a state must also exist in the individuals that compose it."[7] He argued that the struggle among *reason, passion,* and a third, more difficult to define, *spirit* element in *all* individuals was mirrored in the struggles of any polity. For Plato, reason, passion, and spirit competed at large with each other in a form, incidentally, that is not far from Freud's depiction of the battle among the id, superego, and ego. Yet the battle was for a singular notion of justice in both the citizen and the city. As one commentator saw it, Plato was "concerned with morals and not with psychology."[8]

As Plato was not concerned with psychology, so too he was not concerned with what *each* human psychology might bring to an organic political whole. In contrast, a psychologically relativistic theory of politics, if it is to portray "a scientific analysis of the mind," will begin with the commensurable differentiations of human nature.[9] It will be grounded, at least in part, on what each of the commensurable natures contributes to the polity. As a relativistic theory assumes that different human natures embrace different perspectives on a polity, it will describe why different human natures have different visions of what constitutes a just political society. A theory based on relativism will, therefore, have a place for more than one exemplar of Plato's just man. It will have a place for differentiated visions of a just society.

The description of a psychologically relativistic theory of politics will come from the vastly improving evidence of human differentiation that exists in modern psychology. If Plato's vision failed to include the "scientific analysis of the mind," a political theory based on the relativity of human psychology will include what we now know about humankind's principal psychological differentiation.

Modern psychology's revelations about human differentiation have simply not had an effect on political philosophy. The most prominent psychological perspective that has lately affected political thought is still overwhelmingly singular in its perspective. Abraham Maslow's *needs* theory relies on the alleged existence of certain universal human necessities. It then places those necessities in a hierarchy of psychological states. But there are at least two difficulties with needs theory. The first is empirical: A hierarchy of needs may well not exist at all. The second is normative: A hierarchical framework for understanding human psychology evidences a clear ideological bias.

Maslow suggests that five needs, arranged along a ladder in which the satisfaction of one need necessarily promotes the next, make up the human psychological progression. Maslow's needs are physiological, safety, belongingness or the need for love, esteem, and self-actualization. Maslow declared the self-actualization stage to be the highest order of human psychological development. This was the stage in which a strong and independent human psyche ostensibly directed its energies toward healthy pursuits.[10] It is a stage that is not much different, incidentally, from what Carl Jung described as individuation.

In their comprehensive review of Maslow-related studies, Mahmoud A. Wahba and Lawrence G. Bridwell found that, at best, only a smattering of empirical evidence confirmed the hierarchy. Not only did ten factor-analytic studies and three ranking studies lend but limited evidence for the reality of a needs hierarchy, but the same studies demonstrated no support whatsoever for the so-called gratification/activation proposition that ostensibly moved each psyche to the next level of need once each prior level was achieved.[11]

But damning though they are, the empirical difficulties of the needs thesis are not its most troubling problem. A more severe problem grows out of needs theory's ideological biases. These biases are mainly a product of needs theory's lack of psychological differentiation. Though needs theory is ostensibly liberating in its purpose, it clearly does not take into account the possibility that differentiated needs exist within different psychologies. As a consequence, some have argued that needs theory includes a strong potentiality for authoritarianism.[12]

Ross Fitzgerald, in particular, describes the authoritarian potential of needs theory by focusing on the writings of Herbert Marcuse and Christian Bay. Marcuse, in his extension of Marx and Freud, differentiated between what he called true needs (food, clothing, shelter, and so forth) and those needs that evidence the enjoyment of a higher state of living. Fitzgerald notes, however, that this higher state becomes possible for

Marcuse only when society is able to forestall the manipulation of needs in the postindustrial state.

Fitzgerald's commentary on Marcuse may be a bit overdrawn, as Marcuse at one time said that what true needs are "must . . . be answered by the individuals themselves,"[13] but his argument still has merit. In Marcuse's work, and particularly in *One Dimensional Man*, his assumption concerning the singularity of human needs, and hence the ostensibly objective manner of achieving those needs, is a prescription for a singular political orthodoxy.

Fitzgerald concluded his critique of needs theory by noting another of its singular interpretations. Commenting on Christian Bay's conceptions of human needs, Fitzgerald notes that Bay differed only slightly from Marcuse in his differentiation of political from what he described as "pseudopolitical" or merely "private interest" needs.[14] Bay, like Marcuse, adopted his Maslow-like psychological singularity through his own psychological perspective. In stressing the universality of the five supposedly progressive needs, even though his depiction more pointedly rested in what Bay called needs "areas" or "complexes" that were supposed to exist at each of the five original levels, the designation of Bay's "good self" is nonetheless an arbitrary and singular designation. This designation, ideologically, holds true for all. As Fitzgerald appropriately notes, Bay's assumptions include the "basic biological-psychological unity of the human species."[15] Movement beyond such a universal, singular, and ultimately objectivist perspective is the key to a psychologically relativistic theory.

THE DEVELOPMENTALISTS

Approaches like needs theory are really nothing more than extensions of a long time orthodoxy of psychological perspective. They are simply extensions of the work of those early psychologists who typically pointed toward universal stages of psychological development. Such formal developmental theory, of course, began with Sigmund Freud.

Freudian psychoanalytic theory centered around an understanding of childhood developmental stages. The Freudian perspective, like the early Marcusean perspective, was generally pessimistic, as Freud held out little hope for the successful resolution of conflicts that bound every child to their developmental impediments. Accordingly, Freud's attempt at a social theory based on his human psychology *(Civilization and Its Discontents)* depicted the agony of the repressed adult psyche as it strained under the pressure of instinctual denial.[16] In fact, Walter Kaufman persuasively argued that Freud was not a scientistic purveyor of a brittle academic psychology but was a nonmaterialistic and creative disciple of the true intellectualism of Goethe and Hegel.[17] It is still clear, however, that Freud created a singular, linear form of developmentalism (much as Hegel did) and did not build his psychological theory on human psychological differentiation.

The writings of such recent influential psychologists as Jean Piaget have clearly followed Freud's developmental path. Piaget's studies of children were directed toward an understanding of any child's process of learning.[18] After amassing a mountain of experimental evidence, Piaget concluded that children developed certain cognitive skills at predictable ages and, like Freud with the psyche, had little concern for differentiation among those learning patterns. Much like Freud as well, the differentiations that Piaget did recognize were largely matters of the impediments to movement along a singular, developmental hierarchy. Piaget, like Freud, neither began with nor concluded with a relativistic vision.

More recently, the writings of Lawrence Kohlberg have received a good deal of attention among political psychologists.[19] Kohlberg's emphasis on moral as opposed to cognitive development, locked in what he calls his "cognitive-development theory," describes stages that ostensibly occur during periods of socialization. Though depicting such notions within a rich context of morality in attitude and behavior, Kohlberg's work, like Freud's and Piaget's, unfortunately seeks only singular and universal patterns. It too is not relativistic.

THE FOUNDING PRINCIPLE

As described earlier, a relativistic theory of politics begins with an understanding of a known, bounded, and commensurable range of human psychologies. A relativistic political theory should respond, in a Bernsteinian sense, to the derelictions of both absolutism on the one hand and nihilism on the other. In doing so, the theory must describe how a known and a bounded range of human natures has an impact on preferences for both differentiated cognitions and the structures and processes of a political system as it shapes those cognitions.

In prescribing for a psychologically relativistic theory of politics, therefore, one must be particularly wary of those attempts to prescribe for a choice among psychological perspectives. In an influential article, the Nobel laureate Herbert Simon, improperly I think, delineated what he considered to be the key linkage between psychology and politics. In describing antecedents to political behavior, Simon differentiated between what he called "procedural" rationality and "objective" rationality. He sought to separate "behavior that can be adjudged objectively to be optimally adapted to the situation" from what he labeled as the behavior of "bounded" rationality. Bounded rationality behavior was what Simon described as "adaptive within the constraints imposed *both* by the external situation and by the capacities of the decision maker."[20]

Simon's dichotomy might have been apt as a preface to a relativistic theory but, unfortunately, he went on to favor one rationality over the other. Ignoring the possibility of differences among knowledge forms, Simon argued for the explanatory superiority of the procedural or bounded definition of rationality. Though he properly claimed that a restricted sense of what is rational could forestall the false claims for objectivity that traditional organizational theorists have used, he replaced them with his own singular subjectivity.

Simon's need to make one organizational vision superior to another is particularly unfortunate in that he properly recognized that "the barriers are down" to better understandings of how organizational structures are perceived. The charge of "mentalism," as he phrases it, should no longer deter a psychological understanding of structures. Simon also understands that "considerable empirical knowledge about the decision maker" surely leads to better knowledge of how institutional decisions are made.[21] But like the needs theorists and the psychological developmentalists before them, Simon still finds it necessary to come down on the side of a singular, in its own way objective, perspective on how individuals ought to perceive organizations. He avoids the possibility of natural, psychological differences among decision makers as well as natural, psychological differences among preferences for different ways of understanding political issues.

Just as Simon's organizational vision is no more relativistic than the developmental psychologists's vision of human psychologies, so too his competing notions of bounded rationality and objective rationality only utilize the cognitive differentiation that he sees as running *among* social science disciplines. Simon suggests, for example, that the bounded rationality perspective is dominant in the field of cognitive psychology, while the perspective of objective rationality dominates neoclassical economics. A relativistic perspective on cognitive psychology, however, requires a different conclusion. Though cognitive preferences can indeed dominate *sub*disciplines, the relativity of human cognitions exists *within* each social science discipline rather than among them (see chapter 3). Each social science has its own cognitively related range of perspectives within it.

Herbert Simon has, nonetheless, contributed at least one insight that may be useful for relativism. Simon has fairly described fundamental differences between cognitions as they exist within institutional settings. When outlining "auxilliary assumptions" (or those assumptions that are necessary to a position of objective rationality), Simon did properly contrast them with "empirical validity" assumptions, the latter questioning the "plausibility of the auxilliary assumptions" in the achievement of any objective position.[22] Simon, in other words, knew that the structure of any institution affects the manner in which that institution addresses its task. He was also aware that preferences for the kinds of cognitions that are permitted into a discipline's consideration make up the crucial introductory step for each discipline's agenda. Simon, however, declined to link those cognitive preferences to differences among human psychologies.

The psychologically relativistic position, I think, advances the understanding of Simon's objective rationality versus bounded rationality argument. If the mentalist barriers are truly down, as I think they are, then it is appropriate now to examine how consciousness about relative preferences for different ways of thinking contributes to the building of a psychologically balanced political structure. Consciousness about the cognitive preferences that are derived from a known and bounded psychological relativity will make up the core of a relativistic theory. Within a political context, psychological relativism will depict that known and bounded spectrum of commensurable personality characteristics that influence the interpretations of politics of different psychologies.

Psychological relativism, a static concept, thus begins with the permanent differences among psychological dispositions and the impact of these dispositions. Relativism, unlike Simon's choices, never demands resolution into a singular cognitive position. It does not resolve itself into an assumedly rational perspective but simply exists as relativism, seeking balances and equities among different perspectives. It exists as a result of the differentiated psychologies that generate different cognitions and, in its search for political equity, balances the perspectives of those psychologies and the political system that houses them (see chapter 6).

One final issue that Herbert Simon has raised deserves attention. Simon argued for an understanding of the theoretical importance to psychology and politics of the distinction between normal and abnormal psychologies. Abnormal psychologies evidence what Simon appropriately calls "passion and unreason" as opposed to the supposedly dispassionate behavior of normal psychologies. This distinction recalls Harold Lasswell's notions of the relationship of psychopathology to politics, reminding one that not all of psychology and politics is understandable from a perspective of a normal human psychology. Simon is correct when he argues that one must "attribute to passion" much of what goes on in politics. One must indeed attribute what has often been the brutal and inhumane politics of both this and previous eras of history to "powerful impulses that do not permit the mediation of thought."[23] Hitler and Stalin, this century's wars and persecutions, and the awful lessons of centuries of political history teach nothing if not this.

Yet granting the importance of Simon's depiction of nonrational political activity, a relativistic perspective on politics does not grant equal status to abnormal psychological motivation in its prescription of political equity. A relativistic perspective on politics begins with an understanding of the range of human normality; it reserves the pathologies of abnormality for a secondary place. Regardless of the arena of controversy, normality and abnormality have never been of equal theoretical significance. Normality is the standard, abnormality the deviation. Normality will always define abnormality and not the other way around.

THE POSTMATERIAL AGE

What, then, of normal psychology is available to support a better theoretical perspective? The recent writings on postmaterialism have a psychological ring to them but so far they have been rooted in no philosophical foundation. But evidence that postmaterial human subjectivities have a large real world impact on political attitudes and behaviors is increasingly convincing and within the past twenty years, sound research has defined what is called postmaterial political values. These values have been found almost exclusively in the post-World War II generation, the hypothesis of such postmaterialists as Ronald Inglehart being that those born into "unprecedented levels of economic and physical security" have been freer to generate an entirely new category of political concerns.[24] Though I do not believe these concerns to be as novel as Inglehart claims, they do indicate, as the term *postmaterialism* implies, a certain transcendance of the desire for material wants among an increasing share of an advanced society's people. This advancement manifests itself in a desire for what some call a more meaningful human existence.

Though Inglehart's and others' research represents an uncovering of a new political perspective for at least some citizens of economically developed societies, these early studies are, by themselves, not useful for political theory. For one thing, they are limited by their one-sided ideological flavor, Inglehart's writings being steeped in the terminology of the 1960s and of the New Left. But beyond his ideological limitations, a far more serious difficulty with Inglehart is his assumption of the existence of a singular, universal political orientation once the postmaterial stage of material development is reached. Predictably, Inglehart's model borrows heavily from Abraham Maslow, and the absence of differentiation in Inglehart's findings reflects the same singular, developmental progression of human psychology that Maslow described.

To be sure, subsequent writings on postmaterialism have moved away from ideologically singular perspectives. James Savage has noted convincingly that a postmaterial perspective may have emerged in the postwar generation, but a full ideological range is evident in those populations. Savage, in contrast to Inglehart's implicit assumption of an ideologically neutered postmaterial politics, argues that ideological conflict will continue within the politics of prosperous nations. Such conflict, he suggests, will have a great deal of psychology to it.[25]

But Savage's revisions of Inglehart's postmaterialism, unfortunately, do not speak to the most serious impediment to postmaterialism's potential contribution to theory. Specifically, Savage argues that a psychological relativism surely exists among what Maslow called "higher order needs." But Savage, like Inglehart, still defines postmaterialism in terms of materially distributive concerns. His definitions of postmaterialism still only deal with the psychology of politics from the perspective of how psychology plays a role in distributing material rewards among its citizenry. He does not deal with psychology and politics from the perspective of how reasonably static, different adult personalities impose psychologically differentiated *forms* of meaning on political reality. The psychological costs or the psychological benefits of different political arrangements as they exist apart from material costs and benefits are not discussed.

Postmaterial research, as far as it has gone, is therefore still largely atheoretical. It does not psychologically differentiate nor does it relate psychological differentiations to the deeper issues of politics. Also, insofar as it has theoretical assumptions within it, these assumptions are still epistemologically rational. They embrace only real-world causes for why human psychologies are what they are, and they are also biased in an epistemologically, not substantively, material way. They do not describe how different psychologies cause different things to happen in politics and, most importantly, they do not describe, in a relativistic but not randomly relativistic mode, how the cognitive balance of political structures and processes affects how political issues are understood and processed. As its epistemological roots are still rationalistic, postmaterialism can contribute little to a psychologically relativistic theory of politics. The exclusively substantive postmaterialism of Ronald Inglehart, James Savage, and others, although noteworthy for its recognition of the importance of psychology to politics, does not place postmaterialism into its appropriate epistemological context.

Oswald Spengler's reflection on the "more than one style of knowing" ably defines what can be the core of relativistic theory. Spengler's definition saw the issue of knowing as acknowledging the perspective of all who seek to understand something. Similarly, in the context of psychological relativity, the study of politics must now consider the relative preference for different forms of thinking about politics. Such preferences must describe not only someone's objective political condition but also what styles of knowing each citizen brings to the issues of politics.

Questions concerning styles of knowing can not be answered in a relativistic way by the strain of developmental psychology that runs from Freud through Piaget to Kohlberg. A psychologically relativistic theory of politics will begin with a description of the range of normal but differentiated perspectives on a variety of political considerations. As such a theory grows out of the relativities among human psychology, it will build its prescriptions for political equity on the psychological balances that exist along the principal human-nature range.

Chapter Two

RELATIVISM AND POLITICAL THEORY

When the political theorist Carl W. Friedrich wished to chasten G. W. F. Hegel with as much severity as he could muster, the disapprobation he chose was "relativism."[1] The entire corpus of Hegel, Friedrich claimed, was essentially relativistic, and though he chastened Hegel for many things, even calling him "the philosopher of war and the national authoritarian state," it was Hegel's relativism that most fired Friedrich's indignation.[2]

Friedrich no doubt considered Hegel's relativism to be of Bernstein's nihilistic or random type. Hegel's alleged blurring of Western standards 6f morality, along with his alleged stealing away of stable criteria for differentiating between right and wrong in Western thought, added up to nihilism for Friedrich. Predictably, Friedrich gave his approbation to Immanuel Kant, at one point notably grounding that approbation in Kant's freedom from the "subjective relativity of judgments."[3]

Hegel certainly was a relativist, but his relativism was far less nihilistic than Friedrich claimed. Also, Hegel's relativism was hardly immoral. It was merely historical, an attempt to regain the reason on which morality could be founded and which morality had lost in the Garden of Eden. As a consequence, it first concerned itself with the path of intellectual history and only then with real history. Hegel focused his historical relativism on stages of human knowledge, wrapped, as they always seemed to be for Hegel, in a package of ever-growing understandings of self and then circumstance. In its intellectual form, Hegel's relativism was unquestionably organic. Its dialectical structure borrowed from Zeno, Plato, and other classical dialecticians. Above all, it undertook a sequence of contradiction and resolution, replayed over and over as it climbed the ascendant levels of human understanding.

Hegel's dialectical catalyst for the progress of understanding and history was structured in three stages, each corresponding to a different attention to what needed to be known. The first stage was a knowing of only the thing "in itself." This was a knowing of something in its own state alone, that state existing for a time outside of the human consciousness. It was a knowing, therefore, in a remote sense, the first stage of the dialectic thus also being remote. As it was a knowing of an existence only in that existence's isolation, it was self-contained, self-referrent, for Hegel. It had not yet engaged the general consciousness.

It was therefore only in the confrontation of the objective, external, or the thing in itself with the general consciousness that the dialectic's second stage was engaged. This second stage, the stage of the "for itself," was the meaning, or what Hegel, and others before him, called the contradiction of the thing in itself with the current pattern of consciousness. This stage of the contradiction, the for itself stage, was the point of confrontation wherein the purely external or objective reality confronted the subjective consciousness. Naturally, as the previously externalized object confronted the consciousness, it contradicted what consciousness had previously understood. In doing so, the new existence, the for itself, confronted something that was not of the same intellectual quality as the current understanding. This difference of intellectual quality is the core of the Hegelian contradiction.

The resolution of the contradiction in the second stage of the dialectic made up Hegel's third dialectical stage. This was the stage of reconciliation. It was the stage wherein what was previously so contradictory was brought into a reconciliation with the previous understanding. The final stage, then, the stage of being "in and for itself," brought what was previously outside the understanding of the consciousness (or what had existed merely in a state of objectivity) into consciousness. In doing so, the consciousness could embrace a wholly new, necessarily more complex, *quality* of understanding. The second stage's contradiction had been transcended. But the transcendence succeeded only by an expansion of the very framework of understanding.

For Hegel, very simply, the dialectic marked a progress toward ever-better understandings. Though Hegel defined a final perspective, or a final understanding that included complete knowledge through complete self-knowledge, Hegel's notion of the Absolute did not, at least in the first instance, have anything to do with politics. Though Friedrich and others have incorrectly charged that Hegel's position necessarily leads to authoritarianism,[4] the fact is that it need not do so at all. Hegel's position is not one of political absolutism, though Hegel's relativism was misused by those who wished to glorify the state in extraordinarily inhuman ways. Hegel's relativism, again, was merely historical. It was not based on the simultaneous holding of different, much less psychologically generated, political perspectives in society, any more than it was based on an authoritarian imposition of a singular political orthodoxy.

Although Hegel was not a psychological relativist, it would be improper to say that Hegel had no appreciation for whatever differences might exist among personalities. Many writers on Hegel, including Judith Shklar, have found a nascent psychological relativity in Hegel, even though Shklar concluded that Hegel "does not explain the differences among people." Shklar saw that Hegel's differences among individuals were not the result of differences in environment, culture, climate, religion, and the like. As Shklar put it, the above factors did not adequately explain Hegel's "differences between people, each one of whom seems to act in his own way to a common environment."[5]

J. N. Findlay, who was most responsible for the resurrection of Hegel in the English-speaking community, also witnessed a nascent psychological relativity with Hegel. Hegel was responding to Kant and to the skepticism of Kant's writings, yet Hegel acknowledged the separation between the mind and reality. Findlay noted, for example, that Hegel, responding to the skeptical mode, spoke of how the "mind adapts reality unto itself." Hegel, however, argued that the dialectic thus drove each mind to "follow the bent of his own inclinations, affections and emotions and carry off thence what is of particular and special moment for itself."[6] In doing so, each mind made "what is objective conform to reality." Findlay interprets Hegel's perspective here as including what different individualities, dealing with a world that "impinges" on them, naturally do. It is a world, according to Findlay, wherein "the knowledge of that individuality" is certainly of no small importance.[7]

Even in the above writings, however, there is no evidence that Hegel ever placed his understanding of different human psychologies at the core of his metaphysics. Yet Hegel is still the best precursor of a psychologically relativistic theory of politics because his metaphysics describe the single most significant relativity among human cognitions. Although Hegel did not mean to lay the groundwork for a relativistic theory, his cognitive descriptions do so. This cognitive relativity lies in differentiations among cognitions that Hegel described in the *Logic* though Hegel had already used them without explanation in the *Phenomenology*. I will describe Hegel's cognitive differentiations both in the context that Hegel used them as well as in the context of what leads to a psychologically relativistic theory of politics.

HEGEL'S ANALYTIC AND SYNTHETIC COGNITIONS

In order to place Hegel's notions of a psychological relativity into a theory of politics, Hegel's exposition of the most basic differentiation among human cognitions should be considered first. Hegel's description of the differences among human cognitions grew out of his critique of Kant. It should thus be no surprise that the context of Hegel's response to Kant was lodged in Hegel's discussion of the nature of knowledge. Hegel responded there to Kant's argument on the limits of human knowledge.

To emphasize the vast distinction between Kant's and Hegel's notions of mediation (or knowledge), I will focus, as I think Hegel did, on two key elements of distinction. These elements, roughly stated, include Hegel's view of cognitions (as these cognitions differentiate among the cognitive *qualities* of variables) and the relative contributions that these cognitive qualities make to the progress of human understanding. Placed in terms that both Kant and Hegel used, the first element (the distinguishing among the qualities of variables) differentiates between what both called the *analytic* and the *synthetic* cognitions. Hegel, placed into a context that distinguishes his position from Kant's, assigned a superior role to the synthetic cognition both in the operation of the dialectic and in the advancement of human understanding.

The distinction between the analytic and the synthetic cognition for Hegel appears in *The Science of Logic* (1812–13), the second of Hegel's four major works and the first after his *Phenomenology* (1807).[8] Hegel's response to Kant specifically disagreed with the intellectual distinctions that Kant had made between what could and what could not be known. The Kantian position, of course, was itself a response to his predecessor Gottfried Liebniz, who had argued that synthetic a priori knowledge could not exist at all. Liebniz contended that synthetic knowledge, that is, knowledge of two or more different *qualities* of things, invariably required empirical evidence. Whether the room was warm or the wormwood bitter could not be known simply by reason, a priori. Kant's response to Liebniz was tantalizing, even ironic. In its limited way, it argued for the possibility of synthetic a priori knowledge.

Yet Kant's restriction on *what kinds* of a priori synthetic knowledge could be known was very confining. It was limited almost exclusively to mathematics and natural science, the only exception being the personal moralities that underpinned Kant's Categorical Imperative. Above all, it discouraged the synthetic cognition's role in speculative, metaphysical understandings. Since Hegel wished to expand such understandings, Hegel later gave this synthetic knowledge a far more robust intellectual role.

Hegel's argument for the expansion of the synthetic cognition disputed Kant's depiction of the equation $5 + 7 = 12$ as synthetic. Kant had contended that because one side of the equation was a compound and the other a single number, the cognitive quality of the two sides of the equation differed. Because of that differentiation alone, Kant argued that the equation was cognitively synthetic.

Hegel was thoroughly unconvinced. Challenging the depiction of the equation as an example of synthetic knowledge, he categorized the logic of it as merely analytic. In his response to Kant, Hegel argued that an analytic cognition was made up of "something *already complete* in the object" (emphasis his). What Hegel meant was that the logic of $5 + 7 = 12$ was a logic dealing with components of the same intellectual quality. Five, seven, and twelve, in the final analysis, were all only numbers. Because Kant's equation did not require the introduction of a qualitatively differentiated variable, the equation did not "pass through any further *middle term*" (emphasis his). The equation, therefore, could "be apprehended without any subjective mediation."[9] As a result, Hegel argued, the equation $5 + 7 = 12$ was not synthetic, as Kant had claimed: it did not need to be brought into the consciousness through the dialectical process.

Hegel's own preference among cognitions could not have been made more clear than through his criticism of Kant. Hegel had little regard for what he perceived to be the restricted vision of the analytic cognition, the cognition of variables of similar quality being a limited cognition.

Hegel considered a cognition to be of significant value only if it led to a better general understanding and thus a "cognition is supposed also to be a progress," as well as an "explication of differences."[10] The analytic cognition neither explained differences nor contributed to a progress of understanding; therefore, it was inferior.

Hegel could not have been more direct about the role he assigned to the different cognitions. His concern with the progress of understanding was so overwhelming that he even denounced the analytic cognition by labeling it "undialectical." Hegel said that since the progress of the analytic cognition took place "solely in the determinations of the material," the analytic cognition could never lead to the progress of ideas. Indeed, Hegel claimed that the analytic cognition "seems to have an *immanent* progress only in so far as the derived thought determinations can be analysed afresh" (emphasis his). The only thing that was gained from such an analytic cognition, therefore, was an "abstract subjective identity." What was gained was only a categorization, a something that occurs in a qualitatively similar mode. As Hegel said, such an analytic mode was fundamentally different from what was "over against it." That was called "diversity." As Kant's claims for intellectual progress, according to Hegel, were "nothing but the mere repetition of the one original act of analysis, namely the fresh determination as a *concrete,* of what has already been taken up into the abstract form," Hegel's condemnation of the analytic cognition described them as being so *"complete in themselves* that their determination was already found *essentially linked to the other"* (emphasis his). Once more, such cognitions were all of the same qualitative form. The relationships between them were those only of "a mere datum" or of something that, in its form, was *"found already there"* (emphasis his).[11]

Hegel's discussion of the differences between cognitions responded directly to Kant's definition of cognitions. According to Hegel, Kant's method of categorization stemmed *"from formal logic"* only, Hegel feeling that he (Hegel) had demonstrated that purely logical reasoning could never be a part of a "genuinely synthetic progress" (emphasis his). Hegel specifically drew attention to the fact that *"arithmetic,* along with the more general *sciences of discrete magnitude* especially, are all properly classified as *analytical science* and *analysis"* (emphasis his). Hegel understood that within such analysis, the "method of cognition is immanently analytical in the highest degree." There the "material of arithmetic and algebra . . . is something that has already been made wholly abstract and indeterminate and purged of all pecularity of relationship." Purged of its peculiarity, all that can be done with "[t]his relationless atom [is that it] can be increased to a *plurality,* and externally determined and unified into a sum (emphasis his)." For Hegel, then, Kant's mere *"Magnitude* is in general the only category within which these determinations are made (emphasis his)."[12]

Curiously, Hegel chose to conclude his argument on the inferiority of the analytic cognition by chiding Kant directly, scoring his philosophical predecessor for Kant's misunderstanding of the synthetic cognition. Returning to Kant's equation, Hegel said, "Kant, it is true, has declared the proposition $5 + 7 = 12$ to be a *synthetic* proposition" (emphasis his). But Hegel scoffed that "if the analytic proposition is not to mean the completely abstract identity and tautology $12 = 12$ and is to contain any advance at all, it must present a difference of some kind." To Hegel, "12 is therefore a result of 5 and 7 and of an operation which is already posited."[13] Prophetically, he suggested that such a cognition is an "act completely external and devoid of any thought, so that it can be performed even by a machine."[14] With mere analysis, "there is not the slightest trace of a transition to an *other,* it is a mere continuation, that is, a *repetition,* of the same operation that produced 5 and 7" (emphasis his).[15]

Hegel's synthetic cognition is, therefore, the catalyst of intellectual "transition." But, as Hegel put it, that transition could only be accomplished as the result of what he called "an underlying *qualitative* determination of magnitude" (emphasis mine). Hegel's synthetic cognition was in direct contrast to what Kant saw as central to the dialectic. The transition from an analytic determination to a synthetic determination, for Hegel, permitted a movement away from a mere "magnitude as such": "transition is not of a mathematical nature" because movement "from [the] analytic to [the] synthetic cognition lies in the necessary transition from the form of immediacy to mediation, from abstract identity to difference."[16]

Referring again to the argument over the nature of knowledge, Hegel further distinguished the analytic from the synthetic cognition by saying that the analytic device is "good only for the *apprehension* of the object while the synthetic cognition is responsible for the *comprehension* of it" (emphasis his). The diverse is dealt with in the synthetic cognition which "passes over" from *"abstract identity* to *relation* in the understanding of things" (emphasis his).[17] This is the unique part of Hegel's differentiation between the analytic and the synthetic cognition.

MEDIATION

Differences between Kant's and Hegel's beliefs concerning the impact of the analytic and synthetic cognitions are significant in three central areas. These areas are knowing, or mediation; the dialectic; and the progress of understanding or history. I will turn to the differences in these areas next because a theory of politics founded on a relativistic understanding of human psychology will first need to make clear the nature of psychologically differentiated perspectives on knowledge, the improvement of knowledge, and the progress of history in their appropriate epistemological context.

Earlier, I contrasted Immanuel Kant's obstructive, skeptical perspective on knowledge with the facilitative, speculative view of knowledge that Hegel championed. The Kantian position, as a matter of intellectual history, completed David Hume's skeptical notions concerning the separation of mind and object and the Copernican Revolution in metaphysics. Kant is appropriately recognized for building on Hume's skepticism and, specifically, Hume's understanding of the separation between the mind and the object. Kant, of course, went beyond Hume to suggest that the mind and the object were not merely separated, insisting that the mind preceded the object. The mind, therefore, imposed its meaning on the object rather than the other way around. This, of course, is the epistemologically idealist view.

The so-called Copernican Revolution in metaphysics insisted on the skeptical perspective. It insisted on the primacy of the mind in imposing meaning on reality rather than on the mind's simply comprehending what was assumed to be an objective reality. Kant's skepticism was grounded in the sense that it restricted what could be known by reason alone to things other than the great metaphysical truths. Though there was a rationally based transcendentalism to Kant, a transcendentalism that was powerful in the arena of personal morality and the Categorical Imperative, there was no Bernsteinian middle ground between objectivism and relativism in Kant's metaphysics. Metaphysical knowledge, for

Kant, would never be agreed to by different people, and therefore it could not exist.

The Hegelian response to Kant was far more speculative, far less obstructive than was Kant's skeptical view, building on the belief that the mind-object chasm could be surmounted. Dealing with that chasm principally in the *Encyclopedia* (1817), his third major work, Hegel contended that intersubjective agreement on metaphysical truths could in fact be reached.[18] Hegel argued, in brief, that the necessary intersubjectivity (or commonality of understanding) among different observers was more available than Kant had claimed. The link between the perceiver and the perceived, between the mind and the object, was more *immediate* for Hegel than it was for Kant, even though Hegel, like Kant, was not a psychological relativist. Hegel never defined the understanding that may or may not exist among different perceivers as a product of a range of psychological perspectives. He still defined this understanding as singular, but, as his acceptance of the reconciliation of the mind and object assumed an easier road to a uniformity of understanding, he at least aspired to a broader metaphysical reason than did either Hume or Kant. Hegel's attempt to regain the lost reason of the Garden of Eden through the dialectic was what made history and the inevitability of its march of improved understanding so important.

What, then, does the perspective of psychological relativism bring to the issue of mediacy or knowledge that Kant, and even Hegel, did not? How can there be a *greater* element of mediacy or knowledge if different perceivers perceive reality in different ways? Knowledge in a relativistic framework rests on an understanding of the nature of the differences in perspective. In a relativistic theory, mediacy is attained relativistically by an understanding not of a single, objective truth, even with Hegel's arguing that such an attainment is easier than Kant allowed. It is attained, rather, by an understanding of the range of perspectives on truth, a range that is more psychological in its nature than historical, though history does play a role in developing the relativistic perspective. Although understandings of the positions that different perspectives hold on reality will never be the same, what properly lies between Bernstein's singular objectivity on the one hand and his random or nihilist skepticism on the other is the reasonably well bounded and reasonably well known relativity of different perspectives on knowledge itself. An understanding of a bounded relativity of perspectives on knowledge, of course, can underpin a relativistic theory only if the range of perspectives on knowledge is available. But a relativistic form of understanding is possible there, whereas a singular, intersubjective understanding is not. Bernstein's notion of the commensurability of different perspectives can, and should, embrace psychological relativism. It can account for different perspectives.

Perhaps a serendipitous circumstance is at work in this search for a relativistic understanding. It is that psychologically differentiated perspectives on reality may best be adapted to political philosophy through an understanding of the minds of Kant and Hegel themselves. If one looks beyond the arguments of these two great idealists' differences on the questions of mediacy or knowledge, in other words, it may be that the contrast of their own psychologies, and the contrast between their different but commensurable ways of thinking, stand as the best exemplar of relativism.

To repeat, the juxtaposition of Kant's and Hegel's own positions on knowledge reveals far more than just the details of their metaphysical argument. Their positions reveal the differences between Kant's and Hegel's own psychologies and the cognitive differences that will underpin a relativistic theory. Kant, in his cognitive preference for the qualitatively similar variable (as revealed by his judging $5 + 7 = 12$ to be synthetic) and Hegel, in his cognitive preference for the differentiated variable (revealed by his wanting more of a differentiation for the quality of a synthesis than $5 + 7 = 12$ provides), I think, depict the principal cognitive range (chapter three).

Also, just as Kant and Hegel may best illustrate something like the Weberian "ideal types" of the cognitive range that run between analytic and synthetic preferences, so too any random population will also embody that cognitive range. Preferences for the analytic or the synthetic cognition, that is, psychological preferences that manifest themselves among preferences for the different degrees of differentiation that are required for something to be considered synthetic, are available for our observation in any population. They lie within the different psychologies of each population and, as a result, just as different psychologies possess different preferences for cognitions, the psychological preferences for those different cognitions reside with some predictability in the membership of any polity.

I pointed out earlier that Hegel seemed to have had at least some sense that differences existed among personalities. It is clear, however, that he did not place those differences at the core of his metaphysics. Even the considerable contrast between his own cognitive preferences and those of Kant was not considered by Hegel to result from any psychological difference between Kant and himself. Hegel, like Herbert Simon today, simply considered one cognitive perspective to be superior, and he chose to elevate it in his writings.

Thus, though Hegel's chapter on cognition in *The Science of Logic* fairly delineated the most fundamental distinction between the principal methods of reasoning that metaphysics provides (the analytic and the synthetic cognition), there is no evidence that Hegel understood, and he surely did not make use of the fact, that different psychologies possess different preferences for the cognitions that they wish to use. Hegel understood the differences between the analytic and the synthetic cognitions, yet he did not understand that the *locus* of that difference resided unevenly among different psychologies. I will refer to Hegel's nonrecognition of the psychology of cognitive preferences as Hegel's *omission* throughout this work. The correction of Hegel's omission is central to a psychologically relativistic theory of politics.

THE DIALECTIC

With the above understanding of psychological relativism's relationship to the difference between Kant and Hegel's view of cognitions, I will examine how that understanding contributes to a relativistic understanding of the dialectic. If the differentiated Hegelian and Kantian perspectives on knowledge were tied to their own psychologies, as I think that they were, then the differentiations between Kant's and Hegel's respective preferences for cognitions were also tied to their different perspectives on what will improve human understanding. The differentiation is important for Kant's and Hegel's very different view of the dialectic.

For Kant, as with so much else, the dialectic was largely categorical. It was a method whose purpose was to place objects in their appropriate setting in relation to other objects. It was a scheme of classification, an ordering of considerations that, for Kant, were always moral at their root. Hegel's view of the dialectic could not have been more different. His vision was necessarily evolutionary, for it was inevitably a matter of intellectual progress. It specifically criticized Kant's use of the triadic form within a nondynamic, nonprogressive categorical framework. Hegel once depicted Kant's dialectic as something "reduced to a lifeless schema."[19] Current writers still cite the formalism of the Kantian perspective. Steven Smith, for example, claims that Kant was "more interested in the form or structure" of things than in "their content or direction."[20]

For Hegel, then, the dialectic was where progress or the improvement of understanding began. It was, of course, the synthetic cognition that propelled Hegel's dialectic to better understandings. Jean Hyppolite, in his discussion of Hegel, explained the nature of Hegel's dialectic, although he did not utilize a cognitive, much less a cognitively relativistic, perspective on the differences between Hegel's and Kant's dialectic. But Hyppolite still reflected on mind-object mediation. He quoted Hegel's depiction of nature before consciousness as "only a concept in itself." This concept was curiously appropriate for Hegel to that contradictory for itself, or second stage, of the dialectic.

Hyppolite's language is suitable for a notion of relativism for the self-consciousness that Hyppolite found Hegel to be seeking in the dialectic was ultimately judged to be "reflecting upon life." It reflected on life in such a way, Hyppolite said, that "one can begin with the separate individual . . . for whom the whole is an external unity."[21] As Hegel's relativism was only historical and not psychological, and as it demonstrated only "that unity [is] the immanent nature of the individual," Hyppolite properly points out that Hegel failed to differentiate among perspectives on truth in the dialectic. Only a singular perspective was permissible in the Hegelian dialectic. That singular perspective, granting its superiority to the synthetic cognition, forces Hyppolite to acknowledge that for Hegel "history is [only] the concrete self-development of such consciousness and the realization of the life of the spirit in a profound unity of the individual and the universal."[22] The synthetic cognition permits that development, but it still only works for Hegel in movement toward a universalistic, singular understanding. Further, as the role of the analytic cognition was not helpful to Hegel's second or contradictory stage of the dialectic, that is, as the $5 + 7 = 12$ cognition was to have no role in Hegel's dialectic, a relativistic perspective (which would include *both* the analytic and the synthetic cognition) was no part of Hegel's dialectic. This, too, resulted from Hegel's omission.

Hyppolite's analysis of Hegel's dialectic and its role in the progress of history properly represents the absence of relativism in both Hegel's views on knowledge and his dialectic. The synthetic cognition alone carries Hegel's progress toward understanding. But Hyppolite's commentary does not describe an even more serious cost of Hegel's omission, failing to note that as cognitive preferences do not fall evenly within all psychologies, so too, from a relativistic perspective, the dialectic is not cognitively neutral at each of its variant stages. What is significant about the dialectic is that different stages of the dialectic rely on different psychologies and on the different forms of cognition that different psychologies prefer. That the dialectic is not cognitively neutral, as a whole, and that the dialectic is not neutral in each of its stages, different cognitions being dominant within each stage, were never part of Hegel's scheme for the improvement of understanding.

What then, is the cognitive nature of the dialectic? Better stated, what is the cognitive nature of *each stage* of the dialectic when it is examined from a relativistic perspective? Recall that Hegel described the second stage of the dialectic as that movement from the first stage, the in itself stage, where the idea exists only outside of the consciousness, to the stage of the contradiction. As I described earlier, the contradiction is where the idea for itself confronts the consciousness. Recall also that this second stage of the dialectic, for Hegel, necessitated a juxtaposition of the existing form of understandings with not just a different understanding but with a *qualitatively different form* of understanding. This different form of understanding was never, therefore, simply an addition to a present understanding but was an addition of a different (and always more complex) framework of the understanding itself. Each new understanding could not fit into the old.

At the point of the first dialectical stage, of course, the being in itself had yet to enter the consciousness. It thus required only an analytic cognition in order to achieve objective knowing. But to progress from the thing in itself to the thing for itself, it was necessary, according to Hegel, to engage in the contradiction of those "explication of differences" that were presented by the new *form* of object that would enter the consciousness. As that contradiction, or that new cognitive form, could only come into existence at the second or "for itself" stage of the dialectic, it represented an extension beyond mere objectivity or beyond what until then had only existed outside the consciousness. Most important, it was a product, and it could never be anything but a product, of the synthetic cognition.

The third stage of the dialectic (the stage of the in and for itself) was one of intellectual reconciliation or rationalization. It was the stage wherein a routinization of understanding was to be restored after the dialectic had successfully engaged the new, contradictory form of understanding. A kind of intellectual homeostasis returns in the third dialectical stage, and that homeostasis imports the incorporation of the previously differentiated form into what then becomes a more easy form of understanding at the new historical stage. Obviously, the third stage of the dialectic necessitates a return of the analytic cognition. The key point is that the cognitive form of *each stage* of the dialectic is different. Each stage reflects different cognitions, and if Hegel's omission is to be corrected in the context of a psychological rather than a historically relativistic dialectic, each stage of the dialectic can only be worked through if it reflects the right cognition at the right time.

RELATIVISM AND HISTORY

The way of knowing, or mediation, and the way of the dialectic, or the way in which knowing is improved, leads ultimately to a way of understanding how history moves. Just as specific perspectives on the essence of knowledge have reflected different cognitions and different psychologies, so too different paths for the progress of history have also reflected different cognitions and different psychologies. Hegel's perspective on history was vastly different from Kant's, for Kant saw history as a vision "without dialectical logic."[23] For Kant, history was at best "a moral task," never a "cognitive object."[24]

If there was only a limited consciousness in history for Kant, the "blind, natural teleology" or the "cunning of nature," as Kant called it, being only marginally assisted in the movement of history by an ostensibly rational will,[25] then the Enlightenment which supposedly facilitated that will would be understood by Kant as exaggerating the claim of rationality.[26] Kant saw history as a reconciliation, but it was a reconciliation only of nature and of nature's progress as that progress was but marginally assisted by enlightened humanity's historical impact. Importantly, Kant did not "have a coherent theory to account for the rigorous duality of the empirical and the *a priori*," or the historical reason of the mind. Neither did he have a sense of how a priori reason affected the empirical world historically. Kant did not have such a sense of history precisely because he did "not have a dialectical logic."[27] In sum, though the Kantian design of history was not simplistic to be sure, it certainly reflected Kant's cognitive preference for the qualitatively similar variable and for the analytic cognition.

In contrast to Kant, Hegel's position on the progress of history marked a greater role for a priori or nonempirical knowledge. Hegel's history was idealistic too, though not in the subjective sense. It was a collective, singular, but conscious movement through those stages of knowledge that heralded the ascendance of human reason. As I have said, Hegel's *Phenomenology* is a grand portrayal of the journey toward the reestablishment of reason in which each of the identifiable stages marks a higher human consciousness. Historical progress for Hegel thus proceeded from the first stage of consciousness through the intermittent stages of self-consciousness, reason, spirit, and religion to the final, Absolute stage. In this progression, Hegel referred to specific events in the development of human history, even though they are developments that J. N. Findlay properly suggests we read in an illustrative rather than a literal way.[28]

It is the *method* of the historical progress in the *Phenomenology*, then, that is significant for relativism. Each of Hegel's stages is purely dialectical in its form, portraying a sequence from an original homeostasis, through a challenge to that homeostasis, to a return to homeostasis with a more complex level of understanding. The first grand stage of the *Phenomenology*, Consciousness, marks the elemental human understanding. It is concerned merely with a sense certainty, that is, a knowing of what senses tell us.[29] The challenge to the homeostasis of consciousness introduces differentiations, which are among the things perceived but are in opposition to the unity of what is already perceived. Such prescriptions are not as yet part of the understood, sensual world. The third stage of the first grand level, the resolution, is the Understanding. It represents the integration of what was not defined previously into a unity of sense perceptions. Homeostasis returns, at this third stage, the analytic cognition taking over again.[30] The routinization of the Understanding of the sensual world marks the close of the first phenomenological stage.

Hegel's second grand stage transcends consciousness and enters Self-consciousness. It begins with the conscious Ego, which, as Findlay says, is more concerned with desire than with intellectual interpretation. Nonetheless, early self-consciousness finds the world arranged not as the Ego would have it. There are contradictions between the real world and the thinking of that world. But those contradictions are resolvable, and they are resolved, for Hegel, in an awareness of the conscious Ego. This awareness comes only from human subjectivity turned back on itself.[31]

An awareness of self-consciousness leads to the third grand stage: Reason.[32] Reason begins with the homeostasis of an observation of nature. It is simple empiricism that is confronted with an awareness of the subjectivity on the empiricist perspective. That subjectivity is known to be arbitrary, wishing to impose a reason and a style of living on the world that is essentially selfish. It becomes objective, or reconciled, when everyone does what one is good at. It affirms the Kantian consistency of each person's working in his or her own proficiency. It is, necessarily, self-consistent and universal. True universalization, which is understood or conscious, is required for reason. Only true universalization can lead to the fourth, Spiritual stage.[33]

The spiritual stage begins with the homeostasis of the Greek family and family life. It incorporates the Greek culture and, in particular, such Greek dramas as *Antigone*. It is consistent, roughly, with the state as it is represented in the simple polis.[34] But this stage is contradicted by the rise of the latter form of states, which include bureaucracy and the regulation of economic life. Modernity (in a way that is wonderfully predictive of Max Weber incidentally) is a threat to the self-contained stage. This fourth stage brings contradiction to a kind of utilitarian atomism. Its resolution comes only from a reflection on morality. It comes from what Findlay calls "the individual's own deep reflection on conduct."[35] Through such reflection, one ends the alienation of the spiritual stage, preparing one for the stage of Religion.

The stage of religion evidences the same in itself, for itself, and in and for itself of the dialectic as do the previous stages. Early Christianity represents the first, still homeostatic, stage of human spirituality.[36] That early period is contradicted by the different periods of Christian history, with the Middle Ages, the post-Renaissance, and the Enlightenment marking greater periods of discordance. The contradiction, because of the nature of the synthetic cognition, is capable of resolution, and religion is thus capable of reaching a period wherein reflectiveness on morality permits movement to the final stage, the Absolute. The Absolute stage represents the grand reconciliation of subjective consciousness. It is nothing less than the full reconciliation of the subjective and the objective in a marvelously self-reflective way.[37]

All historical stages for Hegel, again, were predominantly stages of the mind. As they were also stages of the intellectual and, not incidentally, moral progression of humankind into ever-higher ethical states, the substantive content of these stages is of less importance than the *form* of the dialectic with which Hegel ensured the historical advance. The dialectic, in its three stages, represents distinct cognitive preferences: it is always analytic to synthetic and back again. But Hegel did not see the movement of history as an alternating dominance of different cognitions, much less of different psychologies. Steven Smith wrote that, for Hegel, "history as a whole expresses a sort of force or cause that must be distinguished from the purposeful plans and deeds of individual actors." It is only a "totality of human deeds" that "expresses a plan, plot or rationality of its own." [38] This position is wrong, however, for the very reasons that a theory of relativity suggests.

What happens when psychological differentiation is added? When psychological differentiation is added, the in itself of each grand stage's first level is internally consistent, almost Kantian, in its mathematical nature. But the contradiction, the second stage, is a stage of qualitative differentiation. This stage marks movement from an abstract identity to what Hegel himself called "differences." Contradiction is only resolved, as it must be for Hegel, by a successful incorporation of the synthetic or differentiated variable into the conscious mind. Only then can the differences of the contradictory stage be assimilated and the next grand stage allowed.

Hegel, as did the principal dialecticians before him, emphasized the second stage, the contradictory stage, as the key to the dialectic. This contradictory stage, after all, is what the synthetic cognition served. But, recall, the Hegelian vision is psychologically incomplete. Hegel saw the significance of only the cognitive dissimilarity, the differences. He did not understand the cognitive differences that exist between each dialectical stage and the importance of cognitive similarity, not cognitive differentiation, to the first and third stage. Further, Hegel's omission, no matter how expansive the *Phenomenology* may have been in its detailing of the progress of understanding and history, precluded the role of psychologically differentiated perspectives on the advance of understanding or history. The *Phenomenology* simply cannot be interpreted to show that Hegel understood how *different* psychologies played different cognitive roles in advancing their respective stages of the dialectic through the stages of history.

That absence of a relativistic perspective on human psychology, I suggest, meant that Hegel's perspective on history was bound to a particular form and that form, inevitably, was linear. History existed without oscillation or cycle or, as Judith Shklar described it, it was never more than a "whole quest for certain knowledge" on the part of all. Shklar appropriately depicts the progression toward knowledge as a "single, ordered whole," an improvement of understanding, all of a piece again at each historical stage.[39] Hegel's nonrelativistic vision of each historical stage, his failure to understand that the cognitions he described in the *Logic* varied within the internal dynamic of the dialectic itself, doomed his history to linear patterning. A psychologically relativistic pattern, in contrast to Hegel's, views the progress of history within the context of its appropriate, differentiated, psychologies. This is what a relativistic theory adds to Hegel's notion of history and it is the core of a relativistic theory of politics.

THE RETURN OF THE IDEAL

I have contrasted the perspectives of Kant and Hegel on the essential questions of knowledge, the dialectic and the progress of understanding (or history) within a broadly skeptical and idealist, as opposed to a rationalistic and materialistic, epistemological framework. The skeptical vision, in keeping with Kant's Copernican Revolution, places the observer apart from the observed, the perceiver apart from the perceived. Even Hegel, in his response to skepticism as stated in the context of a belief in gathering rationalism, acknowledged the chasm between the perceiver and the perceived. A relativistic perspective is skeptical, recognizing the differences between the location of many perceivers and whatever is perceived. It is also idealistic, for the mind of the perceiver is not only imposing meaning on reality, but its imposing of such meaning is viewed as the principal engine of history. This is the idealist vision.

Let me say again that what is so serendipitous about the contrast between Kant's and Hegel's skeptical idealism is that their own metaphysical perspectives so well reflected the cognitive differentiation that is central to a theory of relativism. Their differentiation, I suggest, is serendipitous because it is not adequate merely to say that Kant and Hegel represented psychological preferences for the analytic or the synthetic cognition. In order to ground an epistemologically postmaterial or idealist vision in the relativism of different psychologies, the cognitive perspective of Kant *and* Hegel combined on the causes of history is essential. These two grand cognitions, much better thought of along a range and not as two discrete points, are what can create the intellectual alloy that makes a relativistic theory possible.

Recall that Kant insisted on strict, identical intersubjectivity as a standard for metaphysical knowledge. He, like Hegel, may well have sensed that people actually thought differently about things, apart from their objective or external circumstances. But Kant used whatever differences that existed among people's thinking to bolster his metaphysical skepticism. It was grist for his mill concerning the inaccessibility of metaphysical knowledge. Though it was obstructive in its own context, Kant correctly represented the contemporary limits to metaphysics in his time. Hegel wished to extend those limits and, in so doing, he accomplished even more. He not only represented a cognition that was different from Kant's, but by focusing on knowledge itself and arguing for the ultimate reconciliation of the mind and object, of the perceiver and the perceived, he developed a metaphysical response to Kant's skepticism that enshrined cognitive differentiation.

But, again, Hegel's purpose was overwhelmingly historical. It was, hopefully, an assist to that universal, linear collection of greater understandings that sought to respond to Kant's metaphysical and historical skepticism. Hegel sought to trump Kant's skepticism with the superiority of the synthetic cognition, but the irony of relativism is that the barrier of intersubjectivity that Kant built for metaphysical knowledge is best responded to by the necessary usage of *both* the analytic and the synthetic cognitions.

It is, therefore, the usage of both the analytic and the synthetic cognitions—as those perspectives are commensurable in Bernstein's prescription for a nonnihilist relativism—that permits a triangulation of different perspectives on knowledge. It is the very going beyond Hegel's formula for the improvement of knowledge over time, a permitting of greater knowledge *at any time,* that includes the simultaneous perspective of multiple perceivers on what they perceive. Relativism permits a depiction of history that responds to each of the different stages of the dialectic. Relativism is therefore both a more accurate and a more robust vision for history than any vision that describes historical progress as linear. It is also a more robust vision for a theory of politics.

THE SUBJECTIVE AND THE OBJECTIVE

A final point. Of course, no psychologically rooted political philosophy should be guilty of what social scientists call reductionism. Psychology has never accounted for, and will never account for, the entirety of any observer's political perspective. The external, objective circumstances of each political observer will continue to color political perspectives, even in a postmaterial world. Yet in a modern, developed, or postmaterial state, the understanding of differentiated human psychologies reveals the relativity of cognitions that exist within any objective circumstance more clearly than ever before. Relativistic subjectivity must now be a part of political philosophy. To place it there is not reductionism because for every objectivity, there is a subjective or a psychological differentiation. For every objective circumstance—whether class, gender, nationality, or the like—a variety of psychologically generated perspectives both on the issues that concern that circumstance and on a variety of other political issues, exists among the members of that objectivity.

Recall that both liberalism and Marxism, the two political philosophies of the modern era, are derived from rationalistic, materialistic, not psychological, assumptions. Their foundations are external, the economic, legal, and political circumstances whose alleged reality is assumed to be knowable objectively by all. Neither of these political philosophies are responsive to the profound metaphysical idealism of Kant, Hegel and the latent subjectivities that lie fallow in their writings. Neither suggest a political theory that is skeptical in its origin and that encompasses the range of perspectives that best responds to skepticism through its inherently idealistic, epistemological roots.

What is important for political philosophy today is no different from what has always been important for political philosophy. It is what we bring to political philosophy that can, and must, change. A relativistic perspective on knowledge itself, along with a relativistic perspective on the dialectic, the process of knowledge's improvement, and a relativistic perspective on the nonlinear progress of history, are now possible. In its definition of political equity, as in its descriptions of reality, a relativistic perspective on politics can grow out of the understanding of the differences among human natures and the differences between those human natures' "knowledge forms." A relativistic perspective on human natures, and a relativistic perspective on the principal spectrum of knowledge itself, can define equity in the context of postmaterial politics.

Chapter Three

THE PSYCHOLOGICAL DIFFERENTIATION

From the time of Herodotus' distinction between the hedgehog and the fox, or from the time of the distinction between the Apollonian and Dionysian visions of the world, differentiations have been made concerning the human perspective. A modern, oversimplified distinction like that between the Type A and the Type B personality is but a recent typification of the way that different personalities approach the world. But such differentiations have not become a part of political philosophy. Further, so many of them have unfortunately described human differentiation as a duality and not as a range.

I will review typical research on the principal range of normal human psychology here, briefly depicting human affective and cognitive psychological differentiations among normal personalities and describing how these personality differentiations relate to the principal differentiation among political views that subjective considerations account for. Although the human personality surely reflects the environment that it has lived in, patterns of personality are still reflected within and across classes, cultures, nationalities, and the like. The differentiations that I review here are far from the only psychologically related differentiations that can and should eventually be included in a psychologically relativistic theory of politics, but they should make up the roofbeam of a psychological theory. They are the most prominent and consistent differentiations that psychological indicators currently describe and they must be where the theory begins.

Spengler's *Decline of the West,* with its call for a "comparative morphology of knowledge forms," was published in 1922.[1] In the previous year, Carl Jung had published his descriptions of different human psychologies.[2] Jung, though a far less attractive figure politically than Freud, distinguished between the extroverted and introverted personality that still guides research on psychological differentiation. The Myers-Briggs test, perhaps the most widely used personality and occupational preference inventory, is based on Jung's psychological categories. Although Jung's classifications incorrectly placed a number of subcategories of psychological traits into both principal classifications rather than the correct general category, he accurately depicted the most fundamental range of personality traits. As his depictions of thinking and feeling, sensation and intuition, and the like were bracketed under their correct principal classification, his framework was well-confirmed.

Jung's interest in human psychological differentiation included both affective and cognitive distinctions. He focused on how differentiated personalities both felt and thought. Jung did not attempt to link psychological differentiations with differences in political beliefs, but some early twentieth-century writers had begun to link psychological and political attitudes. The observations of Graham Wallas, Emory Bogardus, and Harold Lasswell,[3] all searched for the importance of psychology to political behavior. These early writings, unlike Jung's, stressed affective (feeling) variables almost exclusively.

Lasswell, at least in his early writings, spoke to the politician's psychological need for power as a nearly universal trait. In his later work, however, he began to search for differentiations among normal psychologies as well. He began to differentiate, for example, among what he called "varieties of character and personality," finding that "agitating" as opposed to "bureaucratic" personalities corresponded to what he labeled respectively as the "dramatizing" or the "compulsive" role in politics.[4] His later work moved away from singularity and linked differentiated psychological traits with differentiated political attitudes and behaviors.

Lasswell's work, however, also focused almost exclusively on affective rather than cognitive traits. It dealt with the feelings of political figures and largely ignored the cognitive or "ways of thinking" classifications that Jung had described. Affective variables are instructive for the determination of attitudes toward politics, but the cognitive variable in psychology is more likely the key to a relativistic theory. Let us look briefly at the affective variable, however.

THE AFFECTIVE VARIABLE

The most renowned empirical study that linked psychology to politics was exclusively concerned with affective psychological orientations. *The Authoritarian Personality* marked the culmination of a monumental post-World War II research effort that attempted to explain the horrors of the Nazi holocaust. The so-called Berkeley Study isolated specific personality traits within a PEC (Political and Economic conservatism) scale, an A-S (Anti-Semitic Attitudes) scale, and an E (Ethnocentrism) scale. Most prominently, *The Authoritarian Personality*'s F scale, which measured what were labeled as "pre-fascist" personality traits, made up what the authors called the "authoritarian" personality. The Berkeley Study found the authoritarian personality to naturally identify with positions on the far right of the political spectrum, the authoritarian psychology being found to favor sharply delineated political jurisdictions, as well as steeply drawn hierarchies and clearly defined channels of political authority.[5]

The Authoritarian Personality generated substantial criticism. Methodological shortcuts plagued the research, as sampling errors, response-set errors, and the fact that personal interviewers had prior access to written test scores all clouded the study's acceptance. Nevertheless, *The Authoritarian Personality* had more than a ring of truth to it. Its impact on the study of psychology and politics was enormous, and its specific linkage of an authoritarian personality to right-wing political attitudes and behaviors spurred further research. Hundreds of scholarly pieces, many using the F scale in all of its subsequent variants, followed. The Berkeley Study supported the position of Lasswell and others who had argued for the importance of psychology to political attitudes and behavior.

There was little in *The Authoritarian Personality*, however, that dealt with a full spectrum of psychological traits. Though its findings encouraged the development of a political theory based on an understanding of differentiated human natures, it did not provide sufficient data for a full-range, relativistic theory.

Before a psychologically relativistic theory of politics could be constructed, the difficulties that plagued the early psychology and politics literature, including *The Authoritarian Personality*, needed clearing up. Most important, there needed to be a description of the full range of personality differentiation. But criticisms beyond the methodological critiques also dogged *The Authoritarian Personality*. Critics contended, for example, that the Berkeley Study, as with so much of the authoritarian research that followed, failed to distinguish among two very different *kinds* of personality traits.[6] Hans Eysenck, a much-scarred veteran of the nature-nurture debate, argued that the growing literature on authoritarianism still did not make a crucial differentiation between what William James labeled "tough-minded" and "tender-minded" personality traits. Such traits, Eysenck argued, had little to do with differences in left-to-right political attitudes and behavior. Instead, Eysenck argued, they signaled how rigidly or flexibly different people held to their ideological views, regardless of what they were.[7]

Another researcher, Milton Rokeach, agreed that a second dimension of politically relevant traits existed.[8] He, too, felt that this set of traits did not correlate with traditional left-to-right ideological perspectives. Accordingly, he argued that a two-dimensional rather than a one-dimensional psychological map was needed. If one dimension depicted the correlations between psychology and left-to-right ideological orientations, the other, running roughly perpendicular to that spectrum, depicted what he called the "stylistic" dimension. In *The Open and Closed Mind,* Rokeach argued that such stylistic personality traits as rigidity, intolerance of ambiguity, and dogmatism represented the workings of the closed political mind. Such a state, Rokeach argued, was apparent whether that mind was affectively predisposed to ideologies on the right or on the left.

In response to the Berkeley Study, and particularly in response to the biased scoring of the F scale, Rokeach found that dogmatism, rigidity, and intolerance of ambiguity could exist anywhere along the left-to-right ideological spectrum. Rokeach, like Eysenck, added that such stylistic rigidities as "tough mindedness" existed more prominently at the extremes of the right to left political spectrum.[9] In essence, both Eysenck and Rokeach argued for a U-curve relationship of construct and style variables. A combination of the extremes of both left-to-right construct and exaggerated stylistic traits best describe the kinds of pathologies that Harold Lasswell, for example, had examined.

THE PSYCHOPOLITICAL SPECTRUM

A second substantive criticism that haunted *The Authoritarian Personality* noted that the authoritarian research dealt almost exclusively with the relationship of psychological traits and the political right. Some research had specifically investigated the linkage of psychological variables with left-wing political views, but none had attempted to discover whether a single, commensurable spectrum of authoritarian to nonauthoritarian psychological characteristics in the Bernsteinian sense corresponded to the left-right ideological spectrum in politics. A relationship between a full spectrum of psychological variables and a corresponding spectrum of left-to-right political attitudes needed to be clearly established before a psychologically relativistic theory of politics could be developed.

In 1956, Christian Bay's *The Structure of Freedom* began to define a personality that fit along such a full-range psychopolitical spectrum. Bay described a constellation of psychological traits that he labeled as "antiauthoritarian." Although he too relied on developmental, Freudian terminology, Bay suggested that his antiauthoritarian personality evidenced a reasonably permanent "defensive predisposition to oppose uncritically standards and commands supported by authorities." Bay depicted an antiauthoritarian as one who "sees all authorities as bad and wicked." The antiauthoritarian rejects the hierarchies of overstructured or stratified organizations, as well as clearly defined channels of political authority.[10]

Christian Bay's early definitions were instructive for my own early inquires. Though smaller in scope than the Berkeley Study, *The Anti-Authoritarian Personality* attempted to discover if Bay's psychopolitical linkage on the left fell within what Bernstein would call "commensurable" findings in tune with the authoritarian personality's conclusions on the psychopolitical right.[11] I tested for whether the precise reverse of the principal psychological traits of the *Authoritarian Personality*—specifically a *negative* orientation toward power, a *negative* orientation toward order, a *positive* orientation toward the expression of impulse, and a *positive* orientation toward introspection—correlated with left-wing political views.

Finding that personality traits that were conceptually opposed to authoritarian traits did in fact correlate with left-wing political positions (and also that the strength of these correlations increased as they moved toward the psychopolitical poles), I suggested that the full spectrum of affective authoritarian to antiauthoritarian traits correlated with the full spectrum of left-to-right political views. I tentatively concluded that at least with regard to affective traits, the development of a psychologically relativistic theory of politics, based on the full-range psychological spectrum that *The Authoritarian Personality* and *The Anti-Authoritarian Personality* defined, was possible.

THE COGNITIVE VARIABLE

As I mentioned earlier, affective traits will be of some significance for a relativistic theory of politics, but cognitive traits will be more important. The suggested linkage of the spectrum of affective psychological traits with the spectrum of left-to-right political ideology did not, of course, address the relationship of cognitive psychological traits to political attitudes and behaviors. If the differentiation between Kant's and Hegel's definitions of the analytic and synthetic cognitions are to underpin a relativistic theory of politics, then the analytic-synthetic cognitive distinction needs as much empirical verification as did the affective authoritarian-antiauthoritarian distinction.

Beyond the need for the verification of a cognitive differentiation, however, evidence is also needed for the idea that psychological preferences for the analytic or the synthetic cognition fall along a commensurable psychological spectrum. If Hegel's omission in fact does bridge the gap between both Kant's and Hegel's cognitive distinctions as well as the psychologies that underlie different cognitions, then a relativistic theory must describe that full range, analytic-to-synthetic, cognitive differentiation. In addition, of course, it would be useful if the full spectrum of cognitive traits existed in rough parallel to the spectrum of affective traits. If both of these conditions are met, then an understanding of the range of differences among how people both feel and think would certainly further a relativistic theory.

The early writings of Jung described cognitive differences and accurately predicted the results of subsequent empirical work on cognitive differentiation. One of the most convincing confirmations of Jung's cognitive differentiations came from the research of Herman Witkin. Witkin's findings in *Personality Through Perception* grew out of a variety of perceptual tests that demonstrated how some cognitions relied more strongly than others on a clear definition of the structure of the environment.[12] Witkin demonstrated that some individuals needed a far clearer delineation of what it is that they were attempting to understand than did others. *Forms* of understanding, or the cognitive casements in which understandings are couched, are different for different persons.

Witkin's research was significant for its methodology and for its description of the relative psychological need for cognitive clarity. His studies, not based on either survey research or on such faulty, intrusive techniques as those used in *The Authoritarian Personality,* included such creative clinical techniques as the rod-and-frame test (a stick tilted in various directions within a frame that may or may not be level with the floor); the tilting-chair test (an assessment of the angle of wall figures in a darkened room as seen from an upright or tilted chair); and the rotating-room test (an alteration of a perceptual environment in relation to an observed object). All of these tests required the subject to arrive at a judgment concerning the true location of a visual object. Each test noted the degree to which a subject was either more dependent or less dependent on external definitional cues in the assessment of that object's location.[13]

Beyond the above techniques, however, Witkin developed what he labeled an embedded-figure test. This instrument, recalling Kurt Lewin's notions of field theory, differentiated between what Witkin called "field dependence" and "field independence."[14] The test required the subject to locate a simple figure or design within the context of a complex and purposively confusing configuration of other designs. As Witkin predicted, the test separated those who took a longer time to locate the hidden figure from those who found the figure more quickly. The text, Witkin suggested, distinguished once again between those who were either more dependent on the field that surrounded the figure and those who took a shorter time and were thus judged to be less field dependent.

The ability to cognitively differentiate was central to Witkin's experimental findings in the embedded-figures test. Witkin, however, concluded that the ability to readily locate a hidden figure within a morass of confused markings was the result of being cognitively more predisposed toward variables of a dissimilar nature. Accordingly, the relative inability to locate the hidden figure among the surrounding lines existed among subjects who were less cognitively predisposed toward qualitatively dissimilar variables.

The cognitive differentiation between an affinity for similar or dissimilar variables as Witkin described it is much the same as the differentiation among analytic and synthetic cognitions that Hegel described in his discussion of Kant's equation. The Kantian preference for similar variables contrasted with Hegel's preference for "the explication of differences" in a way that reflects a relative preference for the similar or the dissimilar cognitive qualities that Witkin tested.

If Herman Witkin's findings are to be useful in the development of a psychologically relativistic theory of politics, his linkage of relative cognitive preferences to differentiated performances on a variety of functional tasks is hardly adequate. But Witkin's research is useful to a relativistic theory for at least two additional reasons. First, although Witkin did not consider the theoretical implications of his work within the context of political attitudes and behaviors, he clearly understood that his cognitive differentiations existed along a spectrum and not within two discrete categories. Throughout his findings, Witkin dealt with *ranges* of cognitive responses, ranges which described a full, commensurable spectrum of cognitive preferences. These cognitive preferences are as available to a relativistic theory of politics as the full spectrum of affective traits described by the authoritarian-antiauthoritarian personality findings.

Beyond the development of his cognitive spectrum, however, Witkin understood that his descriptions of cognitive differentiations would be reinforced if the cognitive range were parallel to the affective range of the authoritarian-to-antiauthoritarian personality. Again, Witkin was not directly concerned with the political implications of his findings, but the fact that his affective and his cognitive test scores correlated strongly within those groups that had undergone both his perceptual regimens and a variety of affective trait tests is significant.[15] Subjects who scored as field dependent on the embedded-figures test almost invariably scored higher on affective tests for such things as the repression of impulse and extroversion. Those who scored as field independent on the perceptual tests conversely scored as both more introspective and as more prepared to express their impulses.[16] Field independent cognitions were consistently found to be closer to the antiauthoritarian pole of the affective spectrum. Field dependent cognitions were closer to the authoritarian pole. Writing in the wake of *The Authoritarian Personality*, Witkin's spectrum of field dependent-to-field independent cognitions fully described the cognitive spectrum that a psychologically relativistic theory must build on. Witkin's evidence of the intrapersonality parallels between the principal affective and cognitive spectra only further encourage the development of such a theory.

A good deal of subsequent research on human cognition has confirmed Herman Witkin's conclusions. More recent research has also displayed an awareness of the potential theoretical implications of knowing the full cognitive range. Perhaps the most perceptive researcher with regard to the theoretical implications of what he worked on was the psychologist Joseph R. Royce. Like Oswald Spengler, Royce recognized early on that "the question of knowledge is inextricably bound up with the question of reality and meaning." Royce understood that it was "what and how we know" things that was at the core of our perception of the world. In determining what and how we know things, Royce believed that our "epistemic styles" were "key manifestations of what we are."[17]

Royce, along with other cognitive psychologists and philosophers, was pleased that the 1960s exhibited a revival of interest in human cognition. Royce wrote that "as the decade of the sixties unfolded, it became increasingly apparent that the psychological study of epistemology might not be the 'irrelevant' philosophic side trip [that] it looked like in the midfifties."[18] Royce also commented on what he called "the many manifestations of a paradigm shift toward a more cognitive psychology." He saw such a shift as evidence of "a greater willingness on the part of contemporary psychology to form alliances with philosophy."[19] Royce sensed that what he called a "new interdisciplinary field" was emerging. He was hopeful that what he described as an "epistemological psychology," that is, a psychology that focused on *"processes of knowing"* (emphasis his) rather than substantive theories of knowledge, would result.[20]

Royce's work is deservedly well-known and respected. In many ways, it parallels what a variety of researchers, working in very different fields, were finding. Royce himself was aware of a variety of crossdisciplinary parallels and frequently cited the findings of the cultural historian Pitirim Sorokin and the neuropsychologist Carl Pribram, for example, as supportive of his own conclusions.[21] He noted particularly that Sorokin's sense of cultural cycles revolved around definitions of 'sensate," that is, material, as opposed to "ideational" societies. In a similar way, Royce cited Carl Pibram's understanding of the neural roots of his polar cognitive concepts and their relationship to typical understandings of "induction" and "deduction." These terms mirrored Royce's shorthand for the cognitive factors of "symbolizing" and "thinking" that demarked his own polar positions.[22]

In recent years, the importance of the cognitive dimension within psychological research has been confirmed many times over. The contemporary psychologist Howard Gardner, in spite of his preference for a typology of multiple cognitive predispositions, still emphasized the qualities of "two cognitive styles in normal individuals."[23] Those styles contrasted people who exploited what are often thought of as "right hemisphere processes" as "somewhat more humanistically oriented" and people who exploited "left hemisphere processes" as "more sober, scientific or 'straight'."[24]

Gardner, though again primarily concerned with the multiple intelligences that he thinks we all have, concedes that what has been missing in so much of what has been written on psychology "is a recognition of the ways in which . . . individuals within a culture can still differ significantly from one another."[25] Psychological differences, with due regard for the importance of certain Piagetian universals that have an impact on all human development, and with due regard for the impact of the culture with which each personality interacts, provides a middle ground of perspective for Gardner.[26]

All of the above suggests that modern, experimentally based depictions of the principal, commensurable spectrum of normal human psychologies demonstrate the great theoretical importance of the analytic-synthetic distinction. In its proper theoretical context, I think that this cognitive spectrum, along with its parallel affective spectrum, best fills in Hegel's omission. It also best describes the differences between Kant's and Hegel's own cognitive preferences, as those preferences represent ideal types in the metaphysical arguments over cognition itself and cognition's role in metaphysics.

RELATIVISM AND THE EPISTEMOLOGICAL DEBATE

If the above research and commentary on human cognitive relativities provides the basis for a psychologically relativistic theory of politics, then the psychological differentiations that I have reviewed over the last pages may, with caution, be linked to understandings of differentiated political attitudes and behavior. But something is still missing: the evidence that would link the psychological spectrum to the specifics of the way that citizens feel and think about politics. Part Two below describes the cognitive structure of a variety of politically relevant concerns within the context of the American political system. But in my own testing of the proposition of whether the psychological spectrum is related to political attitudes and behaviors, I thought it best to first examine whether the psychological spectrum described above has in fact accounted for ranges of attitudes within a variety of intellectual concerns.

In a book that attempted to describe the importance of cognitive differentiations within the history of Western thought, I researched the cognitive nature of the principal epistemological debates within both metaphysics and a number of the social sciences. *Relativism and the Natural Left* demonstrated, I think, that the principal epistemological debates of a variety of intellectual areas in fact did reflect the cognitive differentiations discussed above.[27]

Something very significant for a psychological theory of politics happened in the evolution of Western thought. What happened, I think, was that a fission occurred within both what had been the classical rational and the classical skeptical metaphysical positions, a fission that reflected the cognitive differentiations that already existed within each of the two grand, rational and skeptical, schools. What also happened was that by the late eighteenth century and early nineteenth century, the two grand classical schools of metaphysics realigned themselves according to their cognitive affinities. A fusion occurred, in other words, along cognitive lines.

Although it is frequently overstated, it is generally fair to say that within meatphysics, the classical rationalist position contained a differentiation between the essentially organic view of Plato and the somewhat more mechanistic view of Aristotle. That difference was in large part a cognitive difference. Similarly, within the classical skeptical school, a contrast existed between the bearing of a figure like Protagoras and a figure like Thrasymachus. In the skeptical divide too, the differentiation was largely cognitive. Thrasymachus's argument, for example, showed a cognitive predisposition for the qualitatively similar variable in such positions as its demand for a "clear and concise statement" from Socrates on the question of political authority. That position contrasted significantly with the Protagoran form of skepticism, wherein Protagoras suggested that man should be "the measure of all things." Though both positions were broadly skeptical, Protagoras attacked the rationalists for prescribing an overordered world, whereas Thrasymachus attacked the rationalists for not requiring enough order. Cognitively, they represent polar positions.

What has happened through the centuries of Western thought, again, is that a fission, a cognitively differentiated fission, occurred. But, in the long strain of Western thought, the fission of the rational and the skeptical position resulted in a metaphysical realignment that was consistent with the cognitive differentiations of, among others, Kant and Hegel. Note that the differentiated metaphysical positions of these two figures do not reflect a pure affinity or lack of affinity for a rationalist or a skeptical view. Kant's more vigorous skepticism was tempered by a strong, transcendental, moral rationalism. Hegel's gentler skepticism was tempered by a historically developing metaphysical rationalism. The differences in their positions reflected different kinds of cognitions.

Relativism and the Natural Left, which tested a relativistic perspective on the course of Western intellectual history, amply demonstrated that the differentiation between the analytic and the synthetic cognitions of Kant and Hegel have now emerged as the principal benchmarks of the Western metaphysical divide. The Kantian and Hegelian positions, I suggest, are still the broad umbrella of the epistemological debate that underlies so much of the Western metaphysical argument.[28]

In an attempt to confirm the above, *Relativism and the Natural Left* examined the epistemological debates within the principal fields of social science. It argued that just as the writings of Kant and Hegel marked the realization of cognitively relativistic perspectives on metaphysics, a cognitively based realignment of the epistemological argument within social-science fields emerged in the modern period as well. In law, for example, the struggle between the *verum* of the law, or the legal inclusion of philosophical values that underlie principles of justice and equity, now contrasts clearly with an emphasis on the *certum* of the law, or the requirement that law be internally consistent and predictable before it is anything else.[29] Latter-day natural-law writers like Lon Fuller, who chastised the legal positivists for never "letting the green fields of life lure them from the gray path of logic," evidence the *verum* view of law.[30] Fuller, of course, was responding to the positivists who were the cognitive heirs to John Austin and Jeremy Bentham as well as to Austin's

and Bentham's intellectual predecessor, Immanuel Kant. Kant's jurisprudential position could not be better expressed than by his wish to "make
completeness my chief aim" in the law.[31]

Within the discipline of economics, the preference for the qualitatively
similar variables of price theory, for example, as well as the acceptance
of the importance of microeconomics generally, contrasts cognitively
with the qualitatively dissimilar variable perspectives of Joan Robinson,
G. L. S. Schackle, and others who have criticized economics' epistemological narrowness.[32] Those who descended from the marginal utility
theorists like Walras, Menger, and Jevons have drawn criticisms from
Sherman R. Krupp and others concerning the "scope" of the discipline
and the degree to which noneconomic "affairs" are to be studied as part
of the "spectrum of human concerns."[33] As with law, the inclusion or
the noninclusion of the qualitatively dissimilar variable correlates predictably with the degree of cognitive preference for such variables.

Within sociology, the plea for a normative science in the work of
Georg Simmel and contemporary writers like Ralf Dahrendorf contrasts
with the positivism of Max Weber and the even more rigid positivism of
Emile Durkheim and modern, quantitively oriented sociologists.[34] Anthropology, too, reveals a clear cognitive differentiation between the
early, culturally relativistic work of Ruth Benedict, Melville Herskovits,
and Margaret Mead and the quantitative methodologies of the logical
positivists and the Vienna Circle as well as the English positivists.[35] The
culturally relativistic authors preferred to deal with what Franz Boas
called the "just noticeable differences" among peoples, while the positivists clearly preferred the collection and assimilation of fungible social-
science data.[36]

In sum, I believe that *Relativism and the Natural Left* supports the
notion that differences in the ways that relative psychologies have preferred to think about epistemological questions across several disciplines
are essentially similar. These differences have not been restricted to
various intellectual fields, as Herbert Simon has improperly suggested.
Further, the evidence of preferences for either qualitatively similar or
qualitatively dissimilar variables is itself similar to the preferences for
the analytic cognition and the synthetic cognition that Kant and Hegel
exemplified. If there is a degree of permanence to the relativity of human
psychologies, and I believe that there is, and if the psychological relativity that I have described satisfies the theoretical requirement for a static

understanding of human psychologies, then Hegel's omission of relative psychologies within the context of mediation, of the dialectic, and of the progress of understanding or history requires an understanding of psychological relativism to rectify it.

Incidentally, in recent years some social science research has centered around what is called schema theory. Those who have written on schema theory have concerned themselves with cognitions, broadly defined, and to a degree they have developed their own sense of the differences among cognitions. Unfortunately, however, schema theory's purpose of understanding those differences is usually devoted to the finding of objective truth rather than the finding, and ultimately the balancing, of different subjective perspectives on truth. Michael A. Arbib has described both the "coherence and [the] conflicts within a schema network" as part of a static view of personality, but that attention to coherence and conflict is still centered on an allegedly objective reality. There are faint understandings of personality difference within such schema-theory writings as Arbib's, but a theory of relativity, based on commensurable differences in cognitions, must go beyond a mere "understanding of the diversity of value systems" and "how they interact and how they may change."[37]

In closing, let me restate my belief that the only appropriate epistemological perspective on the above considerations of relative cognitions or relative states of the mind is the perspective of a moderate skepticism and of a robust epistemological idealism. Only an understanding of how different people's imposition of meaning on politics denies the existence of an objective, rational reality within politics, along with an understanding of how different personalities propel history, can permit a psychologically relativistic theory of politics to exist. As Hegel prescribed for it, the idealist position places the mind first and battles toward rationality from a position of Kantian skepticism. Important though the apparent realities of the world seem to be, minds impose meaning on cultures, economic arrangements, politics, and the like. If the arguments of postmaterial politics in fact reflect the primary relativistic spectrum of known and bounded human cognitions, then a psychologically relativistic theory of politics should now be able to build itself on that spectrum.

Chapter Four

HEGEL AND THE DECLINE OF THE IDEAL

POLITICS AND THE DIALECTIC

Two issues concerning Hegel and the development of a relativistic political theory need further clarifying. First, Hegel's intellectual position, and particularly his writings on cognition, needs to be placed into its appropriate political context. Second, Karl Marx's revisions of Hegel, which not only did not mark any further progress toward the development of a relativistic perspective but in fact retarded progress in that direction, need to be examined carefully.

Hegel's epistemological perspective, described in the *Logic* though evidenced in the earlier *Phenomenology*, was clearly idealistic. It is still the finest exemplar of the mind-first notion of causation and response to the historical challenge. Ironically, however, Hegel's work also signaled idealism's demise in the practical, postivistic, nineteenth century. Hegel's writings were followed by a dramatic shift in epistemological orientation toward the materialistic assumption. That shift must be reversed before a theory based on a relativity of human psychologies can emerge.

As Walter Kaufmann has argued, the writings of Hegel forged a unity that carries into his last major work.[1] In his most political writing, *The Philosophy of Right,* Hegel's perspectives on mediation, the dialectic, and the progress of history were placed into their appropriate political context. In *The Philosophy of Right,* Hegel reviewed the prepolitical and political considerations that are necessary for what he called the "ethical state."[2] Though much of that work is not of particular importance today, at least for its substantive position, it is of great importance for its attempt, not always successful, at placing epistemological idealism into politics.

At one level, *The Philosophy of Right* is a traditional political tract. It is a collection of attentions to roughly the same institutional and procedural matters that political philosophers have always written about. At another level, however, it is a unique piece, in part because of its prescient considerations of the middle class, the bourgeois state, and the approaching modernity of the early nineteenth century. More significant, however, is the *Philosophy of Right*'s concern with the political mind. It is, more than any work of political philosophy, not simply a lecture on the considerations of politics, but a lecture on how one should think about politics. The synthetic cognition, as one would expect, is dominant throughout.

Hegel's notions of the political role of the synthetic cognition brought a certain unity to Hegel's political argument. That unity, however, reflected nothing like a relativistic perspective. At the outset of *The Philosophy of Right*, Hegel defined the primary issue of government as a matter of the individual within a larger, inexorably political world. Predictably, that self began in Hegel's *Phenomenology* with the gift of self-consciousness.[3]

The seeing of oneself as part of the world was a beginning which eventually reached, as Hegel explained it in the *Phenomenology*, beyond simple sensory consciousness. Self-consciousness required recognition of the human desire or spirit. *The Philosophy of Right*, appropriately, depicted the citizen as far more than a human spirit who lived solely at the first stage of the dialectic or as a thing in itself. Each being could, or at least should, live through the other stages of the dialectic. Each citizen's life should be lived both for itself and finally in and for itself within the ascending human consciousness.

Hegel's political dialectic, of course, included the dialectical contradiction in its political context. The dialectic saw the political individual as naturally in opposition to the universal of the state. Only by introspectively looking back on oneself could an individual overcome that contradiction. Hegel wished for the creative consciousness that links each citizen to history to flower out of that contradiction's resolution.[4]

For Hegel, the cognitive process that brought that flowering to the political world was, again, the synthetic cognition. In his preface to *The Philosophy of Right*, Hegel, without hesitation, dismissed the "forms and rules of the old logic, of definition, classification and syllogism, which include the rules of discursive thinking." Still borrowing from the

Logic, Hegel believed that these old and inhibitive rules had long "been recognized as inadequate for speculative science." With specific reference, saying that "since I have fully expounded the nature of speculative knowing in my *Science of Logic,*" he attacked those, like Kant, who would not take the speculative view. Puckishly, he offered that "we may of course hear from those who seem to be taking a profound view that the form is something external and indifferent to the subject-matter.[5]

Hegel's early political prescriptions took a predictably dialectical form. Specifically, his sense of the contradiction in a political context was properly embedded in the dialectic's logic. To Hegel, "external" thinking was never more than a limited thing. Rather, Hegel defined "the basis of right" as "in general, mind," and he condemned what he called "the old method of cognition" as a procedure that "was extracted, in the manner of the old empirical psychology." The progress of politics, he argued, could therefore only grow "from the various feelings and phenomena of the ordinary consciousness, such as remorse, guilt and the like."[6] There is, of course, no relativity within such a consciousness.

Hegel knew that cognition went beyond remorse, guilt, and the like. In his attempt at reconciling the in itself with the for itself, or in his attempt at transcending the mind-body distinction in a manner that was far easier for him than for Kant, he referred again to his *Encyclopedia.* He wrote, quite prophetically, that "scarcely any philosophical science is so neglected and so ill off as the theory of mind, usually called 'psychology.'"[7]

In discussing governments and their institutional arrangements in relation to the mind, and the political forms that would best maintain the historical progress of understanding, thereby continuing political progress, Hegel first argued that politics should be organic. Politics must emulate nature or at least be in a place wherein "nature's eternal harmony" was evident. This eternal harmony must be evident "in the sense of the law and [the] essence immanent within it."[8]

Essence was overwhelmingly subjective for Hegel. It too was a matter of the mind and, to further the contradiction, Hegel argued that essence must be contrasted to existence. It must be contrasted to the external "ethical world" or, eventually, to the state that is "not allowed to enjoy the good fortune which springs from the fact that it is reason which has achieved power and mastery within that element."[9]

It is reason, therefore, that must be brought to government, just as it is reason that must be brought to Hegel's broader notion of the ethical state. To do that, one must know what "lies between reason as self-conscious mind and reason as an actual world before our eyes." One must, in particular, know "what separates the former from the latter and prevents it from finding satisfaction in the latter." Reason, in this sense and in a sense that is very different from Kant's, is "reason as speculative knowing." Further, "content is reason as the substantial essence of actuality, whether ethical or natural." For Hegel, as we would expect, "The known identity of these two (ethical and natural) is the philosophical Idea."[10] Only through the Idea can the speculative perspective, which in turn moves from natural to ethical political harmony, be attained.

Profound though Hegel's introductory political commentary may be, the overbearing influence of the synthetic cognition in Hegel's dialectic, or Hegel's failure to link his analytic and synthetic cognitions to different human psychologies, caused Hegel to make no differentiation among all who hold a political will. Presumably, when Hegel described how the political "Right" was to be brought into fulfillment, he argued that the Right would be fulfilled only "through the [entire] particular national character of a people."[11] That national character is never differentiated and, though Hegel's political writings surely distinguished the national character of one people from another, they never distinguished among subjectivities within one objective state.

There was, of course, a historical relativity, as distinguished from a psychological relativity, within each nation's progress for Hegel. As he put it, each nation periodically achieved a different "stage of historical development."[12] The Hegelian historical development inevitably led to what Hegel called "the universal concept"[13] as it was adapted to "particular, externally given characteristics of objects and cases."[14] Again, cultural and historical relativism existed for Hegel; psychological relativism did not.

One overriding theme in Hegel's *Philosophy of Right* is the dialectical tension between the particular and the universal. In dealing with the problem of the self within the larger world, Hegel said simply that "every self-consciousness knows itself (i) as universal, as the potentiality of abstracting from everything determinate, and (ii) as particular, with a determinate object, content and aim."[15] Hegel still did not acknowledge anything like psychological relativism in his discussion, but the psychology, or more specifically the cognition, of his own linkage between the particular and the universal could not be clearer. As it is the "will or that part of psychology which is not formal logic" that finds itself "in the abstract opposition of its subjectivity of external immediate existence," so too it is the "will" that finds "its purpose actualized and achieved by means of the activity of translating its subjective purpose and objectivity." [16]

The cognitive process that achieves this form of actualization is what Hegel called "the task of logic as purely speculative philosophy." [17] By the adoption of this speculative process, according to Hegel, "man discovers within himself as a 'fact of consciousness' that right, property, the state &c., are objects of his volition." [18] As is often the case with Hegel, this speculation is only achievable through the synthetic cognition. Also, the synthetic cognition is very much a universal notion, at one point Hegel criticizing Jean Jacques Rousseau who Hegel said wrote of the "will of a single person in his own private self-will, not mind as it is in its truth." Predictably, Hegel argued that Rousseau's "view is devoid of any speculative thinking and is repudiated by the philosophic concept." [19] Political speculation for Hegel, as well as all of the progress that comes from it, therefore, must follow the prescription of Hegel's *Logic*. This prescription, again, incorporates the universal usage of the synthetic cognition.

HEGEL AND POLITICAL UNIVERSALIZATION

Hegel's rich notion of philosophical speculation has always given his political writings their naggingly totalitarian political tinge. When Hegel wrote that "the will is the universal, because all restrictions and all particular individuality have been absorbed within it," he gave the Carl Friedrichs and Karl Poppers among his modern-day critics an opportunity for an interpretation that left little of individuality outside the state.[20] Although Hegel did not mean it literally, his statement on universality, particularly in the context of a discussion of Abstract Right, does say that "individuals and nations have no personality until they have achieved . . . pure thought and knowledge of themselves." [21] Hegel granted a degree of political protection to the individual personality wherein the "capacity for right [thus] constitutes the concept and the bases . . . of the system of abstract and therefore formal right." But he promptly reverted to the universal conclusion that the "particularity of the will is [but] a moment in the consciousness of the will as a whole."[22]

For Hegel, therefore, "there is no question of particular interests, of my advantage or my welfare, any more than there is of the particular motive behind my volition, of insight and intention" in the universal state.[23] This, of course, is not the language of the particular, or the self, much less the language of a balancing of differentiated selves. Hegel borrowed generously from his metaphysical writings in his work on politics. His preference for the synthetic cognition in applying mediation, the dialectic, and the progress of history to politics is consistent throughout. In doing so, however, Hegel argued that political progress was achieved only through a compiling of individuated qualities into a universalized, ethical state. He argued this even in his discussions of such typically individualistic notions as property and contract, purposefully distinguishing his view from bourgeois notions, which dealt only with the externals or objectivities of political things.

Another political impact comes from Hegel's psychological preference for the synthetic cognition. Hegel's preference, of course, had had an impact on both the sweep of the ideational history that was confirmed in his *Phenomenology,* as well as the form of thinking utilized in his *Logic.* But Hegel also wished to incorporate his mediation of the mind and object in the *Encyclopedia* into his view of history. He knew that he could only create a dialectical understanding of human progress if his description of the resolution of each dialectical tension was imprinted on the political tension between the particular and the universal.

It seems that Hegel's oft-repeated political assertion that the particular could only be realized through the universal was consistently a matter of the second or contradictory stage of the dialectic for him. But as that contradiction, in politics as in metaphysics, could only be achieved by the synthetic cognition, it was therefore only that cognition, as it incorporated the qualitatively dissimilar variables of the particular and the universal, that fostered the dialectic in its political context.

Hegel's almost exclusive utilization of the cognitive form of the second stage of the dialectic, or his insistence on the political need to bring the thing in itself into confrontation with the thing for itself, was translatable in politics into a contradiction between the condition of the individual mind and the condition of an evolving ethical state. Hegel argued correctly that the synthetic cognition and its corresponding political position favors the facing of the qualitatively differentiated and as yet unconfronted political difficulty. This is what moves political history. Hegel's "explication of differences" in the *Logic,* put into its political context, requires the political confrontation with the routinized political understanding. Hegel's preference for engaging in the qualitatively dissimilar cognition assures historical confrontation with each significant political issue as it comes along.

Appropriately, of course, each such issue in the Hegelian political tradition is made up of a different cognitive *form.* Hegel argued that Kant's analytic cognition, the cognition of the similar variable, was not able to understand the form of any novel, more complex, political understanding. Most important, he argued that the analytic cognition was not able to resolve the historical contradiction that led to the new political understanding through the synthetic cognition and the dialectic. The state that adapts to the repeated facing of the contradiction, through the synthetic cognition for Hegel, will of course have a better chance of transcending history's crises.

HEGEL AND THE STATE

Hegel used both the analytic and the synthetic cognitions in his prescriptions for politics, but his bias in favor of the synthetic cognition, along with his omission of the linkage between relative cognitions and relative human psychologies, I believe, impedes the creation of a standard of psychological equity within the Hegelian mode. To be sure there were attempts at institutional and other political balances in Hegel's *Philosophy of Right.* In the matter of private property, for example, Hegel's cognitive preference for having each person "translate his freedom into an external sphere in order to exist as an Idea"[24] was balanced with the view that everyone "has as his substantive end the right of putting his will into any and everything and thereby making it his."[25] Yet Hegel invariably came down on the side of the synthetic cognition and its preference for the political universal, saying, "I hold property not merely by means of a thing and my subjective will, but by means of another person's will as well." He said that he would only hold it "in virtue of my participation in a common will."[26]

Hegel's preference for the reconciliation of the particular into the universal was not only evident in his view of property, but also in his view of ethics and the state. He said that "the right of individuals to be subjectively destined to freedom is fulfilled [only] when they belong to an actual ethical order."[27] For Hegel, that ethical order had three levels: (1) the family, (2) the civil society, and (3) the unity of the Constitution of the State.

The family represented what Hegel called "the immediate substantiality of the mind," Hegel asserting that the "self-consciousness of one's individuality within this unity as the absolute essence of oneself" resulted in one's being with the family "not as an independent person but as a member."[28] To sustain marriage as part of the necessity of the universal, Hegel said that persons must "renounce their natural and individual personality," as well as renounce the "identification of personalities, whereby the family becomes one person and its members become its accidents."[29] Aggregation within the family was the essence of the "the ethical mind" for Hegel.[30] What went on in marriage, or what went on in what Hegel described as an "ethical transaction," was similar in its absorption of the particular into Hegel's sense of an individual's appropriate relationship to civil society.[31]

Without differentiating among the perspectives of different individuals, Hegel described the "particular person" in civil society as "so related to other particular persons that each establishes himself and finds satisfaction by means of the others." With an unmistakable tinge of communitarianism, Hegel went on to argue that such satisfaction came into existence only "by means of the form of the universality."[32]

Aware of the incipient modernity of the nineteenth century, Hegel was aware as well of the new role of the burghers, the emerging German middle class. But he was frightened of the middle class because he saw it merely as a collection of private citizens "whose end [was only] in their own interest." To remedy the political atomization that he feared, Hegel wanted the burghers' interest to be "*mediated* through the universal which thus *appears* as a *means* to its realization" (emphasis his).[33] Hegel argued that only through such a mediation would a citizens' "singularity," as well as his "natural condition," be raised. It would be raised as a result of the necessities imposed by nature, as well as by things ranging from "arbitrary needs, to formal freedom and formal universality of knowing and willing."[34] With regard to such needs, Hegel placed the "satisfaction of subjective particularity" at a place that he called the "social moment."[35] This moment, most significantly, was the moment of the dialectical contradiction, the point at which the particular met the universal, and it was achieved, of course, through the synthetic cognition.

THE DESIGN OF HEGEL'S STATE

In Hegel's ethical state, the individual or the particular, as absorbed within the universal in the political progression of history, sought out the universal in dynamic ways. It did so in the form of the dialectic or by seeking the contradiction of the dissimilar variable at the second stage of the dialectic. Naturally, at the moment of each contradiction, the qualitatively dissimilar variable of history's newest challenge was to be both confronted and resolved. The political place for that confrontation and resolution was the place where "the actuality of the ethical Idea" occurred. It was the place where the singular "will manifest" was to be found, and it was where that singular "will manifest" was "absolutely rational inasmuch as it is the actuality of the substantial will which it possesses in the particular."[36] The singular will was thus only a "self-consciousness once that consciousness has been raised to conciousness of its universality."[37] Again, such a consciousness was never relative for Hegel. As a result, the state and the confrontation of its particular and universal contradiction was not relative either. As the state was "mind objectified," it was "only as one of its members that the individual himself has objectivity, genuine individuality and an ethical life."[38]

If Hegel's philosophical prescriptions for the particular and the universal, as well as his political prescriptions for the individual and the state, are aligned by the synthetic cognition throughout the governmental order and its march through history, the cognitive form of Hegel's prescriptions for specific governmental institutions is synthetic, too. Once again, Hegel's omission plays a deciding role in Hegel's political prescriptions, for as Hegel's absorption of the particular within the universal lacked relativity, Hegel offered that the task of building reason into the political world "has been the task of the world during the whole course of history."[39] Such a view of reason, of course, defines a particular kind of public institution.

The most vigorous criticisms of Hegel, the Friedrich and Popper kinds of criticisms, have centered around the overtly collective nature of Hegel's public perspective. Hegel's structural prescriptions were indeed collective, although they were not as collective as they at first appear. Hegel's prescription for government greatly reflected the influence of Montesquieu, and his governmental design depicted a well dispersed, three-cornered government, complete with its full measure of separated powers.

But Montesquieu's influence on Hegel was reflected in more than a separation of powers. Hegel recognized that "the constitution of any nation depends in general on the character and development of its self-consciousness." His design for a three-cornered government came as much from an expectation about the universalizing of an aggregative role as from a sense of how each public institution would play a balancing role among governmental institutions.[40] In keeping with Hegel's dialectical view of history, his political institutions were appropriately charged with furthering the achievement of the universal among the particular, as well as furthering the progress of history toward the ethical state.

In Hegel's political design, for example, the first institution, the Crown, was the essence of the state's sovereignty placed in an appropriately idealistic framework. The Crown had as its principal charge the capturing of "the universal *thought* of the ideality" (emphasis his). With that charge, sovereignty was something that came into "existence only as subjectivity sure of itself."[41] As a result, the allocation of power to the Crown "concerns the absolute universality which subsists subjectively in the conscience of the monarch and objectively in the whole of the constitution and the laws."[42]

The second institution of government, the executive, was charged consistently with the Crown with the "power to subsume single cases and the spheres of particularity under the universal."[43] Declaring the "circles of particular interests [to be] subordinated to the higher interests of the state," Hegel concluded that "the state's universal interest, and of legality, in this sphere of particular rights [are] require[d] to be superintended by holders of the executive power."[44]

The third principal institution, the legislature, was granted the least important governmental role. The legislature, according to Hegel, must only be able to "determine and establish the universal," a task that Hegel recognized as requiring a direct participation of the Estates.[45] Valuable as they are "as a mediating organ," therefore, the Estates existed only in order to represent "the subjective moment in universal freedom."[46] This was surely a collective moment. But that moment was to come into existence only as it was "integrally related to the state." As the "organic unity of the powers of the state itself implies that it is one single mind," this mind "firmly establishes the universal."[47]

It is clear from Hegel's description of the legislature, as well as from his description of the remainder of the governmental order, that Hegel understood the process of the universalization of the particular in a historical way. Hegel never perceived that the questions of *to what degree* the particular should be made a part of the universal, nor to what degree the personal self might gather property or even be part of a marriage, would be different for different citizens.

In retrospect, the difficulty with Hegel's political prescription is not only that particulars are inevitably absorbed into universals. The difficulty is that though the mind was to be the instrument of progress, the real world pathway to the absorption of those particulars, or of subjective freedom in a political society, wound its way through the collectivizing Estates. With the Estates alone, Hegel said, was there a "guarantee of the general welfare and public freedom." Although he said that "the highest civil servants necessarily have a deeper and more comprehensive insight into the nature of the state's organization and requirements," Hegel maintained that deputies of the Estates possessed what he called an *"additional* insight" (emphasis his). This insight, rather than the insight of their differentiated, individual members, would allow the Estates to understand "the more pressing and more specialized needs and deficiencies which are directly in their view."[48] Only in this way was there any small concession to particularities in the forming of the collective or the universal.

If there was only one place, the Estates, through which particularities could mold the Hegelian governmental design, then the evolving universality of the ethical state left only a small place for subjective freedom. Once more, disagreement over the degree to which subjective freedom should exist within the ethical state had no place in Hegel's political prescriptions. Hegel did not comprehend how there might be differences over how much subjective freedom should be allowed. I argue that Hegel did not comprehend the possibility of these differences, at least in part, because he did not comprehend the psychological origin of such differences. Hegel assumed that political progress, as a part of dialectical progress toward the understandings that propelled it, was invariably a matter of the "single, ordered whole" march to the political universal. As reason, or the Absolute Spirit that propelled history, was singular in its political design, it could afford to rely exclusively on the synthetic cognition.

In sum, Hegel's nonunderstanding of psychological differentiation, along with his political imbalance between an individual's and a state's interests, is most evident in Hegel's structural prescriptions. Hegel's particular cognitive preference, his own synthetic mind, is radiantly clear throughout his political prescriptions. Hegel's perspective on both the tensions among institutions of government and the tensions among interests in the larger society come down to nothing more than what for Hegel was a *necessary* reconciliation of individual interests in the state.

Hegel's epistemological perspective foreclosed his coming to a relativistic political theory or to any theory that would balance the imposed meanings of political reality and, in the first instance, design public institutions according to a balance among cognitive preferences. Even before the Marxian revisions, Hegel's intellectual design precluded a relativistic, psychologically balanced theory of politics. What Marx did to further deter the development of a relativistic perspective is what I will turn to next.

THE ROAD TO MARX

Hegel's last writing, composed in the wake of the July Revolution of 1830, not surprisingly decried the encroaching liberalism of the early nineteenth century. Hegel denounced the Revolution and, for good measure, denounced Peel and the English Reform Bill that the British Parliament went on to adopt in 1832, the year following Hegel's death. What has often been labeled as a later-life conservatism in Hegel was little more than an extension of Hegel's lifelong fear of bourgeois social atomism. It was a legitimate fear of that social, and ultimately political, disassembling that as Hegel predicted, has typified the liberal age.

The road to Marx as it led from Hegel, explaining why the Marxian revision of Hegel's dialectic further precludes a relativistic perspective, begins with the fate of the idealistic epistemological perspective of Hegel. Something fundamental happened to that epistemology under the materialistic revisions of Ludwig Feuerbach, Arnold Ruge, Søren Kierkegaard and, finally, Karl Marx. The overthrow of the idealist perspective was no mean accomplishment. It took years to achieve, and it happened only because of a deeply rooted attack on the metaphysical foundations of idealist epistemology. But it did happen.

In its infancy, the nineteenth-century materialistic epistemological perspective as it was propounded by Feuerbach and others deprecated Hegel's skeptical but aspiringly rational position on the very availability of mediation, or knowledge. Such a determination, of course, had been central to Hegelian and idealist thought, Hegel defining mediation in order to discover what Karl Löwith has described as the "mid-point" between subject and object.[49] This midpoint, as explained in Hegel's *Enclyclopedia,* attempted to ease the barrier between mind and body. It sought to bridge what lay "between the internal and the external."[50]

The materialistic epistemology, in contrast to the idealistic, describes a world made up of the sensual self alone. Whereas Hegel witnessed the idea as the process of the spirit or, in a corollary sense, as the process of that "dialectical movement of the spirit" that strives for Absolute knowledge, the materialists pondered only the real world causes and results of the dialectical process. The materialists wanted to know about the economic and political realities of what they claimed to be an objectively understandable world before they wanted to know anything else.[51]

Whether the existence of a psychologically based relativity within Hegel's idealistic perspective on mediation, the dialectic, or the progress of understanding would have forestalled the materialist revisions of Hegel can never be known. Hegel's singular, linear vision of historical progress, however, in keeping with his singular perspective on the final or Absolute stage of history, did not impede the ascendance of materialism.

The real world changed mightily in the nineteenth century, encouraging a political perspective that embraced the bourgeois, industrial class. It also brought forth the writings of those like Charles Fourier, Pierre Proudhon, Louis Blanc, and Ferdinand LaSalle, who spoke to the economic and political injustices of the new order. Before the criticism of that order could be detailed within a suitable intellectual framework, a revision of Hegel's idealistic epistemology was necessary. As a result of this need, Karl Löwith argues that "in place of Hegel's mediation, there appeared the demand for Christianity, God and the world, the internal and the external, being and existence."[52] All of these elements were seen in a more immediate and real-world context by the time of Marx and

Kierkegaard. Note that the above elements were all the product of material realities. They were not products of the mind.

Again, one cannot say whether an early appreciation of the relativity of skeptical perspectives or an early understanding of the relativity of how different minds impose meaning on the world would have forestalled the dismissal of epistemological idealism. Löwith, of course, does not address the issue of how an idealistic perspective, taken from the *combined* cognitions of Kant and Hegel, would have addressed the realities of the new industrial order. Löwith correctly reports, however, that, as a result of the nature of the then-current perspective on idealism, Hegel's cognitive prescriptions for mediation which relied on the superiority of the synthetic over the analytic cognition were lost.

Put simply, knowledge itself or, from a relativistic perspective, the matter of the cognitive balance of one *kind* of knowledge with another was never the burden of epistemological materialism. For materialism, the issue was a matter of existence, not essence, and that existence, as Löwith suggested, was for both Marx and for the Christian existentialist Kierkegaard a matter of something to be "realized." Of course, Marx sought to achieve his realization through the "brain of the proletariat," whereas Kierkegaard achieved his through the perspective of the "existential thinker."[53] But no matter the origin, the catalyst was existential. It was objectivist in the form of its own mediation and the Hegelian sense of mediation, and the Hegelian sense of cognition with its idealistic, mind first premise, was no part of it.

THE BREAK WITH HEGEL

At the beginning of the post-Hegel period, the materialistic path of departure from Hegel occurred along two distinct avenues. Roughly, the first was the path of the Young Hegelians, the second, the path of the Old Hegelians. The Old Hegelians were the right wing. They argued, in a Panglossian way, that the real was rational. Whatever existed in the world was the way the world should be.

The Young Hegelians were the left wing. Dissatisfied with things as they were, they argued that only the rational should be real. Their perspective on rationality, as the political left still generally views contemporary society, necessitated revision of the real. Löwith has argued that the concept of mediation or knowledge in Hegel, which sought a balance between mind on the one hand and existence or reality on the other, kept the place of the rational and the place of the real about even. Hegel's description of the rational, however, left him open to what Löwith labeled "dissolution." Dissolution was a kind of intellectual dismantling that originated in a very different perspective on the relationship of the real and the rational.[54] It should be no surprise that Feuerbach and Ruge, in the spirit of the Young Hegelians, found it so easy to alter Hegel's philosophy in order "to bring it into agreement with the spirit of the changing times."[55]

Of course it was Marx, in step with and in some ways marching ahead of his materialist predecessors, who drew what Löwith called "the extreme conclusions from the changed [real-world] situation."[56] Marx's emphasis was overwhelmingly on the immediate, and he left "the domain of the history of philosophy" for others. Western philosophy generally still feels the impact of that redirection.[57] Accordingly, as modern philosophy was to become only a product of theology (Kierkegaard), or as modern philosophy was to become only a handmaiden to the overthrow of the bourgeois order (Marx), these existential visions also became a part of the new epistemology. From then on, the role of the mind in metaphysics was preempted, and philosophy, as Löwith put it, evolved into only those things that were "tangible" and "finite."[58]

MARX, MATERIALISM, AND MEDIATION

We should not forget that the philosophical writings of Feuerbach, Ruge, and others did not by themselves initiate the erosion of Hegel's epistemological idealism. These writers, who attacked Hegel over the questions of knowledge, only followed the writings of Hegel's own students. These students, though concerned with abstract levels of understanding to some degree, began the pursuit of mediation, the dialectic, and the progress of history from a wholly different perspective only a few years after Hegel's death. Not viewing the dialectic as a matter of the contradiction of ideas, the vision of these students was never a vision of what Hegel knew as speculation. It was a philosophical, or dialectical, vision only in the sense of the contradiction that existed between any idea and any existing reality. Their dialectic, as a result, lost the perspective of Hegel's cognitive "explication of differences" that had challenged the then dominant (Kantian) analytic cognition. As it surrendered the kind of contradiction that grows out of different *forms* of ideas, it lost the synthetic cognition that was the catalyst to that contradiction in the beginning.

For Hegel's students, well before Marx, the principal contradiction was no longer a cognitively synthetic contradiction in its form. As it was only a contradiction between the ideal and the real, it was only concerned with "the 'real' state and with 'real' Christianity."[59] From this post-Hegelian perspective, the dialectic was principally used to show up the real or, at least, the perceived deficiencies of a newly industrialized world. Predictably, those deficiencies could not be placed into an exclusively intellectual, much less epistemologically idealistic, framework. They were placed, rather, into a relationship with what the real world could and eventually would become. Later, as both Marx and Kierkegaard argued that "the purpose of philosophy is to be realized," the post-Hegelian *form* of that realization, excluding the synthetic cognition, had already been made available to them by Hegel's own students.[60]

Karl Löwith has argued that the true nature of Hegel's mediation was such that the intellectual division between the rational and the real, or even the ideal and the real, was never as great as some have made it out. Just as there was more of a balance within Marx between essence and existence than vulgar Marxism acknowledges, so too there was a fairer balance between the mind and the real world within Hegel than has typically been attributed to him. Hegel was not a sterile metaphysician. He was concerned with the real world and, because of that concern, Löwith argued that "for Hegel, the [politically] conservative and the revolutionary components . . . were given equal weight."[61] Hegel's successors, just as Hegel had differed with Kant over the quality of mediation, differed with him over what the appropriate structures and procedures of the modern state should be. Their form of disagreement, however, their displacing of the contradiction of speculation into a contradiction between the rational and the real, had a monumental impact on the cognitive nature of the argument. Their differences turned back toward the only cognition that a contrast between the rational and the real requires—the analytic cognition. In insisting on seeing the contradiction as existing only between the rational and the real, or not seeing the contradiction as the speculative contradiction as Hegel had, Hegel's successors, almost certainly unwittingly, assured the dominance of the analytic cognition in the materialist dialectical form. In the matter of discovering the *form* of how one knows things, nothing could be known again in the synthetic cognitive context that Hegel had used.

Nonetheless, if the epistemological positions of Feuerbach, Ruge, and others were a significant, indeed necessary, prelude to Marx, it was still Marx who accounted for the thorough reversal of Hegel's epistemological idealism into a epistemological materialism. Lucio Colletti has said that Marx sought to unite "the worlds of sense and reason," whereas Hegel had only prescribed for the "identity of being and thought, or of the real and the rational."[62] Although the identity of the real and rational within Hegel was temporary at any one historical stage, it was, of course, subject to a process that was energized by a synthetic cognition and that brought about the ever-evolving realization of the rational within the real. Just as reason needed the qualitatively dissimilar variable in order to progress as an intellectual and not a real-world phenomenon in Hegel's hands, so too Marx's reason needed only the qualitatively similar variable for its progress.

Marx's reason was thus never, and never could be, a product of the synthetic cognition. As Marx criticized Hegel's use of reason for its only having made "the realm of empirical truth . . . into an internal moment of the Idea," Marx charged that in so reifying the Idea, Hegel's reason became "an absolute, self-sufficient reality."[63] In one sense, of course, Marx was correct. Reason, within the epistemologically idealistic mode, is self-sufficient. But what Marx did not consider was that in the progression of historical stages, reason required, and still requires, different *forms* of cognitions. As Marx would have had "the empirical world, which is the true subject" turned into an "external phenomenal form of the 'Idea,'" so too Marx, just as with Christianity and with Kierkegaard, would make the cognition of the materialist epistemology singular.[64] Marx's sense of reason does not invite, and indeed it cannot endure, the cognitively dissimilar variable that is at the core of the speculative Idea.

From a purely substantive perspective, it is only fair to remember that Marx's criticism of Hegel's epistemology no doubt prescribed for a healthy diversity of both a people and their enterprises within the real world. Those rich prescriptions of Marx, however, were only substantive, not epistemological. They were relevant at the historical place in which Marx was concerned with bourgeois property, fetishism, and the alienations that he discussed in *The Economic and Philosophical Manu-*

scripts and his other early writings. They were, no doubt, relevant at other historical times and are certainly still relevant today for when Marx spoke of the state, for example, he was justified in criticizing Hegel for proceeding "from the state and conceiv[ing] of man as [merely] the objectivized state."[65] But though this depiction is not an unreasonable one in light of Hegel's purely synthetic political prescriptions, it negates the importance of cognitive differentiation altogether in designing the intellectual framework of a better world. It does so in great part because it negates consideration of cognitions as such. It does so more certainly because it moves away from and not toward the nascent relativity that is contained in Hegel's understanding of cognition.

The dominance of the analytic cognition within Marx's dialectical prescriptions, indeed his tacit if not patent rejection of the very consideration of cognitions, is just as important to Marx's view of governmental structures as Hegel's singular cognitive assumptions were to his view of governmental structures. Marx specifically criticized the abstractions of Hegel's governmental prescriptions, particularly Hegel's assumption that the subjectivity of the state is characterized within the monarch.[66] "Hegel's purpose is [only] to narrate the life-history of abstract substance, of the Idea," he claimed.[67] He is not, for Marx, sufficiently concerned with reality.

Marx wanted more than narration and abstraction. As a consequence, the transposition of the subjective and the objective that Marx imposed on Hegel, with the attendant cognitive ramifications in favor of the analytic cognition, is evident within Marx's commentary on Hegel's governmental structures. His scolding of Hegel for the assumption of organic unity in governmental structures, something that Hegel "failed to justify logically," had Marx seeing Hegel as one who fled from "the genuine conflict between" political institutions.[68] Marx, referring specifically to Hegel's assumed unities of the legislature with the constitution and the legislature with the executive, said that this "mystical evasion" contributed to a false assumption concerning political conflict within the real-world society.

But Hegel's most damaging error, for Marx, lay not in the assumed organic unity of his political institutions or in the ordering of the subjective and the objective realms. More pointedly, Marx chastised Hegel for his assumptions about the Estates, these being what Hegel assumed would reconcile differences in the polity. For Marx, the "*knowledge* and *good will* of the Estates are . . . partly superfluous and partly suspect (emphasis his)." Marx preferred what he called representative constitutions. Such constitutions were "a great advance over the "constitution based on Estates," because they were "the *open, logical* and *undistorted* expression of the *situation of the modern state* (emphasis his)." Only such a constitution was an *"undisguised contradiction"* (emphasis his).[69]

Where Hegel saw reconciliation, therefore, Marx saw conflict. But Marx's conflict was just as analytic in its cognitive form as Hegel's reconciliation was synthetic. Neither form was relativistic. Whereas Hegel's cognition encouraged reconciliation and the progress toward the universal, Marx saw any such reconciliation as false because "the *Estates* were transformed into social classes" in the advance of history.[70] They would therefore be a part of the class conflict. Marx saw the power of the bourgeois class as manifesting itself in bourgeois governmental structures. The *"arbitrariness"* of those classes, with their "chief criteria" of *"money* and *education,"* would, according to Marx, not be enhanced by Hegel's governmental design because Hegel's *"constitution based on the Estates,"* was nothing more than an "attempt, partly within the political sphere itself, to plunge man back into the limitations of his private sphere" (emphasis his).[71]

Marx's epistemological materialism, of course, along with his surprisingly cursory prescriptions for governmental structures, were designed out of a concern for the distributional inequities of the industrial age. They were certainly not concerned, any more than were Hegel's epistemology and his distributional designs, with cognitive equity or, more specifically, with the cognitive equity that political structures and their impact might have on distributional equity. As a result of Marx's emphasis on the class-dominated conflict of the real world, his disapproval of Hegel's facile universalization of ever more synthetically reconciled particulars is understandable. Thus, though there is a *substantive* richness to Marx's political prescriptions, this richness exists only at that level. Marx's justifiable commentary on the economic and political inequities of the early industrial reality should never be construed to include an understanding of cognitively different qualities within an intellectual framework. The transposition of the objective and the subjective, along with Marx's materialistic concern with the conflict between the real and the rational, not the advancing of the cognitively synthetic and more complex understanding that comes through reason, proscribes the nascent relativism that exists within Hegel's cognitive understanding. No epistemologically idealistic prescription for political equity, based on a psychologically equitable balancing of cognitions, can flow from Marx's intellectual framework. As I will discuss in Chapter Six, a prescription for psychological equity in a relativistic theory of politics can be ensured only from an epistemologically idealistic perspective.

Marx, of course, assumed a singularity of the reason that underlay his condemnation of surplus value, exploitation, and the like. This assumption was reinforced by Marx's drawing away from the idealist epistemology, which can explain both the differences among cognitions as well as the differences among minds. Within a psychologically relativistic theory of politics, relativity tells us that if a singularity of psychology does not exist, so too a singularity of reason will not exist. In contrast to Marx and to the Christian existentialists as well, a relativistic perspective suggests, even more certainly within a postmaterial world where the reality of different psychologies is more evident, that different psychologies impose different meanings on the world. It also tells us how different perspectives on the world, and even on such political matters as what constitutes material distributional equity, relate to their psychological roots. But what the relativistic perspective permits that a Marxist perspective does not permit is even more than a recognition of those differences. It is a proper ordering of the considerations that will bring forth equitable remedies, even in the distribution of society's material rewards.

If the above analysis properly describes the essence of the Marxist criticism of Hegel, and if it properly describes why I feel that Marx's analysis excludes what a relativistic perspective provides, what is the significance of the Marxist position for a relativistic theory? If Marx's position in fact does not deal with the construction of a philosophical framework, much less a philosophical framework that specifically includes the synthetic cognition, and if Marx's dialectic is one that only takes its analysis through the historical stages of slavery, serfdom, capitalism, socialism and, finally, a modern form of communism as each stage is marked by progress along a qualitatively similar spectrum, then the richer cognitive frameworks of historical progression that Hegel described in the *Phenomenology* is proscribed by Marx's materialism. This is so because each of Marx's stages is *qualitatively* the same. Each manifests differences in the location of only one element, which is the ownership of the means of economic production. For all of its substantive richness therefore, Marx's epistemologically materialistic revision of Hegel *reduced* the cognitive form of the dialectical progression to only qualitatively similar variables. Again, Marx did more than alter the substance of the Hegelian dialectic. He did nothing less than alter the *form* of the Hegelian dialectic, and in doing so, the role of the synthetic cognition as Hegel understood it was abandoned. The nascent Hegelian psychological relativity that could be placed into its proper political context was never advanced again.

THE NEO-MARXISTS

Among the writings of latter-day descendants of Marxism, *The New Class* by Milovan Djilas is still the most convincing of the works that describe the tragedy of the modern communist state.[72] At the extreme, of course, such states have engendered the likes of Josef Stalin, Kim Il Sung, and Pol Pot. Less dramatically, but far more frequently, modern communist states have until recently subjected their citizens to the woefully inefficient and often self-aggrandizing bureaucracies which are being found out and disposed of as I write. The works of Antonio Gramsci, Georg Lukács, and others, along with the recent reform efforts of such heroic political figures as Mikhail Gorbachev, Lech Walesa, Vaclav Havel, and others acknowledge that Marx's prescriptions did not prevent the exploitation of a modern, industrial society by a large and oppressive ruling class.

Over the years, there have been many attempts by intellectual neo-Marxists to identify the principal difficulty with Marx. They have argued that a better standard of political equity will come from a return to the early Marx. I believe that it will come only from a return to a pre-Marxist or Hegelian position, specifically a position that includes the correction of Hegel's omission and the elaboration of a psychological relativism as it grows out of Hegel's cognitive relativism.

In recent years, those who have attempted to pull away from both the later Marx (and Engels) of *Capital,* as well as the real world perversions of Marxism that have occurred in the Eastern bloc, have returned, again, to the writings of the younger, more humanistic Marx. It was Karl Korsch, drawing on the early Marx after the post-World War I failure of a communist revolution in Germany, who first spoke of the failure of

Marxism to achieve a psychological perspective.[73] Citing the absence of what he called the necessary, "social-psychological preconditions" for that revolution, Korsch, and later William Reich, sought to marry the psychology of Sigmund Freud with the softer materialism of the early Marx and thereby propagate a better Marxist vision.[74]

More recently, the psychologist Erich Fromm also attempted to build on Freud within the Marxist context. Fromm, as John Rickert has put it, wanted to "arrive at a synthesis of Marx and Freud" by extending Freudian psychoanalysis "from an individual to a social psychology."[75] In so extending Freudian psychoanalysis, however, Fromm found it necessary to adopt what must be the prerequisite for the materialist epistemological perspective. Fromm's belief that "the most influential factor in molding the social character is the social and economic situation in which the group members exist" is, of course, still the essence of materialism.[76]

But Fromm's belief is the essence of materialism not only because it places the object before the mind in the flow of human history, but also because it is much a part of the same Freudian, singular, developmental bias that denies the consideration of psychological differentiation. This bias denies consideration of horizontal statics, but it is also inherently material in a third way. Fromm referred to "group members" as an undifferentiated aggregate much as Marx referred to undifferentiated aggregates within classes whereas relativism is defined as a recognition that within every objectivity, there is a subjective differentiation. For every objective classification, there is a psychological range existing within what at first glance appear to be undifferentiated aggregations. The singular Freudian view, even with its neo-Marxist revitalization, proscribes such a relativist vision. It is quite apparent to all who look for it, that Erich Fromm's preference for a materialistic epistemology is akin to the psychologically developmental or environmental bias. Fromm did note on one occasion that what he called "the instinctual apparatus" had "certain physiologically and biologically determined limits to its modifiability." Yet he was still overwhelmingly environmentalistic in his psychological writings.[77] Fromm's position thus reflected the largely social or environmental perspective of Freud. As a consequence, it also reflected an antistatic bias just as it proscribed a relativistic treatment of psychology. Significantly, the same Rickert piece that depicted Fromm's attempt to move beyond Karl Korsch in the development of a Marxist social psychology also reviewed the writing of the late neo-Marxist, Herbert Marcuse. Marcuse's specific contribution to neo-Marxism also relied overwhelmingly on an epistemologically materialistic perspective.

Marcuse curiously criticized Erich Fromm for the half-hearted nature of Fromm's materialism. He chastisized Fromm for being too concerned with the human spirit and not enough with social and economic reality.[78] Like Fromm, Marcuse's epistemological materialism prevented him from assuming anything other than a singular psychology. His *One Dimensional Man* described and deprecated the same kinds of personality traits that *The Authoritarian Personality* did, but his call for an understanding of a universal distinction between "true and false needs" opens Marcuse to the criticism that James Ogilvy dealt him in *Many Dimensional Man*.[79] I agree with Walter Kaufmann that Marcuse's attempt to blend Freud and Marx is both forced and unconvincing.[80] But even should it have been successful, Freud's lack of differentiation would only have reinforced a Marxian cognitive singularity.

Finally, though I have purposely not concerned myself with the so-called linguistic turn as it currently dominates so much of the writing on the left, a word must be said about two figures who were products of and were contributors to the neo-Marxist position and the political left: Noam Chomsky and Jürgen Habermas. Though Chomsky, with his insistence upon the innateness of human existence, and Habermas, with his "ideal speech situation," no longer consider themselves to be neo-Marxists, they nonetheless represent the unwillingness of even the most prominent writers on the current left to create a relativistic theory.

Chomsky's discussions of language have laudably attempted to include more and more variables, but they still deal with the deep structures and the universals of languages without attention to differentiated psychological proclivities for different language forms. Because Chomsky finds commonalities within the grammars of all languages, his insistence on the biological innateness of the human essence, much in contrast to Marx's minimization of the innate, generally supports the somewhat exaggerated position of Antonio Gramsci that human nature for Marx was only the "totality of historically determined social relations." It is not a relativistic position.

Habermas, in partial contrast, finds language to be interactive, external, and not the product of something innate to the human essence. For Habermas, the distortions of the "ideal speech situation" that he has sought to identify are invariably distortions of economic, social, cultural, and other politically relevant circumstances. They are not the result of differences in psychology and thus, though there is variance in Habermas, it is the variance of existences, not essences.

In sum, so much of the problem of the neo-Marxists and the latter-day linguistic-turn thinkers comes from the fact that they have not come on to the possibility of human relativity. Something more needs still to be conquered before their understandings of either communicative injustices or material political injustices will be complete.

Chapter Five

LIBERAL DEMOCRACY

RELATIVITY AND JOHN LOCKE

Marxism's chief competitor in Western political thought has been liberalism. Fundamentally English, liberalism had its intellectual origins in the rational empiricism of Newton, Bacon, and those who felt that both the physical and metaphysical orders of the universe were discoverable by observation. English liberal thought began with Thomas Hobbes, although Hobbes was more frightened of the evolving individualism of early seventeenth-century England than latter-day liberals would be frightened of latter-day individualism.

Modern liberal thought fully embraces individualism, just as it embraces the modernity of the evolving postindustrial world. It is not coincidence that liberalism took hold in England, the appendage to Europe that was least touched by feudalism and most adapted to that yeoman class of private, landed citizens. The political evolution of the British citizenry parallels the evolution of liberalism. Thus liberal thought, though it rarely addressed the class nature of English society directly, was true to its liberating promise. Its pluralism, at least formally, tolerated broad differences within the citizenry. Its individualism, though competitive, was at least nominally egalitarian. Politically, it encouraged such levelings as the British Reform Bills, which ended the most patent political debilities of class. It provided for fairer economic opportunity, if not for distributional equity.

Liberalism, like Marxism however, never anticipated an understanding of psychological differentiation. Liberalism never reflected a relativity of cognitions, nor did it utilize relativities generally in its descriptions of intellectual or real-world history. Most important, liberal theory, which broadly defined a theory of knowledge, did not contain either a dialectical sense of how knowledge was improved or a Platonic sense of forms. It certainly did not contain a Hegelian sense of the progress of understanding as that progress moved history. Liberal theory, like Marxism, prescribed for nothing with regard to the structures and processes of government from a cognitive, much less a relativistically cognitive, perspective. Liberal thought, however, is still significant for a theory of relativity.

After Thomas Hobbes, the development of liberal thought fell almost exclusively to John Locke. Locke, a man of affairs in English commerce and politics and a political philosopher, is best known for the *Two Treatises on Government*.[1] Earlier, however, Locke had written *An Essay Concerning Human Understanding*, in which he spelled out what he believed knowledge to be.[2] Locke began the *Essay* with a denial of the possibility of innate ideas. His epistemological position was what Gottfried Leibniz replied to, in turn prompting Kant's response to Leibniz and Hegel's response to Kant. In his *Essay*, Locke described the mind as a "white paper void of all characters," a position which thereby permitted knowledge to come only from outside the mind.[3] As his biographer Alexander Fraser put it, "it is no dialectic deduction of what knowledge in the abstract *must be* that he promises" (emphasis his). What Locke promised was only "a matter-of-fact accounting of what seem to be the resources of human understanding".[4]

For Locke, then, the *tabula rasa* was ready for all that the senses brought to it. As Locke said, the "senses at first let in particular ideas and furnish the empty cabinet."[5] Locke's theory of knowledge, however, was more than one of naked empiricism. Locke was much influenced by Richard Hooker and, like Hooker, he had a sense of how a person could improve his or her understanding. But his sense of that improvement borrowed too much from the one who thought of it as merely a reaching out for the knowledge of the angels.

Locke's progress of understanding came neither from the capacity of innate ideas, nor, as Fraser pointed out, from anything like a dialectical progression of speculative principles. The first chapter of Locke's *Essay*, "No Innate Speculative Principles," begins with a rebuke of the "established opinion among some men, that there are in the understanding certain *innate principles*" (emphasis his).[6] In the first chapter of book 2 of the *Essay*, Locke says it again: "I know it is a received doctrine, that men have native ideas, and original characters, stamped upon their minds in their very first being."[7] But Locke had no sympathy for the doctrine.

From an epistemological standpoint, Locke was not an idealist, even though some have argued that there is a hint of idealism there.[8] It is curious, therefore, that Locke's descriptions of the progress of knowledge approximates the Hegelian distinction between analytic and synthetic cognitions. Essentially, the similarity between Locke's and Hegel's forms of knowledge can be found in Locke's differentiation between what he called "simple modes" and "complex modes." Simple modes were defined as "only variations, or different combinations of the same simple idea, without the mixture of any other." Everything within a simple mode was "contained within the bounds of one simple idea."[9] This is not much different from Kant's and Hegel's definitions of the analytic cognition.

Locke's "complex mode," in contrast, was made up of what could be "compounded of simple ideas of *several kinds*" (emphasis mine). These ideas, according to Locke, were "put together to make one complex one; —v.g. beauty, consisting of a certain composition of colour and figure."[10] Locke contrasted this complex mode with things that were "made up only of that simple idea of an unit repeated. The mode reflected repetitions of this kind joined together to make those distinct simple modes, of a dozen, a gross, a million."[11] The choice of a mathematical example, similar to Kant's equation, occurs again when Locke speaks of physical lines to which we can "double the length" or take from them "one half, one fourth, and so forth."[12] Complex modes consist of "several combinations of simple ideas of *different* kinds." (emphasis his).[13] Locke even sensed that the complex mode may be somewhat more engaging of the mind, saying at one point that whereas the mind only received simple modes, it "often exercises an *active* power in making these several combinations" add up to complex modes (emphasis his).[14]

There is a hint of relativity, therefore, among the structure of Locke's forms of knowledge. But even if this hint were fully a matter of different cognitions, which it is not, Locke suggests nothing about how such cognitions might relate to different states of the mind. Also, as with Hegel unfortunately, there is nothing in Locke that describes how different cognitions are linked to different psychologies. Locke has no nascently psychological relativity at the core of his theory of human understanding. It should come as no shock, therefore, that even sympathetic biographers of Locke like Alexander Fraser find nothing of the "dialectical deduction" in Locke.[15]

Not only is there no dialectic in Locke; there is no dialectic in liberal thought generally and, not unexpectedly, there is no dialectical theory of history within liberal thought either. There is no notion of how increasing levels of understanding, even of understanding that might only respond to Hooker's "approaching of the angels," might rely on a particular form of cognition or propel a cognitively driven, dialectical progression of history.

LOCKE AND POLITICS

Locke, of course, was a man of affairs as well as a philosopher. His ties to Shaftesbury, along with his role in the Glorious Revolution of 1688 and the accession of William and Mary to the English throne, are well-documented. What was not known until recently, however, was that Locke's *Two Treatises on Government* were written well before their 1690 publication. Locke was no fool; the imprisonments and exiles that took place during the last days of the Stuarts and that had encouraged Locke's own extended *vacances* in Holland, discouraged the immediate publication of such writings.

The argument of the *Two Treatises* is no less combative for its having spent time in a drawer. It pointedly responded to a contemporary work that had apologized for a severe monarchical authority, and it carried much of the argument of the early seventeenth century jurist Edward Coke into the latter portion of the century. Coke was the principal anti-Stuart writer before the interregnum, making much of the necessary limitations to modern monarchy and the kingly abuses by James I of both the law and Parliament. Locke's *Second Treatise* more broadly defined the seventeenth-century liberal position and it remains as much the oracle of political liberalism today as it was when it was published.

Locke's *Second Treatise* revolves around Locke's version of the social contract. Much has been written on both the importance of Locke's social contract, as well as its contrast to other social contracts. There is a subtle, often-neglected element in Locke's definition of the social contract that should be coupled with the political notions he advanced in late-seventeenth-century England. This element comes from the English private law for, without question, the burden of what traditional political scientists have drawn from the lessons of Locke, or indeed from the Glorious Revolution and the advance of democracy that Locke represents, has much to do with Locke's position on private law in a democratic state. That role envisions the private law as sufficiently self-contained to justify limits to state jurisdiction. Locke's advocacy of firm political and legal protections for individual economic liberties follows on accordingly.

The point is no less important for its present obviousness than it is for its uniqueness. So engrained in England that Locke could easily draw on it was the importance of wholly private, yet sacrosanct, legal arrangements. These arrangements ignored government altogether, save for judicial enforcement. What was important for Locke, and what was so available to Locke, was that English governments from the time of the Norman Conquest had not sought to define law from the perspective of what the continental civil law calls the *law giver*. The real corpus of English law did not come either from a government or a philosopher. English governments, particularly early English governments, used public law as a reconciler, or as a ratifier, of a self-regulative private law.

The equities of the English legal and political system found their legitimacy from that collection of English customary precedents that made up the common law. Those precedents had grown through the centuries out of the rulings of a complex of writs and rules of evidence. They well-covered the daily legalities of any English citizen's life, for the common law, and the universality of its acceptance, permitted the English to do something no other political system permitted. It permitted them to create a public order with a minimum of public law.

Put simply, the English, long before Coke and Locke, drew their line between the public and private jurisdictions as far as private law would permit. Even the nature of the English parliament for roughly the first 150 years after William I was almost wholly judicial, not legislative. The early parliament was what the king counseled with as it assisted him in perfecting the legal and political realm. But the parliament, later as much as earlier, only perfected those customs and practices that blanketed the routines of land and chattel alienation and the other legal necessities of English life.

The regularization of the common law accompanied the regularization of the rule of reason within that law. What a king could do, and what Henry II particularly did in the 1179 Assizes, was to engross a universal concept of reason into the underpadding of the common law's quilt. Such a perspective on reason was already common in its origin, for it had grown from its own roots and not from an English Hammurabi, Cicero, or Justinian. By the end of the twelfth century, it would be common as well in its blanketing of the realm.

Two more points help explain the common law's relevance to Locke and early liberalism. They reflect on Locke's prescription for the social contract and, ultimately, on the psychology and particularly the cognition that typically underlies liberalism. The first concerns the *method* of the common law, for if the greatest distinction between common law and civil law, or between the English and the continental traditions, is the relative involvement of government in promulgating that law, then the most significant methodological distinction between the two legal corpuses revolves around the locus of reason in their separate jurisprudential houses.

In the civil law, reason comes from a real or at least what is perceived to be a real source that is greater than the law alone. In the civil law tradition, the law invariably comes from something that is ultimately a political but what was originally a moral or philosophical vision. Within the civil law, the law is invariably subordinate to that grander philosophic bearing. For the civil law, therefore, the question of reason is a matter of the law's being inherently correct in the sense of how that law positions itself according to a moral design. As part of public life or, in a Platonic way, as part of an organic quest for an interrelated private and public virtue, the civil law is clearly a derivative commodity.

The underlying justification for the common law could not be more different. In the common law, the arena of public law was limited largely because the English have considered themselves capable of discovering their own reason rather than importing it from a philosopher or philosopher king. Private English economic law has always revolved around only two legal touchstones and, even in their modern embellishments, the laws of property and contract continue to support private intercourse within England, as they do in other common-law countries. Law within the common-law jurisdictions grew out of the resolution of day-to-day conflicts that in turn grew almost exclusively out of the evolving usages of private property and contract in everyday English life.

The essence of the common law, therefore, reflected nothing more than the principles that defined the alienation of property and the evidences of the contractual transactions that alienated property. If the common law was contractual at its root, it was not only not ordained from a higher authority, but it was engendered by usages of private citizens, not public authorities, who were considered to be of equal legal weight and authority. The golden rule of applying the common law equally in private matters overrode any notion of the natural superiority of the king's law. Even such occasional statutory revisions as the 1677 Statute of Frauds were typically concerned only with matters of evidence. They did not substantively change the rules of contractual alienation.

Thus, if the rationalized buttresses of the common law were nonphilosophical and nongovernmental, the character of the law also manifested itself in the sanctity of the exchange. As the common law defined and adjudicated the disputes that surrounded a citizenry's private transactions, it did so with the assumption that the voluntary transactions of *sui juris* adults would receive the law's protection. The underpinning for that protection came directly from contract law's most significant rationale. It was the rationale of the "meeting of the minds," which concerned the two minds who engaged in the agreement reaching full identity.

The contractual assumption of identity between the position of two common contractors was of course a wholly prepsychological assumption. It was concerned solely with the economic identity, or equivalency, of the commodity and the medium of exchange in the minds of the contractors. Within a psychological context, however, the assumption of identity in the minds of contractors could not be more significant. It meant that the parties had each reduced the elements of the transaction to a place where fungible, qualitatively similar, variables defined the issue between them. And, whereas the law deems a contract reasonable because of the single-mindedness of its signatories, the psychological place of that single-mindedness is clearly with the analytic cognition. As the common law had and still has as its principal decisional burden the determination of the contracting parties' ostensibly identical intent, common-law rules governing the construction of contracts, that is, the rules governing the sale of either personal property or what the Middle Ages called the *enfeoffments* of real property, built their claim for equity or justice on a presumption of the similar-mindedness of the transactors.

As the common law's claim to equity was, and still is, a matter of private intent or *scienter,* that claim still rests on that presumed single-mindedness of contractual intent along with the presumedly just enforcement of the equitable dealing.

LAW, LOCKE, AND GOVERNMENT

The perspective of relativism, in short, clearly refutes the assumed identity of the minds that engage in contractually based transactions. It does so because it refutes the identity that is the underpinning for the philosophical tautology that Hegel criticized Kant for in the matter of Kant's equation. Therefore, if the quest for political equity begins with a balancing of the psychological preferences of *relative* minds, then the assumption of equity within the ostensible meeting of the minds of contractors is what a relativistic theory challenges in liberal thought. As liberal theory upholds the methodology of the transaction through both the English common law and the assumption of that law's single-mindedness, then the equity of a relativistic theory must be assessed from the standpoint of the psychology of the transactional mode.

John Locke's *Second Treatise* embraced a form of *social* contract. That form fit very comfortably, and in great part grew out of, the English contractual tradition. As the Glorious Revolution of 1688 assured the permanence of the British parliament, John Locke's ideas of what one should surrender when leaving the state of nature relied on his confidence in political institutions that respected his notion of the social contract. As the law of private contract was and still is so much a part of English private law, it should not be surprising that Locke argued that the government's principal purpose was only to protect both property and the free alienation of property through contract.

Locke's perspective is understandable, in part because it was that of a man of some position in his day. Locke was most directly concerned with the mercantile position of England in regard to the Dutch, the Spanish, the French, and the other seventeenth-century competitors of England. Locke's position on governmental protection of property and contract, therefore, clearly distinguished the role of productive from unproductive property in England's commercial competition. Locke's criticism of the Church, the Crown, and the landed aristocracy was largely founded on the unproductive uses of those institutions' vast properties.

But Locke's position, and that of liberalism, is more than substantive. Though he argued with regard to the distributional patterns created by liberal property that one should be rewarded for the "fruits of one's labour," the difficulty with his prescription is much like the difficulty with Aristotle's notion of distributional proportionality. Like Aristotle, Locke did not speak to the methodology of the contractual exchange, much less to the cognitive bias of that methodology. Unlike Hegel, who utilized the epistemological assumption of his early work in his later political writings, Locke's early definitions in the *Essay* of simple and complex modes did not contain any reflection on the methodology of the economic exchange from a cognitive perspective. Neither did they reflect on the patterns of material distribution that would grow out of an exchange-based economy.

The advancement of liberalism under Locke did accelerate the political inclusion of larger portions of the citizenry into the public affairs of liberal states. These inclusions grew out of the notions of natural rights and liberties that Locke advocated. But if Locke's political writings presaged political watersheds like the English and American Bills of Rights, the English Reform Bills, and eventually even such things as the American civil rights movement, that is, if they helped to ensure that liberal political institutions included progressively more members of a nation's citizenry in its deliberations, Locke still did not perceive how material distributions would be affected by the dominance of the contractual form in both private law and government.

Even today, the personal guarantees of liberal political theory are only guarantees of political inclusion and freedom from governmental intrusion into private areas of life. These guarantees are of political representation, not of either equitable distributional result or of cognitive equity among the processes that account for distribution. They certainly do not include psychological balances as those balances reflect the cognitive balances that are found in the shaping of public issues by different forms of political structures and processes.

As liberalism, from the perspective of a psychologically relativistic theory of politics, never dealt with the cognitive forms of the structures and processes of government, it did not, in its natural favor for the contractual form, balance the identities of the analytic cognition with the qualitative differentiations of the synthetic cognition. As Locke's law of nature is "the preservation of mankind," and as the power of government has "no other end but preservation," so too the legislative power of Locke's government was "limited to the publick good."[16] But that "publick good" must only be in keeping with the true end of government, "the preservation of private property."[17]

By maintaining a separation among the legislative, the executive, and what he called the "federative" function (dealing with the external relations) of a state, Locke believed that "designs against the Liberties and Properties of the Subject" could effectively be thwarted.[18] Like the presumed balances of private contract, the presumed balances of a government, separated because of Locke's fear of "human frailties," were considered to be a guarantee of political equity. But that political equity was only substantive. It did not weigh the cognitive balances of a government's structures and processes.

Looking back, and particularly given Locke's position on knowledge and particularly complex modes in the *Essay,* the parsimony of Locke's political prescriptions should not be surprising. Moreover, as Locke's theory of knowledge was not dialectical, and as it did not anticipate a cognitive relativism, the distinctions that Locke made with regard to knowledge's simple and complex modes were never linked to relative cognitions, much less to relative psychologies. Though Locke conceded that the mind may be somewhat more active when it is in the complex mode, he never sought to join the complex mode with the task of philosophical speculation. Locke's complex mode, though it was similar to Hegel's notion of the synthetic cognition in its incorporation of different qualities of variables, was simply never understood by Locke to be necessary for speculative thought. Consequently, as his biographer Fraser has said, Locke's complex mode was never made a part of a dialectical form within either Locke's epistemology or his explanation of politics. If there was to be no innate knowledge for Locke, and if there was also to be no speculation for Locke either, there could surely be no role for the dialectic. Ultimately, neither could there be a role for a linkage of the *quality* of thought to the progress of understanding or history.

The transactional methodology of Locke, particularly as it affixed itself to a Lockean utilitarian calculus that adjudged pleasure and pain without the qualitative distinctions John Stuart Mill later included, only facilitated the cognitive bias of liberalism. Using Locke's utilitarian methodology, it was not difficult for Locke's followers such as David Hume and Jeremy Bentham to devolve Locke's natural rights position into an overwhelmingly analytic, utilitarian calculus. Though, again, the revised utilitarianism of John Stuart Mill eventually addressed different qualities of pleasure and pain, utilitarian political prescriptions such as Jeremy Bentham's legislative calculus (in his *On Legislation,* for example) were clearly analytic in their cognitive mode.[19]

The political liberalism of Locke and his utilitarian successors therefore defined a political philosophy that is every bit as inattentive to the relativity of human psychology as is Marxism. Liberalism's methodology, infused into a representative and a structurally dispersed government, imposes its cognitively analytic framework on liberal forms of government. Liberalism's epistemology, as the underpinning for the traditional, English vision of political liberalism, was inescapably rational. This rationalism forbade it from dealing with anything save the objective or existential condition of its citizenry. It dealt with circumstance, borrowing from the notions of property ownership and the freedom to alienate property as the natural rights bases for the objective protections of life, liberty, and property. Unfortunately, it dealt with little else.

From an epistemological perspective, therefore, just as liberalism has been rational and not skeptical, so too liberalism has also been epistemologically materialistic and not idealistic. Just as Marxism's materialistic dialectic could not deal with how different minds imposed different meanings on the world, so too liberalism could not and still cannot deal with how different minds impose different meanings on the world. As a result, no theory of relativism can be built on liberalism, and there can be no role for liberalism in the dialectic, or the progress of understanding or history. Politically, no sense of how different forms of political structures and processes reflect what Oswald Spengler called different "styles of knowing" can ever grow out of liberalism.

THE REVISIONS OF LIBERALISM: JOHN STUART MILL

By the middle of the nineteenth century, England and liberalism had nurtured each other well. England's liberalism, of course, played a crucial role in the emergence of the Western world's dominant state, methodological empiricism and a brawny industrialism complementing each other nicely in an empire that expected to see no sunset. But as the epistemological materialism of the liberal perspective nurtured the real-world wealth of Adam Smith's nation, one Englishman challenged that order, at least a little. This figure's criticisms, intellectually if not ideologically, surpassed even the criticisms of liberalism that came from Ruskin, the Chartists, the Utopians, and others who chafed under the distributional injustices of full-steamed English industrialism.

The critic was John Stuart Mill, the son of one of the two leading utilitarians of the day, as well as the student of James's neighbor and the day's other principal utilitarian, Jeremy Bentham. The young Mill's intellectual progression from the paternalistic clutches of utilitarianism is well recounted. But to understand Mill's relevance to a theory of relativism, let us note how far that progression took him. Written almost as a sequel to his father's *Elements of Political Theory*,[20] Mill's seven editions of the *Principles of Political Economy*[21] chronicled a steady movement away from an orthodox liberal or classical view of the state and its economy. They marked, by the last edition, a very candid prescription for democratic socialism. Mill's final *Principles* marked a clear departure from the kinds of protection for property, as well as from the assumed equities of the contractual exchange, that Locke had argued for.

Society, of course, had changed by the mid nineteenth century. A Dickensian awareness of truly hard times made an impression on Mill that was not far different from the impression that Marx had taken from industrialism. Mill's last edition of *Principles* argued for how modern government might ensure equitable distribution and, though certainly not a Marxist, by 1871 Mill was speaking profoundly to the biases of the exchange methodology in a wage-labor, factory-system setting. Mill was certainly aware of the objective, nonpsychological bargaining inequities of purely contractual relationships. Though not dealing with the psychology of it, or with the psychology of the governmental structures that had an impact on distributional arrangements, his questioning of the transactional mode challenged Locke's early liberal assumptions about transactional equity.

If the substance of Mill's writings on politics and economics are clear, Mill's epistemological position is just as clear and more important. Mill's *System of Logic* is the analogue to Locke's *Essay Concerning Human Understanding*.[22] There, Mill emphasized his disapproval of the deductive method while he confirmed a belief in the progress of human knowledge.[23] Nonetheless, Mill, much like Locke, was wary of speculation on "the Mind's own nature," suggesting at one point that the "phenomena of the mind" were made up of two things, "those called physical, and those peculiarly designated as Mental."[24]

What is extraordinary about his *System,* however, is that despite Mill's unwillingness to speculate on the nature of the mind, he, unlike Locke, evidenced an understanding of differences among human natures. In a statement much like Judith Shklar's observation on Hegel concerning personality differences, Mill suggested that "the commonest observation shows that different minds are susceptible in very different degrees, to the action of the same psychological causes." Incredibly, Mill even hypothesized that perhaps the "magnitude of the hemispheres of the brain" was probably significant in such psychological differences.[25]

Mill assigned the "source of moral and emotional peculiarities" to what he called "temperaments."[26] Quoting Joseph Priestly, he noted that if an individual has "great individual susceptibility, he will probably be distinguished by fondness for natural history" or a "relish for the beautiful and great and moral enthusiasm."[27] If, however, only a "modicum of sensibility" existed within a psychology, then there would most likely be a "love of science, of abstract truth, with a deficiency of taste and fervor."[28] Mill predicted well that "when the general laws of mind are more accurately known, and above all, more skillfully applied to the detailed explanation of mental peculiarities, they will account for many more of those peculiarities than is ordinarily supposed."[29]

Though Mill's prediction anticipated a theory of psychological relativity, Mill did not use psychological differentiations in his writings. Mill's theory of knowledge thus has no relativity to it even though it does have a keen sense of the importance of the human mind in the unfolding of human history. Mill did believe strongly in what Auguste Comte had called a "Science of Society" and he found it to be at the core of historical progress, as well as the progress of social knowledge. He once even called it the organ "by which all the conclusions of the other and more special kind of inquiry must be limited and controlled."[30]

Further, Mill's belief in intellectual progress, as well as his belief in a so-called Science of Society, evidenced at least a fair measure of idealism. At one point in the *System of Logic,* in fact, Mill seemed to be addressing the material and ideal balance when he claimed that "the circumstances in which mankind are placed . . . form the characters of the men; but the men, in their turn, mould and shape the circumstances." [31] Mill may have wished to shift his epistemology into a moderately idealistic context, describing what he called the "dynamic state" by asking rhetorically if "one element in the complex existence of social man is preeminent over all others as the prime agent of the social movement." [32] But he answered his question by saying that "there really is one social element which is thus predominant . . . among the agents of the social progression. This is the *state of the speculative faculties of mankind*" (emphasis his). [33] This speculative vision, quite obviously, is not far from the Hegelian position, and it surely has a good deal of idealism to it. It is a mid-nineteenth-century attempt, in the liberal tradition, at an updating of the notion of incorporation into speculative thought. Most important, it is a notion that Mill deduced "from the laws of human nature." [34]

But two critical elements were still missing from Mill's tepid idealism and his philosophical endorsement of speculation. Both, in contrast, were included in Hegel's sense of knowledge. The first element was the dialectic itself, an element that Hegel had described as the key to intellectual progress. The second was the differentiation among cognitions, this absence being particularly unfortunate since Mill, like Hegel, had evidenced some understanding of different human psychologies.

Although Mill, like Hegel, accepted speculation as essential to the improvement of human knowledge, he did not understand how different cognitions, much less the different preferences for those cognitions that existed in different psychologies, might achieve that improvement. Even without these dialectical and relativistic notions, however, the first epistemological idealism of Mill, with its sense of the progress of history, is vaguely reminiscent of the Hegelian dialectic.

Mill wrote somewhat as Hegel did in the *Phenomenology* of the different historical stages of society, he noting that the progress of society depended on an ability to "find the laws according to which any state of society produces the state which succeeds it and takes its place." [35] These states were "reflective of the degree of knowledge, and of intellectual and moral culture," as well as "the state of industry, of wealth and its distributions." [36] For Mill, the laws of improvement were not simply a matter of the laws of nature. Mind and matter were inexorably linked, and therefore, "the succession of states of the human mind and of human society cannot have an independent law of its own."[37] Instead, historical progress for Mill "must depend upon the psychological and ethological laws which govern the actions of circumstances on men and of men on circumstances."[38] For him, "every advance in material civilization has been preceded by an advance in knowledge."[39]

If John Stuart Mill was closer than any liberal thinker to a position of both epistemological idealism and relativism, his nascent relativism, like Hegel's, was still fundamentally historical. The closest that Mill came to a psychological relativism was to note that "the sciences of human nature and society" were familiar "in a peculiar degree" with the "changeable" subject matters of different eras.[40] Mill recognized that "from age to age" the passage of history meant that "not only the qualities of individuals vary, but those of the majority are not the same in one age as in another."[41] He did not comprehend, however, how different cognitions or different psychologies made different contributions to the progress of understanding and history. He certainly did not comprehend how different psychologies were important at different stages of the dialectic.

In the context of its stage in the development of liberal political thought, the writings of Mill constituted an attempt to reverse the almost purely empirical biases of both the early liberal thinkers and their intellectual predecessors like Newton and Bacon. From an epistemological, and even from a political, perspective, Mill grappled with the sterility of the liberal, utilitarian methodology as he properly understood it, and rebelled against the impact that the nineteenth-century acceptance of that utilitarian methodology had had on the distributional imbalances of industrialized England. Mill understood that the purely inclusionary substantive prescriptions of liberalism, though successful in extending the franchise in the Reform Bills, could never ensure an equitable distribution of wealth.

But the Mill of the seventh edition of the *Principles,* writing even after the sweeping Reform Bill of 1867, still thought political participation to be the principal remedy for economic maldistribution. As Mill's political prescriptions were neither consciously psychological nor relativistic from the perspective of determining what political structures and processes would ensure distributional equity, they did not comprehend distributional equity's relationship to the balances of such arrangements. Though Mill did risk the suggestion, over one hundred years ago, that "when the general laws" of psychological differentiation were better known, "they will account for many more of these peculiarities than is ordinarily suspected,"[42] Mill did not relate his bow to psychological relativity or to the relativity of perspective on knowledge or mediation to a Hegel-like perspective on the different forms of knowledge.

Thus, even with the faintly idealistic epistemological flavor that Mill attempted to give to liberal thought, the resultant or material political equities he considered never fully rested in that epistemologically idealist home. As a result, idealistic epistemology is still mute in liberal thought, and liberalism's contemporary prescriptions do not guarantee either psychological equity, the structural and procedural equity of governmental structures, or material or distributional equity. Modern-day liberalism, in part because of the revisions of early liberalism that Mill and writers like T. H. Green proposed, still speaks to distributive equities only as they might be achieved through liberal, democratically participatory channels.

In that liberalism has sometimes initiated a mildly redistributive political agenda and, helped along by a broad panoply of democratic socialisms, has embraced the modern welfare state, it has been faithful to its broadly egalitarian heritage. In its *form,* however, nothing in the political philosophy of liberalism mandates the abandonment of the contractually based, cognitively analytic distributional methodology that has always been paramount within it. As a result, nothing in liberalism forbids a return to the less-egalitarian perspective and the political arguments of recent political outcroppings like the neoconservatives and the neoliberals, for example, have rested comfortably within the same framework of liberal individualism and transactionalism that redistributional advocates have used. Even avowedly antiredistributive policies such as those of Ronald Reagan's late presidency in the United States fit comfortably into what its advocates never fail to remind us is the classical liberal tradition. Without consideration of the psychologically relativistic balance of *perspectives* on equitable material distribution and without consideration of the structural arrangements that might ensure such perspectives in the public realm, the liberal quest for material equity can never succeed. Just as Hegel's cognitive perspective was undermined by Marx and the other post-Hegelians, so too the fragile cognitive perspective of John Stuart Mill has been undermined by the traditional, cognitive perspective of liberalism. As a result, liberalism, even today, addresses the psychology of public structures no better than it addresses the relationship of those structures to distributional arrangements. Liberalism precludes a relativistic perspective on ideology just as it precludes a relativistic perspective on political cognition and the cognition of political structures and balances.

If the last two chapters have demonstrated that neither Marxist political theory nor liberal political theory are capable of being extended into a philosophy that is based on psychological relativity, then the development of a wholly new political philosophy is necessary. Do not forget that in their epistemological materialism, both Marxist and liberal thought are based on what Hegel called existences or what are often referred to as objectivities. Do not forget either that liberalism and Marxism, as their proponents do not like to admit, are really epistemological first cousins. They are far more closely related in all of their principal assumptions about knowledge, as well as in their principal assumptions about intellectual history, than their modern advocates concede. As neither theory places its prescriptions within an idealistic epistemological framework, even in the postmaterial world, so too neither theory can provide for psychological and, hence, distributive equity in advanced political states. A purely substantive, or resultant, view of postmaterialism cannot describe how different psychologies prefer the differentiated structural and procedural arrangements that ensure distributive equity. It cannot describe how different psychologies prefer different *forms* of understanding political issues, as they are defined by different governmental arrangements. A merely substantive postmaterialism cannot do that because it links postmaterialism only to the substantive political preferences of each citizen and no more.

The remedy for substantive postmaterialism, therefore, must be nothing less than an *epistemological* postmaterialism. It must be a postmaterialism that sees the mind as the catalyst of history and sees that the limitations of both Marxist and liberal thought are, at root, limitations that begin with epistemological, not substantive, materialism. They each begin with the assumption that some objective reality is perceived universally by all, and they each begin with the assumption that objective reality is what moves human understanding and human history. Both assumptions are wrong.

If a postmaterial age is therefore to create understandings that go beyond traditional political theories, it will not be enough for these new theories to describe psychological determinants of political attitudes and behaviors. A new political theory must describe how relative psychologies give different meanings to political reality. The epistemologically idealistic perspective is the only perspective that describes, in the Platonic sense, how differentiated cognitions impose different *forms* of meaning on politics. Further, as neither Marxist nor liberal thought, both of which were born well before the postmaterial age, address the issue of equity from the perspective of an idealist epistemology or a bounded relativism, a new theory must address how a range of normal human psychologies imposes very different meanings on the forms that equity must take.

In retrospect it is not surprising that when Max Weber contrasted the roles of bureaucracy within capitalism on the one hand with what he correctly assumed these roles would become in socialist states on the other, he noted that the "precision of its [bureaucracy's] functioning requires" that both systems adopt the rational mode. Speaking of the modern need for bureaucracy, he suggested that even "a socialistic form of organization would not alter" the fact that such bureaucracies would prosper there too.[43] Weber's prediction, of course, has proven itself over and over again.

What a relativistic theory guarantees is a better chance at political equity within the modern political state than either Marxism or liberalism has guaranteed. Based as it is on the human psychological relativity, and incorporating the spectrum of cognitions that ranges from Kant's to Hegel's, a relativistic theory can help to assure psychological equity within political structures, as well as within the resultant, material equities that such structures produce. The order of these considerations is what is important. It will not work the other way around. It has surely not worked the other way around for either Marxism or liberalism.

Chapter Six

THE EQUITY OF THE THEORY

AN AVAILABLE STANDARD

For Hegel's cognitive differentiation, with its omission corrected, to underpin a psychologically relativistic theory of politics, such a theory must provide for a standard of equity derived from psychological differentiation. Hegel's descriptions of differentiated cognitions foretell how cognitions affect politics; the standard of psychological equity must thus reflect the range of perspectives on equity provided by these cognitions.

A standard of equity that relies on a *balance* along the principal range of cognitions will necessarily be an abstract standard. Nonetheless, it will be a standard that encourages far more fairness in a postmaterial political world than any standard based on undifferentiated classes, races, or other aggregates of citizens, as Marxism does, or on undifferentiated individuals, as liberalism does. Because all objectivities have a subjective range within them, a political philosophy based on the relativity of human psychology provides a more grounded standard of equity than does any philosophy that is solely based on undifferentiated aggregates. The range of psychologies *within* groups and classes, and *across* all of the citizens of any society, permits a definition of equity that does not rely upon an objective, rational standard of political fairness.

In order to ensure equity, however, a relativistic theory must also prescribe for an equitable arrangement of the political structures and processes of the polity. Only an incorporation of psychological differentiation into governmental structures and processes permits a psychologically equitable arrangement of these structures and processes. Such an arrangement is then able to prescribe for equitable material distributions.

ARISTOTLE AND THE MEAN

A psychologically equitable perspective on equity should be based on two standards. The first concerns the intellectual rationale of the equitable standard itself. The second concerns the application of that standard to the forms, or structures, of a political system. Although the substantive standard of equity within a relativistic framework is different from an equitable standard that relies on single, ostensibly objective, perspectives on equity, a psychologically relativistic standard of equity can still borrow from traditional standards of equity. Indeed, a relativistic standard of equity should be derived from the notion of the golden mean, with that mean existing among the subjective, not among the objective, conditions of a citizenry.

Though bringing psychological relativism to a standard of equity is original here, the use of an equitable mean as it exists along a known range dates back at least to Aristotle. Aristotle prescribed for a "middle condition" within "the ownership of all gifts of fortune," a place that incorporated a state of moderate possession of a variety of human qualities.[1] Aristotle was wary of the extremes of such ownership, citing the burden of "the over-handsome, the over-noble, [and] the over-wealthy," as well as the burden of the "over-poor, the over-weak [and] the utterly ignoble."[2]

Aristotle's equity, of course, rested on a sense of proportion. His reference to an equitable standard is not exclusive to the *Politics*, his plea for proportionality being more detailed in the *Nichomachean Ethics*. In book 5, Aristotle said that "justice is a kind of mean, but not in the same way as the other virtues."[3] Aristotle linked proportionality and his concept of the mean in the realm of justice to distributive justice, saying that "this species of the just is intermediate, and the unjust is what violates the proportion." This is true, he argued, because "the proportional is intermediate, and the just is proportional."[4]

As with Aristotle's proportionality, a psychologically relativistic standard of justice will link a standard of proportionality to subjective perspectives on the structural and procedural arrangements of a political system as well as the issues with which that system deals. In so doing, the relativistic perspective will judge a political system in terms of the psychological balance that is either present or absent in the manner in which its institutions first define and then process political issues. Such a theory will thus apply a psychologically proportional standard to the patterns of that system's decision making.

Again, though the theory will not begin with the equity of distributive results, it will judge distributive equities as they flow from either psychologically equitable or psychological inequitable structural and procedural arrangements. It will do so, however, with a consciousness of how psychological perspectives affect the makeup of public institutions. The psychological character of the processes of government thus makes up the key middle step between psychological equity and distributional equity in a relativistic theory.

THE PROCEDURAL BIAS IN RAWLS AND NOZICK

Two contemporary writers, John Rawls and Robert Nozick, serve as the best exemplars of the range of psychological preferences for political decision-making processes. Predictably, these writers prescribe for very different distributional arrangements, using distinctly different methodologies for the determination of distribution. In *A Theory of Justice,* John Rawls argues for a distributional methodology that deals with the issue of distributional equity directly. Rawls believes in the conscious political consideration of any political system's distributions.

Rawls's prescription for a just distribution is certainly aggregational, that is, his plea for "justice as fairness" suggests an a priori consideration of all of the factors that lead to any political system's allocations.[5] Rawls, for example, would have a political system consider the training, the skill, the risks, and the need for any task in the evaluation of that task's fair return. In his description of equity, Rawls therefore relies on the notion of the "veil of ignorance," a state of not knowing where one currently rests in a polity's distributive ladder.

Rawls's veil of ignorance, along with his notion of the "original position" in which there is supposedly a state of "symmetry of everyone's relations to each other," seeks to prevent any objective or real-world circumstance from interfering with judgments on distributional equity.[6] Rawls's position is a response to Aristotle's imbalances of perspective on equity that are caused by differences in circumstance. For Rawls, not knowing where one is located on any existing distributional hierarchy should permit one to be purely objective on the distributional question.

Rawls's position is one of both consciousness and comprehensiveness. In attempting to define a perspective on what constitutes fair distribution, however, his position is still a long way from a relativistic position. Though subjective, Rawls ignores the reality of psychologically driven perspectives on fair distribution, as well as the reality of how different political structures and processes allocate distribution differently. Rawls simply does not account for the role of psychological differences in the preferences for either different resultant distributions or for different methods of considering distribution. He accounts for but one kind of input into the distributional scheme and, although his distributional prescriptions include an awareness of a variety of objective distributional concerns, he still assumes a single subjective perspective, wherein only objective differences need to be removed.

The best contrast to the aggregational distributional position of John Rawls is the position of Robert Nozick. Nozick's *Anarchy, State and Utopia* defines a standard for what he considers to be fair distribution in the context of his interpretations of John Locke and the Lockean ideal of a "state of perfect freedom."[7] Within that Lockean tradition, Nozick prefers a distributive methodology wherein each citizen engages with his or her fellow citizens in purely contractual ways. The aggregate distribution simply reflects the totality of these contracts. Nozick would have citizens sort out their affairs interpersonally rather than as part of any publicly aggregated process. He would, therefore, have each society's distributional arrangements reflect only the "exchange" or the "gift" that each individual has either contracted for or given to each other.[8]

Nozick's *Anarchy, State and Utopia* pointedly criticizes the distributive methodology of John Rawls, saying that he would prohibit public structures from creating what he called Rawls's "pattern" of distributional considerations. In prohibiting any conscious or a priori attempt at realizing a just distributional pattern, Nozick's preference for "voluntary exchanges," or for exchanges that ensured that the distribution was "produced and maintained by a process that in no way had the overall pattern or design 'in mind'," is clear.[9] Of course, Nozick's position is neither subjectively based nor is it an appeal to a consciousness about the final distributional result. It is solely a reification of the distribution that results from all voluntary transactions.

Like the contrast between the cognitive preferences of Immanuel Kant and G. W. F. Hegel, the contrast between John Rawls and Robert

Nozick illustrates fundamentally different cognitive preferences, as well as different substantive positions on distribution. But a relativistic perspective on equity relates to differentiated decision-making processes in the public arena. One invaluable source, the first to broach the issue of psychological equity in a political context, lends a new perspective on this point.

THE CONTRIBUTIONS OF FRED I. GREENSTEIN

For a psychologically relativistic political philosophy to define both a range of perspectives on the arrangements of public structures and processes and a range of perspectives on distributional equity, the theory's prescriptions for political structures and processes must be made clear. John Rawls and Robert Nozick prescribed for very different valuation processes at the same time that each justified the distributional results of his preferred methodology. If the processes that each prescribed, along with the structures in which these processes exist, are to represent the intermediate step between psychological equity and just distribution in a relativistic theory, then the relationship of psychological equity to psychologically equitable decisional processes must be clear.

The first direct contribution to an understanding of how a psychologically relativistic theory might contribute to the achievement of psychological equity can be found in Fred I. Greenstein's article, "The Impact of Personality on Politics."[10] This article pointed the way to two important conceptual understandings that I believe must underlie a relativistic theory.

First, Greenstein's article, written principally as a plea for understanding personality as a significant political variable, took the position that reasonably static adult personalities are identifiable. Greenstein went on to argue that identifiable personalities had an impact on politics in identifiable ways. Greenstein put it simply, "there is a great deal of political activity which can be explained adequately only by taking account of the personal characteristics of the actors involved."[11] Greenstein understood that his position crossed swords with the largely behavioral, environmentally dominated orthodoxies that had long overwhelmed the study of psychology and politics. Greenstein also understood that the rejection of personality as a key political indicator had hindered both political understanding in general and the construction of a psychological theory of politics in particular.

Second, Greenstein went beyond merely arguing for the consideration of personality as a significant political variable. Greenstein also explained how the acceptance of personality as a political variable almost necessarily imported an acceptance of personality differentiation. He knew that "some inner predisposition of the individual" mediated the enviromental stimuli.[12] Different individuals' "psychological predispositions," he said, played a part in each individual's differentiated understanding of politics.

Greenstein's anticipation of a psychologically relativistic perspective focused on the notion that different personalities did not labor with equal satisfaction in the same institutional setting. He also contended that different personalities would attempt to change the forms of structures of the institutions in which they worked over time. His assertion that personalities either "fit" well or poorly within psychologically compatible or psychologically incompatible structures suggested that different individuals not only preferred different structures, but also attempted to mold those structures in ways that were psychologically compatible for them while they worked within them.[13]

The linkage of psychology or the linkage of relative psychologies to what is psychologically comfortable about relative structures and processes was important to Greenstein. But his use of a notion like "fit" demonstrates that the juxtaposition of personality and structure was ultimately significant for the issue of political equity. The conclusion that can be drawn from Greenstein's linkage of structures and equity is that a psychologically relativistic theory of politics can indeed define a standard of psychological equity. It must do so, however, by determining not only the equities of distributional reward patterns, but the psychological equities that surround the structural "fit" of various political arrangements as well.

Greenstein understood the differentiation among preferences for structures and the nature of the linkage of that differentiation to the issue of political equity in a theoretical way. Although Greenstein conceded that institutional constraints may for a time elicit roughly similar behavior from those who labor in an institutional role, he said that "not all of them will be equally zealous or enthusiastic" about that role. That role, over time, would also be subject to political conflict as well as to psychologically driven incentives for change.[14]

Of course, Greenstein's contribution to the construction of a psychologically relativistic theory of politics, his linkage of the considerations of psychological equity with the preference of different psychologies for different structural arrangements, contained an incipient measure of political equity within it. In defining the linkage between psychological fit and political equity, Greenstein borrowed from the terminology of Nathan Glazer and David Reisman and employed what must become a central concept within a relativistic theory. Greenstein employed the concept of psychological "price," believing that the value of any psychological contribution to a structural setting must be defined according to the degree of that psychology's difficulty of fitting into the institutional setting.

Greenstein argued that if a personality fit reasonably well within a structure, the psychological price that that individual paid for laboring there was comparatively small. Conversely, an incompatible fit of psychology with structure exacted a greater psychological price. This description is no more complicated in its form than what Aristotle described twenty-five hundred years ago: Greenstein placed the largely objective Aristotelean concept of proportionality into a subjective, psychological context, and thus made a substantial theoretical contribution of his own. Indeed, had Greenstein done nothing more than link the relativities of personality to the relativities of structures and relate this linkage to a psychological standard of political equity, he would have given a significant boost to a psychologically relativistic theory. But, not satisfied with only linking differentiated psychologies to political structures in the context of political equity, Greenstein also described the importance of the impact that different personalities have on the makeup of political structures. Rejecting the overly simplistic notion that "personality characteristics tend to be randomly distributed in institutional roles," he argued that different personalities gravitate toward different kinds of institutional structures. He wrote, "there is a great deal of evidence to indicate that particular statuses often attract, or recruit preponderantly for, one or another personality characteristic." Significantly, Greenstein also suggested that these preponderant personalities had an impact on the subsequent molding of the structures. He knew that as different personalities preferred different structures, they would have an impact on what he called the "quality of institutional functioning" during their tenure in the structure.[15]

Finally, and apart from the identification of the crucial variables of a psychologically relativistic theory, Greenstein's thinking also marked a clear priority of considerations. There is a hierarchy or an ordering to Greenstein's psychological considerations here, and this hierarchy places the consideration of relative psychologies *before* the consideration of the structures and processes of a government or any other institution. Psychologies over time, therefore, are thought to determine the shape of institutions for Greenstein and not the other way around. Note that from an epistemological perspective, this is the idealistic and not the materialistic view. Though unfortunately Greenstein did not elaborate on his hierarchy from an epistemological perspective, his proper ordering of the elements of the hierarchy is in tune with the requirements of a relativistic theory.

WEBER AND THE MODERN ORGANIZATION

All in all, Fred Greenstein left a great deal for us. His conclusion that different personalities pay different psychological prices in similar institutional roles, along with his conclusion that each organizational worker's attempt to minimize these differentiated prices makes different personalities prefer different institutional arrangements, both support a relativistic perspective. But Greenstein's third conclusion, dealing with the impact that different personalities have on the structures of which they are a part, is crucial for understanding the evolution or the dynamic of structures. Greenstein related how structures change over time to the efforts of the psychologies that labor in the structure. Relative structures and processes exact their disproportional psychological prices within the context of an Aristotelian, proportional standard of psychological and political equity.

As I have said, structures differ in ways that are significant for a political theory of psychological relativity because different structural arrangements both reflect and promote different ways of thinking about the decisions that they render. Different structures import different forms of cognitions and, within the framework of Fred Greenstein's prescriptions for psychological equity, the cognitive nature of both organizational structures and their processes is akin to very traditional notions of organizational theory.

The modern consideration of organizations began with Max Weber. The decline of the Junker class in Prussia necessitated the development of a predictable, routinized set of institutional arrangements. These arrangements were designed to administer a modernized, and recently nationalized, German citizenry in an efficient way. Referring to private as well as to public structures, Weber greeted modernity by asserting that "it would be sheer illusion to think that continuous administrative work can be carried out in any field except by means of officials working in offices."[16]

But Weber's bureaucratic rationality went beyond an embrace of an approaching modernity. He understood that organizational structures varied and that considerable differences existed between orthodox hierarchical structures on the one hand and those structures that he labeled as "collegial" on the other. Within the orthodox, or "monocratic" structures, Weber knew that work patterns typically prescribed for "a clearly defined sphere of competence in the legal sense." Such delineated spheres reflected clear allocations of authority. Within such spheres, a "strict and systematic discipline and control in the conduct of the office" should reign.[17]

In his depiction of the interactions among systematically arranged bureaus, Weber described a "free contractual relationship" as invariably typifying those bureaus.[18] Relatively homogeneous units of responsibility, discrete units that dealt with each other in the contractual manner that Robert Nozick would prefer, typified Weber's monocratic bureaucratic structure. A relativistic theory of politics suggests that such preferences (which Greenstein argued to be relevant for the allocation of psychological price) favor one psychology over another.

Though a rationalist in the traditional meaning of that term, Weber conceded that hierarchical or monocratic structures did not make up the only conceivable institutional arrangement. He did not think much of the alternative, but he contrasted the monocratic structure to a collegial structure, an organizational arrangement that allowed for "functional collegiality" or the spirit of "consultation" among "a plurality" of institutional roles.[19] The business of such collegial structures, according to Weber, was typically performed "without specification of function." It did its work among "formally equal members" who worked indiscriminately on a variety of tasks.[20] A psychological preference for such structures, I suggest, is very different from a preference for rational structures in precisely the ways that Greenstein comprehended.

THE MODERN WEBERIANS

Weber's organizational relativity, even with its preferences, has survived with elaboration until today. Modern organizational theory, dealing with both private and public structures, has placed the contrast between monocratic and collegial structures along a familiar spectrum. Anthony Downs's recent depictions of that spectrum differentiate between those structures that foster "intensive specialization" to the kind of jurisdictional arrangements that encourage the "overall perspective" throughout the organization.[21] Intensive specialization, according to Downs, brings about a "loss of overall perspective," because "each task is fragmented into tiny parts."[22]

But Downs, like Greenstein, gives us more than a mere description of structures. He goes on to typify the personalities that prefer different structures and procedures, defining the "zealot" as the one who is "loyal [only] to narrow policies or concepts" and contrasting such zealots with what he labeled as "statesmen" (the "advocate" being in the center).[23] Statesmen, understandably, are more naturally concerned with "society as a whole."[24] Within these variant structures, however, differing processes of negotiation and bargaining exist along a spectrum running from Nozick-like exchange forms of negotiation and bargaining to Rawls-like aggregated or "patterned" forms.[25] Like Weber, Downs knew that isolated units were more likely to be dominated by loyalists or zealots. These personalities prefer to deal with each other in an arms length, contractual manner. Overlapping, nondiscrete jurisdictional units, however, embrace the larger perspectives of those who collegially counsel with each other across ill-defined jurisdictions. This is typically done through other than contractual means. Downs knew that statesmen generally eschew the exchange processes that exist among decentralized structural elements.

Howard Aldrich, another student of modern organizations, has described the structural spectrum and Aldrich's notions of bureaucratic and collegial organizations in a way that parallels Weber. The principal distinctions among organizations for Aldrich exist along the range of "inclusive or exclusive" institutions. Such institutions, not surprisingly, are distinguished for Aldrich by "vulnerable" or "impervious" organizational boundaries respectively.[26]

What is significant about Aldrich's typology, much like Greenstein's and far more than either that of Max Weber or Anthony Downs, is that Aldrich specifically related his understanding of a structural spectrum to the range of psychologies that prefer to work at different places on it. Aldrich, for example, emphasized the role of what he called "boundary personnel" in the maintenance of jurisdictional separations. He contrasted the preferences of such personalities with those who prefer to work "with streams of heterogeneous elements." Aldrich thus had a keen sense of what kinds of cognitions were more likely to dominate the interactions of differentiated structures. He also had a Greensteinian sense of each personality's attempt to alter the structural environment. He writes from the idealistic epistemological perspective of what makes up the hierarchy of personality-to-structure relationships. As he knew that individuals over time affect the forms of structures he also knew that relative cognitive preferences for either "homogeneous" or "heterogeneous elements," or for qualitatively similar as opposed to qualitatively dissimilar cognitive variables as a relativistic theory would see them, reveal what Hegel differentiated in his discussion of analytic and synthetic cognitions.[27]

The writings of those who study modern organizations today thus reveal an increasing awareness of the role of differentiated psychologies, as well as preferences for institutional structures. Downs's zealot's ability to negotiate and transactionally interact across well-kept, decentralized structural boundaries evidences a preference for one psychology's natural cognitive favor for the exchange, or the Nozick-like transactionally based interaction. This, of course, is the cognition, as Hegel understood it, that is purely analytic. It is made up of qualitatively similar variables. The statesman, in contrast, prefers overlapping structures and the heterogeneous depiction of bureaucratic tasks. This cognition is synthetic; in Hegel's usage it is the cognition, in an organizational setting, of the "explication of differences."

Weber's "free contractual relationship" implies a cognitive similarity of variables; so too the Weberian notion of "consultations" implies that the elements brought to such consultations from disparate places are more likely to be heterogeneous.[28] But just as differentiated personalities affect the forms of the structure with which they interact, so too the form of those structures, in turn, affect the cognitive form of the issues with which they deal. The equities among the forms of the issues with which any polity deals returns to the Aristotelian-like sense of the allocation of the equities that are found along the range of organizational alternatives. To further identify those equities, the psychological prices that different personalities pay in different political structures must be examined.

THE AFFECTIVE PSYCHOLOGICAL PRICE

If psychological biases are reflected in the differentiations among forms of organizational structures, as well as in the differentiations among the decisional processes that these structures utilize, psychological biases exist within any decision-making arena, public or private. To illustrate these biases, let us posit a simple exchange transaction between two individuals and consider the psychological bias of this contractually based transaction. The opposite psychological price, of course, is paid within "patterned" decision-making processes by those who prefer the contractual decisional form.

If A were to sell a fountain pen to B, setting the price in a simple one-to-one transaction, and if all the external or objective relationships of A and B such as their relative wealth were otherwise equal, a psychologically relativistic theory will contend that a psychological inequity still exists within that transaction. The inequity results from the transactional method of determining the pen's value. The transactional method of sale, with its contractual form of assessing the value of the pen, affects both the valuation of the pen, as well as the equities of the relative psychological prices that the parties to the valuational process pay. This latter inequity is reflected within both the affective and the cognitive psychological prices that are paid in the contractual mode.

With regard to affective equity, Margaret Hermann's and Nathan Kogan's review of the research that has dealt with the affective price of transactional bargaining found the dichotomy of the "authoritarian" as opposed to the "less authoritarian" negotiator to be illustrative. Hermann and Kogan found that the spectrum of affective personality traits that stretches from the authoritarian to the "less" authoritarian correlates well with a preference for what the authors label as "hard" and "soft" bargaining strategies. Though Hermann and Kogan were concerned only with the material equity of the bargaining results between soft and hard bargainers, that is, with the material allocation that results from their bargaining, their evidence also describes the imbalance of what they labeled the "orientation to a negotiation situation."[29]

With regard to that orientation, Hermann and Kogan concluded that the authoritarian personality is more naturally oriented to a one-on-one, contractual bargaining situation than is the less-authoritarian negotiator. The reason for this preferred orientation is that the authoritarian personality is more comfortable with the "hard," confrontational psychological behavior that presses for advantage in the one-on-one contractual framework. Conversely, the less-authoritarian bargainer is less comfortable with the negotiating behavior of the direct exchange. Apart from the distribution or allocation loss that the "soft" bargainer suffers in the exchange bargaining situation, therefore, an affective psychological price is paid by the nonauthoritarian bargainer in the transactional mode. A patterned or nontransactional method of bargaining, of course, would conversely favor the antiauthoritarian negotiator. The *form* of the valuation process, in either case, determines the incidence of the affective psychological price.

THE COGNITIVE PSYCHOLOGICAL PRICE

An affective psychological price is not the only psychological price that the form of decision making exacts on different psychologies. A cognitive psychological price is paid as well, and the allocation of that price among the participants to a decision also grows out of the form of the decisional process. Just as the analytic cognitive structure prefers qualitatively similar variables and, conversely, just as the synthetic cognitive structure prefers the variables of Hegel's "explication of differences," the very nature of the arms-length exchange between two bargainers exacts a form of interaction that qualitatively homogenizes the elements of the exchanges. If the elements of the exchange itself, that is, the value of the commodity and the value of the medium together, are made into an identity, or what Hegel called a tautology in his taunting of Kant's $5 + 7 = 12$ equation, then there is a psychological bias in that transaction in favor of the psychology that prefers the analytic cognition. As processes within organizational structures reflect cognitive biases in favor of transactional or "patterned" decision-making processes, a cognitive price in addition to an affective price is paid within that structure.

Evidence for a linkage between relative decisional processes, their cognitive biases, and the psychological prices that different processes impose generally comes from what is known as "small group" literature as well as from research on the formation of coalitions. Harold Kelley and John Thibault have best described the processes of group decision making,[30] their findings, like Hermann's and Kogan's in the area of affective costs, being concerned with the material distributional outcomes of various bargaining structures. Kelley and Thibault have never directly addressed the issue of the cognitive *form* of bargaining, and they have never addressed the issue of the psychological prices of differentiated bargaining forms. Nonetheless, Kelley's and Thibault's descriptions of the structures of bargaining and coalition formation ably depict the psychology of these processes, and they can readily be extrapolated to the psychological prices of such processes.

Kelley and Thibault's descriptions of coalition building principally distinguish between the bargaining processes of dyadic (two-person) relationships as opposed to the bargaining processes of nondyadic (more-than-two-person) bargaining relationships. The distinction between dyadic and nondyadic bargaining relationships is significant for a relativistic theory since, by definition, dyadic interactions import a transactional form of relationship between the two bargaining parties. A nondyadic interaction, in contrast, generally imports an aggregative or "patterned" relationship as it exists among more than two parties. As Kelley and Thibault put it in their contrasting of two-person and three-person bargainings, "The greater number of possible bargaining positions and settlement points for the triad compared with the dyad reflects the greater number of different structural relations and dynamic processes [that are] possible in the triad."[31] Kelley and Thibault leave no doubt as to the significance of the difference between the transactional nature of a dyadic interaction and the nontransactional nature of an interaction that contains more than two people. As they say, "the greater variety of possible events in the triad compared with the dyad" fundamentally affects the bargaining situation.[32]

A relativistic perspective insists, in the determination of the psychological price of various structural forms, that no decision process is cognitively, any more than it is affectively, neutral. Transactional decision-making processes, typified by dyadic interaction, favor the psychology of the analytic cognition. Patterned decision-making processes, typified by triadic or more-than-triadic interactions, psychologically favor the synthetic cognition. As with the allocation of affective psychological price, the cognitive price paid by the parties in any decisional process depends on the form of that process. In the Aristotelian mode, a psychologically relativistic theory of politics must prescribe for a balance of psychological prices as that balance is assured by a weighing of structurally dictated decisional processes. A conscious balancing of decisional processes is the key to psychological equity in a relativistic theory of politics. Only with such a balancing of decisional processes, and only with a conscious balancing of the structures that contain such processes, a relativistic theory will argue, can psychological equity be achieved.

In sum, the above descriptions of both the affective and the cognitive biases of institutional arrangements evidence the psychological relativity of both decisional structures and their corresponding decisional processes. These relativities reflect the principal known and bounded psychological spectrum, just as they reflect preferences for either the contractual processes of Robert Nozick or the patterned, aggregative processes of John Rawls. These processes, as Weber predicted, are fully a part of the modern bureaucratic life, but they are still dictated by the forms of the structures in which they rest.

The cognitive spectrum that contains the Weberian ideal types of the analytic cognition of Kant to the synthetic ("explication of differences") cognition of Hegel at its poles is also the cognitive spectrum that originates in psychological relativity. An understanding of this relativity, along with an understanding of the equitable balance of the cognitive preferences that it represents, is essential for the achievement of psychological equity. An Aristotelian-like mean can serve as the core of such a definition, but it is Greenstein's notion of psychological price that defines the contribution that relative psychologies make. Aristotle's mean must be placed into a modern political context, just as Greenstein's notions of relative psychological contribution and relative psychological price belong at the core of a psychologically relativistic theory of politics.

IDEALISM AND MATERIALISM

This brief description of psychological equity and, specifically, the affective and cognitive prices that different psychologies play in different structural settings make it clear than an understanding of psychological price can only rest within an appropriate epistemological context. The philosophical contribution of Greenstein's psychological price, understood within the context of proportional political contribution much as Aristotle first described it, is potentially enormous. But if Greenstein never placed his notion of psychological price into an epistemological setting, a full theory of relativity must now do so.

For a psychologically relativistic theory of politics to describe a subjective standard for political equity, grounding itself in an understanding of how differentiated personalities interact within a variety of structures, at least one philosophical prerequisite must invariably be satisfied. This prerequisite is that the standard of equity, which a psychologically relativistic theory of politics suggests, must be idealistic, rather than materialistic. The goal of achieving psychological equity among differentiated personalities is achievable only when the issue of psychological equity is addressed directly. The issue of psychological equity, in the context of an epistemology that places the mind before the body, the imposer of meaning before meaning itself, is inherently idealistic from the beginning.

But three full levels of equity must exist within a relativistic political theory that is epistemologically idealistic. All three of these levels are needed in order to achieve psychological as well as distributional equity. The first level is the psychological level, for psychological relativity is only achieved by ensuring a conscious balancing of psychological price along the principal known and bounded psychological spectrum. The second level of relativity is that of structure and process. Equity is achieved here only by ensuring a mean of psychological price along the spectrums of homogeneous-to-heterogeneous structural arrangements and transactional-to-patterned decisional processes as they exist in their appropriate political institution. The third level of equity exists at the level of resultant or material equity as those distributional results flow out of the political process. In a postmaterial world, resultant or material equities of distribution can be achieved only when there is equity along the psychological range, as well as equity along the structural and procedural range.

Cognitive equity, drawn from a consciousness of the principal psychological range or relativity, can only be defined through a relativistic theory. Such a theory in turn can only grow out of the epistemological position that knows that different imposers of different perspectives on equity exist along what Bernstein called a "commensurable" range. It does not permit an ostensibly objective standard of meaning to define resultant or material equity, as the political philosophies of liberalism and Marxism do in the context of undifferentiated individuals or groups.

It is important to understand as well that a political system's structures and processes are the channels through which structural equity among those of different psychologies ensures resultant or material distributional equity. The three considerations are ordered with material equity last only because *a conscious quest for psychological equity as the perceiver and imposer of what equity is in the first instance* is what ensures the psychological balance of the decisional processes that in turn beget distributional equity. No other ordering of the hierarchy can ensure equity at the other two levels.

A relativistic theory, therefore, insists that distributional equities are sustainable only when the structures and processes of a polity are balanced in a way that reflects the psychological range. It argues that even if a heretofore disadvantaged group or class of psychologically undifferentiated individuals were to succeed in achieving distributional equity for a time, this equity could not be sustained unless the structure of the political system achieves a balance of cognitions, and unless the contractual-to-organizational balance of decision making in those structures that best ensures distributional equity exists. If institutional arrangements are psychologically unbalanced, then what Greenstein has suggested and what Downs and Aldrich have given a great deal of evidence for is that the imbalance of psychologies within these structures imposes imbalanced decision-making processes on those structures. Over time, those imbalances will surely impose distributions that do not reflect either psychological or material justice.

Chapter Seven

STRUCTURES AND CYCLES

THE DYNAMIC OF RELATIVISM

In the preceding chapters, I have described the elements of a psychologically relativistic theory of politics in the context of differentiated perspectives on mediation (knowledge), the dialectic (including the psychological differences among the dialectic's stages), and finally, the progress of understanding or history. In these chapters, I have specifically dealt with 1) the nature of the principal psychological relativity, 2) the inappropriateness of both liberal and Marxist theory for the development of a relativistic theory, 3) a standard of psychological equity for a relativistic theory and 4) the relationship of that standard to the cognitive arrangement of governmental structures, processes and, ultimately, the cognitive shape of substantive political issues.

Throughout these chapters, I have tried to demonstrate how the arrangement of public institutions is not psychologically neutral. In this chapter, I shall argue that just as arrangements of public institutions are not psycholocially neutral, neither are they stable. I will explore the dynamics of public institutions from a psychologically relativistic perspective as I attempt to describe the psychological and political significance of the changes that occur over time within public structures and processes.

In the context of what Fred Greenstein described as a standard of psychological equity, in the context of psychological "price," how institutional changes affect the allocation of psychological and distributional equity over time ought to be better understood.

THE DYNAMICS OF ORGANIZATIONS

The linkage between psychology and organizational structure as seen in the writings of Max Weber, Anthony Downs, and Howard Aldrich explicitly or implicitly tied different psychologies to preferences for differentiated structural arrangements. Weber, in his discussion of charismatic authority, acknowledged the instability of the charismatic mode, for example. Charismatic authority, he said, "cannot remain stable" and it becomes "either traditionalized or rationalized."[1] Similarly, within his discussion of the routinization of personal charisma in bureaucracies, Weber argued that the "process of routinization is thus not by any means confined to the problem of succession." Routinization for Weber meant that "the most fundamental problem is that of making a transition from a charismatic administrative staff, and the corresponding principles of administration, to one which is adapted to everyday conditions."[2]

Anthony Downs updated Weber's intuition concerning the dynamic of all organizations. As Downs described the seemingly inevitable increase of what he labeled "intensive specialization" in organizations, he noted that a distinct "loss of overall perspective" invariably accompanied such specialization. In fact, Downs argued that early, perhaps minimal, losses of perspective in modern organizations contributed to a further specialization until, cumulatively, the organization inevitably fragmented into "tiny parts."[3] Also, because of this dynamic of fragmentation, or because of what Downs called the "rigidity cycle" or the "ossification syndrome," he argued that organizations invariably developed internal processes which he labeled as "bureaucratic free enterprise."[4] For Downs, transactional processes which occur among jurisdictionally homogeneous, highly decentralized subcomponents, typify organizational dynamics.

Howard Aldrich, too, addressed the dynamic of structures. His findings, similar to Downs's, described the inevitable tendency of all organizations to limit what he called the "heterogeneity of the total operation." As Aldrich put it, a tendency was fostered within structures to reduce organizational tasks to "manageable dimensions" over time. This process occurred by the "subdividing [of] work into homogeneous subunits."[5] But Aldrich's descriptions differed from Downs in that he described the organizational dynamic in patently psychological terms.

Aldrich's depiction of those whom he labeled "boundary personnel," for example, highlighted that personality's preference for a "large volume of standardized transactions."[6] Boundary personnel chose this form of cognition over a regimen of more differentiated tasks. The personality that Aldrich depicted is similar to the personality that Downs, without specific reference to psychology, saw as preferring "streams of homogeneous elements."[7]

Just as Downs recognized that structural equilibriums were not stable over time, Aldrich recognized that, over the long term, "strategies for obtaining a more homogeneous population" inevitably won out over strategies that maintained heterogeneity within organizations. Aldrich suggested that, all things equal, the psychology that prefers routinized, homogeneous procedures, or "smoother operating procedures," eventually dominates all organizations.[8]

Again, though Weber and Downs said little about the psychology of what went on within organizations, Aldrich depicted the dynamics of organizations as an essentially psychological phenomenon. If each of these writers was correct about the dynamics of organizations, that is, if what Downs, for example, termed the "rigidity cycle" in fact describes a pattern of the intraorganizational dominance of one psychology over another, then Fred Greenstein's hypothesis concerning the impact of relative psychologies on organizational structures is verified by the increasing psychological price paid by some rather than others in the organization over time.

In the modern writings on organizational dynamics, as Greenstein had predicted, organizations are affected in a similar way by the personalities that work within them. The rigidity cycle, reflecting what goes on in that myriad of interpersonal interactions that makes up an organization's business over time, is reflected in a pattern of psychological dominance within that organization. This dominance, achieved through interpersonal bargaining advantages (such as those described in the "hard bargaining" findings of Hermann and Kogan as well as in the contrast between dyadic and nondyadic interactions that Kelley and Thibault researched), depict the ascendance of one psychology's preferred method of intra-organizational interaction over another's. A dynamic occurs in all organizations that eventually surrenders those organizations to the analytic cognition simply because of the unbalanced organizational influence of those who prefer such cognitions.

More than anything else, what the rigidity cycle demonstrates is not only that organizations are not stable and not neutral but that they are not stable and not neutral in a predictable direction. As the organizational cycle moves irrevocably in the direction of homogeneous jurisdictions and "free enterprise" processes, it favors the psychology that prefers the analytic cognition over the psychology that prefers the synthetic cognition. The former psychology pays a proportionately smaller psychological price within the altered organization.

CULTURE AND HISTORY

In the context of a discussion of organizational dynamics, it is important to recognize that just as psychologically generated changes occur within organizations, so too psychologically generated changes occur in the evolution of both cultures and eras of history. Pitirim Sorokin's studies of the cycles of cultures depict what he found to be a universal dynamic of cultural periods. His *Social and Cultural Dynamics* described a trilogy of *ideational, idealistic* and *sensate* stages that he believed marked different periods in all cultures. The ideational stage depicted a period wherein significant cultural figures consciously implanted novel considerations into the culture. It was a period in which thinking about the world in a creative and increasingly complex way expanded the culture into a variety of different forms. Sorokin argued for the superiority of the ideational as opposed to the sensate vision, contending that the ascendance of what he called the "ultimate reality" was an ascendance of the kind of mind that participated in the "great symphony of life." [9] This is the mind," he said, "that moves in both a "quantitative and qualitative spatial direction." [10]

At the other end of the cultural dynamic, Sorokin's depiction of the sensate culture defined a very different cognitive preference. The sensate culture, or better, the moment of the sensate culture, was made up only of the apparent reality. It was, for Sorokin, a time of mere sensation, a time of reaction that was, above all, not innovative. As one might expect, the sensate perspective was also devoid of introspection and reflection. Most important, it was devoid of consciousness, particularly of the mind's own condition in the sense that Hegel wrote about the mind's conscious role in the progress of understanding.

For Sorokin, the sensate culture's view of the world as nothing more than a "reality" meant that this view included only "the inorganic, the organic, technology, medicine and the applied disciplines and the socio-cultural world."[11] Such a worldview is dominated by individuals who primarily "seek power over inorganic, organic and psychosocial nature," Sorokin suggested, because their perspective, in Hegelian language, is one that seeks to annul "the completed union of the Idea and its reality."[12] From a psychological perspective, Sorokin's sensate vision and its insistence on a linear worldview is the vision of the analytic cognition. While Sorokin's descriptions of the ascendant artistic and cultural periods depict the rise of the synthetic cognition, the decline of cultures, as with the decline of organizational structures, reflects the dominance of the analytic cognition.

Like Sorokin's cultural cycles, Arnold Toynbee's *Study of History* identifies a universal dynamic pattern. Toynbee's pattern describes three well-defined historical stages, beginning with an ascendant stage, typified by a "variety and elasticity, experimentation and creativeness."[13] The ascendant stage is followed by the "zenith" of the civilization. In this stage, a maximum of aggregation, or coordination of the society's rich disparities, occurs. The zenith, however, proves to be unsustainable, and it inevitably falls into a "mimesis" or a "kind of drill" within the waning civilization.[14]

Toynbee noted that the decline of all civilizations is typified by "a kind of mechanization of human life and movement."[15] The political elements of the society in his third stage evidence a predisposition to "check and sterilize each other" through increasingly fragmented governmental structures.[16] Decline and the routinized drill are not guided by "experimentation" and "creativeness," but are guided instead by "the dull ears that are deaf to the unearthly music of Orpheus' lyre." A society in decline, Toynbee suggests, attunes itself only to "the drill sergeant's word of command."[17]

The language Toynbee used to describe the rise and fall of civilizations is richly psychological. The third or mimetic stage of all civilizations is a stage, much like the "rigidity" or "ossification" stage of Downs's organizations, that clearly reflects the dominance of qualitatively similar over qualitatively dissimilar variables. Such a stage, of course, favors the analytic cognition, while the ascendant stage of civilizations is just as clearly a stage of the synthetic cognition.

Beyond Sorokin and Toynbee, similar, psychologically implicit works portray the dynamic of the rise and fall of civilizations. Edward Gibbons' *Rise and Fall of the Roman Empire,* for example, chronicles the structural fragmentation and decay of Rome,[18] particularly noting the progressive formalization of political interactions throughout Rome's public institutions. In *The Decline of Nations,* Mancur Olson, though dubiously assuming a natural political bonding as originating in private economic arrangements, portrays a social fragmentation that is caused by the tugs of disparate political interests. Olson finds "unprecedented quantitative evidence" that describes "the rise and fall of civilizations in a systematic way." He concludes that large groups as well as nations simply "will not act in the group interest" over extended periods of time.[19] As citizens increasingly choose to do things out of what Olson calls their "selective incentives" (a material explanation), structural fragmentation occurs.[20]

With all of the above descriptions, however, it may be that Oswald Spengler's *Decline of the West,* with its inclusion of that "morphology of knowledge forms," describes the rise and fall of nations in the most psychological way. Spengler's book is rich with psychological terminology, he at one point contrasting "the ripest and deepest forms and images" and society's "infinitely-varied external culture" with the "spiritually dead man of the autumnal cities—Hammurabi's Babylon, Ptolemaic Alexandria, Islamic Baghdad, [and] Paris and Berlin to-day."[21] For Spengler, the key indicator of the vitality of nations was the "actualization" of the native culture. Actualization occurs when "an evocation of mind is contemplated, and . . . an assurance of the senses [is] critically comprehended."[22]

Like Sorokin in his view of a nation's culture, Spengler saw the "evocative" vision of a nation's art as best "exemplified in the worlds of Plato, Rembrandt, Goethe and Beethoven." These artists' work marked cultural ascendance while the "spiritually dead" vision, in contrast, was obvious in the works of "Parmenides, Descartes, Kant and Newton." Spengler described the origin of this contrast as "cognition in the strict sense of the word." Such cognition was, above all, "an act of experience."[23] After completing his contrast of "the lived, felt and unconfined 'Nature' of Homer and the Eddas, of Doric and Gothic man" to the "dissected Nature of Aristotle and Kant, the Sophists and Darwinians, modern physics and chemistry," Spengler argued that to "overlook this [contrast] is to miss the whole essence of historical treatment."[24] Spengler reflected sadly, "Tendencies towards a mechanistic idea of the world proceeding wholly from mathematical delimitation and logical differentiation" exist in all civilizations from their earliest time. Inevitably, however, "these tendencies acquire a sterner character" as each society eventually becomes something "that is wrung out of the soul and has to defend itself against human nature."[25]

The above descriptions strike a universal chord of rise and fall, ascendance and decline, over the life of organizations, cultures, and civilizations. But one reflection, concerning the dynamic of historic, cultural, or organizational life cycles, reveals their importance to a relativistic theory of politics. Recall again Judith Shklar's depiction of Hegel's perspective on history, the perspective of the "single, ordered whole." Recall also that throughout Hegel's writings, but particularly within his *Phenomenology,* the notion of the singular, collective step of movement toward understanding seems to confirm Shklar's depiction. But what is clear is that the above portrayals of the history of a variety of entities do not depict the movement of a "single, ordered whole." On the contrary, they portray something that is cyclical in nature, not linear. They portray how different cognitions dominate different periods throughout a variety of generalizable circumstances and seem to show that Hegel was almost certainly wrong about the linear leaps of history. Although history probably does have a pattern to it, that pattern is cyclical, not linear.

I have already described how I believe that Hegel was guilty of a crucial omission by failing to acknowledge the link between different cognitions and different psychologies. Within a dynamic context, now I also suggest that the correction of Hegel's omission mandates that Hegel's singular historical consciousness be extended into an awareness of relative historical consciousness. It is relative historical consciousnesses, working their way through history as history moves back and forth along an identifiable spectrum of cognitive ascendances, that account for the cycles of all civilizations, cultures, and organizations.

LONG CYCLES

The dynamic of the life cycles of organizations, cultures, or political systems does not represent the entire dynamic of organizational structures and processes. Life cycles do not make up the entirety of any structure's dynamic. What are often referred to as *long cycles* depict patterns of alterations that occur over shorter periods than life cycles. Long cycles, as opposed to life cycles, do not carry irreversible changes of direction along with them. Long cycles return, roughly, to an earlier position without contributing, at least measurably, to the life cycle fragmentation of an entire system. Each long cycle creates what are at best minor structural alterations as it progresses back and forth along a known spectrum of oscillation, while life cycles impact mightily on any system's principal structures.

From the perspective of a relativistic theory of politics, the relevance of psychology to long-term cycles has been debated for at least a half century. In economics, the traditional view of cycles is offered by Joseph Schumpeter, among others. Schumpeter's vision had nothing to do with psychology, overwhelmingly ascribing the derivation of long-term growth cycles to the advance of technology.[26] Schumpeter wrote extensively on long cycles, arguing that technological breakthroughs brought about rushes of investment capital and bursts of productive energy. Increases in productivity, real wages, and, accordingly, national wealth reflected the technological surge. Conversely, when the impetus of each technological improvement had spent itself—when the once new technology had had its run of investment applications—economic contraction inevitably set in.[27]

But Schumpeter's description of economic cycles was wholly different from the description of cycles offered by John Maynard Keynes. Cyclical theory in economics is now more frequently identified with Keynes than with Schumpeter, and the contrast between the explanations for cycles of Keynes and his outspoken contemporary is significant for a relativistic theory. The Keynes-Schumpeter dialogue over cycles amounted to more than an academic debate among economic historians. Schumpeter, in the introduction to his two-volume *Business Cycles,* for example, reminded his reader that "I recommend no policy and propose no plan. Readers who care for nothing else should lay this book aside."[28] Schumpeter twisted the knife by adding, "I do not admit that this convicts me of indifference to the social duty of science or makes this book . . . irrelevant to the burning questions of the day." If any suspense remained, he finally named "Mr. Keynes" directly and generously consented to "leave to the reader [any] systematic comparison of my analytic scheme with others."[29] With full assurance that he did not "wish to criticize them" (Keynes and a fellow cyclical theorist, Gottfried Haberler), he went on to explain that he found such a disclaimer to be necessary only because, "in the nature of things, some passages will read exactly like attacks upon them."[30] They still do.

Schumpeter's attack on Keynes is understandable, if less forgivable, in the light of what Keynes was suggesting about cycles and the discipline of economics generally. Concerned principally with unemployment, Keynes's explanation for the joblessness of the Great Depression challenged the long-assumed automatic folding of savings into investment that Jean Baptiste Say had chiseled into the stone of economic orthodoxy. Schumpeter and Keynes differed over Keynes's contention that zero unemployment was not at the savings-investment equilibrium. Schumpeter and Keynes also differed over to what degree economics was the result of Adam Smith's invisible hand or of conscious systemic decision making. This argument, incidentally, persists with every bit as much vigor today in economics as well as in the other social sciences. Keynes's dividing of those who save from those who invest underwrote something of considerable epistemological significance. It also, quite practically, meant that capital either could or could not be invested. Though interest rates and other objective economic variables surely affected such decisions, the introduction of discretionary and potentially countercyclical decision making on the part of economic actors was a heresy for the classical tradition in economics. The disagreement between Schumpeter and Keynes over the importance of conscious human behavior to economic events was really an argument over the importance of the human, subjective intermediary to all of human destiny.

Keynes, of course, cannot be called a relativist in any psychological sense. He never ascribed cyclical economic change to the alternating ascendances of different cognitions. Neither did Keynes call on a particular psychology to redress the imbalances of overinvestment or underinvestment at the appropriate cyclical point. Nonetheless, Keynes's cycles, or his inclusion of the workings of human psychologies within cycles, is a worthwhile preface to relativism. His linkage of the oscillation of long-term economic cycles to human discretion in the "General Theory," including his belief that "the psychological propensities of the modern world [combined] must be of such a character as to produce these [cyclical] results," presages the importance of psychology for economics.[31] Keynes did not utilize psychological relativity as I have defined it or imagine how different psychologies might alternatively dominate stages of economic cycles. But he did recognize that economic cycles resulted from something more than Schumpeterian, material causes. It was a significant recognition.

Later research on cycles has defined the role of the human intermediary in a variety of cyclical contexts. Frank Klingberg identified the cycles of American foreign policy with what he called extrovertive and introvertive psychological phases, Klingberg's "expansive" phase being typified by wars, armed interventions, and annexations of territory and his introvertive or "contractive" phase being typified by isolationism.[32] More recently, Jack Holmes has linked the Klingberg cycles to what he calls "mood curves."[33] These curves initially drew on David McClelland's distinction between psychological power needs as opposed to affiliation needs, Holmes, with Robert Elder, linking his cycles to the Kondratieff fifty-year waves of international economic expansion and contraction. Holmes believes he has discovered the linkage between phases of economic cycles and periods of international conflict and peace.[34] Finally, Joshua Goldstein has recently analyzed a withering collection of data on the relationship of economic cycles and international conflict. Psychology is not significant in Goldstein's analysis, but his conclusions help substantiate the existence of regularized, cyclical behavior in international relations.

One more reflection on John Maynard Keynes and latter-day cyclical writers may be useful here. It is important to remember that the placing of subjectivity, or psychology, within the equation of economic cycles is not all that set Keynes apart from traditional economists like Schumpeter. Just as significantly for a relativistic theory, Keynes's writings evidence a clear preference for a way of thinking about economics that reveals his own cognitive preferences as much as Kant's and Hegel's views of cognitions revealed theirs. Keynes spent a good part of his early career quarreling with the economic orthodoxies of the dismal science. He focused specifically on the distinction between what was labeled *risk* by many economists and what Keynes claimed was more often merely *uncertainty*. Keynes' position was that orthodox economists frequently mislabeled what were imponderable variables as quantifiable risks. Keynes argued that the assigned quantification of risks was arbitrary at best and that the measure of risk was often unknowable or at least unknown at the time value was assigned to it. With the inclusion of a qualitatively different classification—uncertainty—Keynes was really arguing that quantifiable and nonquantifiable factors needed to be identified as qualitatively different in economics and considered in that light.

The cognitive preference that reveals itself in Keynes's risk-uncertainty differentiation in economics manifested itself throughout his work. It led Keynes, for example, to argue for inelasticities in the interactions of supply and demand, these inelasticities coming from such static factors in the population as levels of skill, work ethics, and the like. Because of the importance of such noneconomic factors in any economy, Keynes argued that supply and demand adjustments simply did not slide along the orthodox economists' utility curves as easily as these economists had contended.

John Maynard Keynes, far more than any economist of his day, dealt with things economic in the mode of the synthetic cognition. It was his perspective on the synthetic cognition that permitted him to be so comfortable with a nascently psychological perspective in what was then, and what is even more so now, a largely quantified field. "Our psychological law must hold good" within the realm of cycles, Keynes concluded in the *General Theory*.[35] Though not referring directly to psychological or cognitive preferences within a relativistic framework, Keynes's observation was significant for his perspective on long-term economic cycles and Keynes's ideas on long-term economic cycles are relevant for political cycles as well. Keynes's ideas are further relevant for life cycles, for the structure of the economy, the culture, the political system, or whatever undergoes fundamental, or structural, change over the life of the entity is part of a life cycle. Understanding the role of the human intermediary in the progression of these life cycles is fundamental to a relativistic theory of politics.

POSTMATERIAL CYCLES

The coming of the postmaterialist age has meaning for the nature of both long cycles and life cycles. Long cycles and life cycles reflect psychological, and specifically cognitive, dominance in their various stages. But the coming of the postmaterial age may mean something even more dramatic for cycles. I have deliberately not placed the discussion of cycles into the context of the epistemological debate between the idealist and the materialist vision so far. I have typified cycles only in terms of their cognitive dimension, but I have not claimed that psychology necessarily *drove* those cycles. There is, of course, some evidence that differentiated psychologies have a role in the progression of the cycles. But the conclusion that psychology has invariably been what social scientists call the independent variable in the movement of either long cycles or life cycles has yet to be proven.

Having conceded this, however, let me point out that what has occurred during the phases of various cycles at least *reflected* differentiated psychologies in the past. The postmaterial age, I suggest, can be expected to do a good deal more than that. Recall that in my earlier discussion of postmaterialism, I suggested that two revisions of existing postmaterial writings were necessary. The first revision insisted on an understanding of a full range of psychologically responsive political ideologies. The second required a leap from substantive postmaterialism, a sense of how a citizenry may increasingly turn to nonmaterial concerns, or to an *epistemological* postmaterialism. It asked for a consideration of political attitudes and behavior from the perspective of the psychology of each citizen as that psychology first defined and, at some later time, brought about a response to political events.

Within a psychologically relativistic context, what this means for the definition of cycles is that the impact of differentiated psychologies in a postmaterial world should be more significant in the progression of cycles than it has ever been. Put another way, if economically developed societies have arrived at the stage where the difference between psychologies is more significant for the debates and definitions of politics than it has been, then both the oscillation of political long cycles and the inexorable movement of political life cycles with their accompanying structural changes should more closely reflect differences among human psychologies. The political analogue of Keynesian-style, subjectivist, or postmaterial life cycles will reflect how personal, psychologically relative preferences affect preferences for how political systems know their political issues. As a consequence, a postmaterial society should be aware of how its political system understands politics according to which cognitive forms dominate that system.

Of course, postmaterialism's life-cycle dynamics will invariably reflect psychologically directed choices for institutional arrangements that know public issues in one way or another. Any postmaterial society should reflect on its choices of structural alternatives in a different way than did societies before the postmaterial age. As postmaterial political cycles, much as with Keynesian economic cycles, will reveal far more than the mere substance of public decision making, postmaterial political cycles will evidence more than long cycle oscillations of perspectives on public issues like budgetary expenditures, taxation, defense, entitlements, and the like. Postmaterial political cycles will include more of psychology than have earlier political cycles, and these cycles will have a more direct impact on the governmental structures that decide such issues than earlier cycles have had.

All of this is to say that if postmaterial cycles have a political impact at the level of altering structures and processes within a postmaterial polity, it is logical to assume that postmaterial cycles will also have an impact on the *form* of the political issues with which the political structures deal. Postmaterial cycles will have an impact on the determination of the very *form* of political issue that different *forms* of political structures and processes naturally consider. A new perspective on politics, placed within a framework that emphasizes the form of governmental structures and processes, will more patently reflect the impact of psychological preferences for various structures and processes, and it will less greatly reflect the importance of purely substantive, materially based issues.

Of course, a consideration of the postmaterialist impact on alternative public structures and processes fits within a psychologically relativistic theory in an epistemologically idealistic, not materialistic perspective. Within the postmaterial world, the imposition of meaning that comes from preferences for different styles of knowing, or for differences in what Spengler called "knowledge forms," is more significant politically now than it has ever been.

Yet even beyond epistemological idealism, the postmaterial consideration fits as well within the idealistic hierarchy of political considerations. If a known and bounded relativity of human psychologies in fact lies at the core of a postmaterial, psychologically relativistic theory of politics, the idealistic hierarchy suggests that the range of psychologies (see chapter 3) determines psychological equity, structural and procedural equity as that equity is defined by the psychological balance of institutions and their processes, and, finally, resultant or distributional equity. Truly postmaterial politics is a product of only this order.

An epistemologically postmaterial perspective on politics, specifically a relativistically based idealistic perspective, is thus the proper perspective for incorporating the mind-first order into political theory. I will now use an epistemologically postmaterial, psychologically relativistic perspective to discuss two final considerations. First, I will suggest how the epistemologically idealist perspective affects the definitional framework of modern political progress. Second, I will discuss how a conscious, Keynes-like counterbalancing of the distortions of political life cycles might be achieved.

MEDIATION, THE DIALECTIC, AND THE PROGRESS OF HISTORY

The political impact of all organizational structures is best revealed by an understanding of their cognitive biases. The biases are best understood, in their turn, within Hegel's notions of mediation, the dialectic and the progress of understanding. All three of these notions are not exclusively intellectual notions. They each reveal themselves in the relativity that exists in the dynamic of everyday organizational structures and certainly in the dynamic of any political system's institutions.

Again, if mediation in the context of a relativistic theory of politics shapes the understanding or "knowing" of issues in institutions, the idealistic perspective on mediation means that the perceiver imposes meaning on what is perceived and not the other way around. The idealistic epistemological vision is, of course, a subjectivist vision. If the notion of mediation, from a relativistic perspective, implies the imposition of relative meanings as they originate in different subjectivities, then the role of the institution in defining individual political issues is central to a relativistic theory. As I have suggested, the *form* of meaning imposed on any issue results at least in part from the institutional structure that imposes that meaning. In a political context, therefore, the relativistic vision will describe how different political structures impose cognitive preferences on the *form* of public issues.

For example, consider the Aristotelean notion of proportionality as it relates to judgments on contribution and distribution. I have reviewed two "ideal type" methodologies for the determination of distributions within political societies: the exchange method, preferred by Robert Nozick, and the patterned method, favored by John Rawls. These methodological alternatives correspond to the principal psychological differentiation. They almost surely evidence the cognitive preferences of the authors as well. Within the institutional setting of modern governments, whichever cognitive preference dominates the arrangements of that government's institutions determines the methodology of allocating contribution and reward. It will do so because the cognitive preference, and the corresponding institutional arrangement, imposes a particular cognitive framework of understanding on the issue of distribution.

As a general rule, if the analytic cognition is dominant, a government's institutional arrangement will prefer the exchange methodology of distributional consideration. The analytic cognition, as it is encased within that institutional setting, will know the qualitatively similar variables of the exchange methodology better than it will know patterned variables. More comfortable with what Anthony Downs called "bureaucratic free enterprise," such institutions will prefer the dyadic form of transaction in their method of doing business, as well as in the working out of the policies that exact the political system's pattern of distribution. Also, if certain interests are more adept at the transactional method of interacting with the government than are others, and if certain issues are more accommodated to a transactional form of understanding and political resolution than others, those issues and interests will be favored by the government.

In contrast, if the synthetic cognition is dominant in the institutional arrangement of the government, the cognitive preferences of public institutions will know the patterned method of distributional activity better than the transactional method. Such institutions, and their ability to envelop a variety of interests and considerations in their public decision making, will more likely consider issues that are not well adapted to the transactional mode of governmental influence.

The above, of course, relates the preferred cognitions of public institutions to the distributional policies of these institutions. But what if the dynamic of public institutions, as with any organization, is altered over time in a predictable direction? What happens to the distributional methodology of those institutions? Predictably, as public institutions become fragmented, or what Weber would call "rationalized," they become more amenable to the transactional form of dealing with public issues. As a result, the increasing institutional favor that is shown to the transactional form of doing business favors those interests that are best able to represent themselves transactionally in the distributional argument. If Downs's notion of the rigidity cycle describes how decisional patterns are altered in a predictable and unidirectional way, a predictable and unidirectional alteration toward not only a transactional methodology of dealing with public questions but an inexorable movement toward greater dispersions of wealth among the citizenry will occur.

But even beyond its direct impact on a government's distribution of biases, the dynamic of institutional change over time is significant in the context of Hegel's dialectic and the progress of history as well. The dialectic, recall, is a method for the improvement of understanding. It is a dynamic concept, much like that of the alteration of organizations, the three stages of the dialectic each reflecting different cognitive preferences. As the first stage reflects the analytic cognition, so too the third stage analytically reconciles what has been dealt with in the contradiction. It is the second stage, the stage of the contradiction, that relies on the synthetic cognition. This contradiction, as Hegel defined it, depends on bringing things into consciousness that represent an "explication of differences." Whether it was the particular and the universal of individuals and the state, or the next stage of history contradicting the present stage, Hegel's contradictory stage of the dialectic invariably engaged the contradiction of the qualitatively dissimilar variable.

The relationship of the organizational dynamic to the dialectic is quite clear, for what the Downsian, rigidity-cycle-driven and unidirectional ascendance of the analytic form of cognition means in the context of the progress of history and of a political life cycle is that in their descending stages, public institutions find it increasingly difficult to know the second, cognitively synthetic, contradictory stage of the dialectic. As time goes on, public institutions, in other words, become increasingly incapable of bringing qualitatively dissimilar considerations, the considerations that cannot be transactionally transmitted, into their fragmented forms. These institutions, as a result, become increasingly incapable of the dialectic and the political system of which they are a part increasingly fails to govern the nation either adequately or fairly.

Recall that each of the systemic failures of political empires that were described by Arnold Toynbee and the declines of cultures that were described by Pitirim Sorokin depicted movement toward qualitatively homogeneous forms of mediation or knowledge. The mimesis or the drill of routinized considerations took over from the experimentation and creativeness of earlier times in each circumstance. Through the mediation of increasingly fragmented institutions or cultures, the analytic cognition increasingly imposed its form of meaning on public issues, and the synthetic cognition was correspondingly denied. As the dialectic requires each of the cognitions to advance beyond the contradictions of any civilization or culture, a unidirectional alteration of institutional mediation in the direction of the analytic cognition inevitably impedes the knowing of the second or contradictory stage of the dialectic there. It impedes a knowing of the "explication of differences" that, through the contradiction, permits qualitatively different considerations to be brought before the public's political institutions.

The progress of understanding and history, of course, was the third and final stage in Hegel's "Idea of Cognition." By progress, Hegel meant an improvement of human understanding, a moving toward the abstract notion Hegel called Absolute knowledge. The Hegelian trilogy ends, as it began, as a strictly metaphysical venture. Yet, as Walter Kaufmann and other Hegel scholars have properly pointed out, Hegel was not a sterile idealist. Though Hegel used his descriptions of the progress of history in the *Phenomenology* largely as allegory, he was deeply concerned with real-world political circumstances. Further, though the progress of history began with an improvement of understanding for Hegel, his sense of mediation and the dialectic promoted a form of understanding that met its truest challenge in the progress of real-world politics.

The role of Hegel's mediation and dialectic within the progress of history was in sharp contrast to Kant's sense of these metaphysical elements. Importantly, Hegel's perspective, unlike Kant's, included a consciousness of the dialectical progression itself. A political philosophy that is based on a *relativistic* psychological perspective ensures the element of consciousness and better promotes the reality of dialectical, historical progress. Mediation, the three stages of the dialectic, and the progress of understanding or history that Hegel described can, and now should be, understood within a relativistic framework. They all should be understood this way because within the postmaterial, organizational state, only an understanding of psychological relativity can ensure the necessary balances of Hegel's three intellectual elements. Ultimately, only such an understanding ensures the progress of history by insisting that all forms of knowing be available to public institutions.

In its structural and procedural setting, the Weberian typology of organizational relativity, if unconsciously, reflected the Hegelian cognitive relativity. But if institutions are not neutral and not stable, as

Downs, Aldrich, and others have shown, so too they will increasingly permit only a single cognitive form of understanding to define the issues with which they deal. This is as true for public institutions in the considerations of an issue such as material distribution as it is for any other institution. If I have properly addressed the largely psychological nature of the dynamic of organizational change in the context of a relativistic theory, and if the life cycle dynamic or the internal dynamic of structural alteration that exists during the life of any set of public institutions evidences a predictable psychological pattern, this pattern of alteration will affect more than the mediation, the dialectic, and the pattern of the history of that institution. It will affect the equity of that political system.

A CONSCIOUS COUNTERBALANCE

John Maynard Keynes is best contrasted with Joseph Schumpeter for his introduction of conscious, subjective understandings to the ostensibly objective realities of economic cause and effect. Keynes was an epistemological idealist. His description of economic cycles, and particularly his description of a consciousness about them, is compatible with his demonstrated preference for the synthetic cognition. But Keynes dealt with long cycles, not life cycles. Further, Keynes did not deal with relative psychologies. Yet, just as Keynes' real-world countercyclical borrowing, investment, and taxation policies were offered as a remedy for business cycles, a psychologically relativistic theory of politics' countercyclical remedies will include a conscious placement of appropriate psychologies, and thus cognitions, into their appropriate countercyclical institutional roles. Such a theory will include a conscious restructuring of the institutional and procedural arrangements of a government in order to reintroduce the synthetic cognition into that government's considerations.

It is possible to turn an understanding of the ascendance of one psychology over another within public institutions into a remedy for life-cycle generated political inequity, as well as life-cycle generated political ossification. It is also possible, I think, to prescribe for the conscious balancing of cognitions within structures and processes, just as Keynes prescribed for the balancing of economic stimulants and depressants in a national economy. A balancing of psychological equities, along with a balancing of the institutional arrangements that reflect those equities, or a balancing of Weber's rational and collegial structures, is now feasible within modern governments. But it is feasible only in accordance with a new sense of political equity and its link to psychological equity. The achievement of this new sense of equity is only possible within an acceptance of the equitable hierarchy that begins with psychological equity, continues with structural and procedural equity, and then proceeds to distributional equity.

John Maynard Keynes was not timid about his concern for economic and political equity throughout his professional life. He was concerned with material equities and though he considered psychology only in the context of how a nation's psychology in a broad and undifferentiated way affected the business cycle, he utilized the synthetic cognition in order to include disparate variables within what he saw as a sterile science. An understanding of the relativity of psychologies can lead to a counterbalancing of not only economic cycles, but a counterbalancing of political cycles as well. But this will happen only when psychological equity becomes a conscious political goal and is placed at the top of the idealistic hierarchy.

II

THE AMERICAN POLITICAL SYSTEM

In part 1, I outlined a psychologically relativistic theory of politics. Beginning with a description of the principal bounded and known differentiation among human natures, as that differentiation has revealed itself in studies of both affective and cognitive personality traits, I have argued that G. W. F. Hegel's theoretical understanding of analytic and synthetic cognitions in the abstract, when linked to the real human psychologies that naturally prefer each cognition and placed along a full range of such psychologies, will underpin a relativistic theory.

As I described how Hegel's cognitions related directly to the relativity of known and bounded human psychologies, I also described how neither Marxist nor liberal political theory can address the question of psychological equity. Utilizing Fred I. Greenstein's notion of psychological price, I then defined a standard of psychological equity as a proportionate allocation of the psychological fit of differentiated psychologies within modern public institutions. In doing so, I suggested that the cognitive balance of those institutions significantly affects the cognitive balance of the issues with which public institutions deal.

In Chapter 7, I described how the impact of different psychologies on public structures over time affected both the psychological equity and the material equity that those institutions create. I have also suggested that that the alteration of public structures that has been brought about by the dynamic of interpersonal interaction within these structures affected both the balance of psychological price and the balance of distributional equities in any political system.

In part 2, I shall apply the theory of psychological relativism that I outlined in part 1 to the only government with which I pretend familiarity. For reasons that should be clear shortly, however, I suspect that the

United States government is a good example of the equitable imbalances, as well as the inefficacies, that a relativistic theory describes. Though the United States was the overwhelmingly dominant nation of the immediate post-World War II era, it has fallen rapidly from that position over the past twenty-five years. The decline of American political and economic influence abroad has been matched, particularly since the 1973 oil embargo, by decline in the living standards of some Americans and a near stagnation in the real income of all but the wealthiest of Americans. Since 1980, America's public debt has risen from less than one trillion to more than three trillion dollars. The imbalance of American trade now regularly runs in excess of 100 billion dollars per year.

Some of America's current political difficulties result from the structural and procedural inadequacies of the original constitutional order. I suspect, however, that more of the decline has resulted from those accelerated structural and procedural alterations of the American constitutional order that have occurred only in recent years. These alterations have resulted in great part from an organizational dynamic much like that that I reviewed in chapter 7. From the perspective of a psychologically relativistic theory, these alterations directly contribute to the inequities that are increasingly evident in the American political system.

Traditional writings on the American constitutional order emphasize the legal and procedural regularities of this unique political system. They describe the American political arrangement in terms of how it has evolved within the liberal democratic tradition. The writings of so many constitutional scholars properly applaud the improvement of individual protections from an arbitrary government that the American Constitution has afforded. They also applaud the steady inclusion of the American citizenry into the public decision-making arena. Though John Locke conceived no theory of history as such, traditional, liberal descriptions of the American Constitution relate the generally successful fulfillment of a Lockean prescription for a government that is both limited and protective of the rights of its citizens.

The most significant challenge to the liberal underpinnings of the American constitutional order has typically come from those who felt that the distributive arrangements of the system were unfair. It came from constitutional analyses such as those of the historian Charles A. Beard, who, in *An Economic Interpretation of the Constitution of the United States,* challenged the system from what was essentially a Marxist perspective.[1] Beard freely conceded in the 1935 introduction to his original, 1913 text that he possessed more than an "interest" in Marx when he wrote the *Interpretation*. Beard noted, however, that Aristotle and all of those whom he termed the "great writers [of the] middle ages and modern times," as well as James Madison, had acknowledged the importance of economics to government.[2]

In reference to the Framers and the Constitutional Convention, Beard asked only, "Did they represent . . . economic interests [that] they understood and felt in concrete, definite form through their own personal experience with identical property rights"?[3] Beard's answer was an unqualified "yes," his view of the Framers being that their new republic must take on "a real form; it must govern actions; it must determine positive relations between men." Such a constitutional mandate, of course, could not be separated from "the social and economic fabric of the country."[4]

But if for Beard the government of the United States was primarily "concerned with the property relations of men," then those relations, or what he called "the processes by which the ownership of concrete forms of property is determined," were the relations of property and contract that Beard generously cited in Madison's no. 10 *Federalist*. Beard specifically noted Madison's allusion to the "diversity in the faculties of men, from which the rights of property originate." He also noted Madison's reference to the "division of society into different interests and parties."[5] Beard, of course, was unsympathetic to Madison's defense of such divisions and he responded in typically Marxist fashion to the American order's jealous protections of property.

A psychologically relativistic theory's perspective on the American constitutional order is altogether different from either the supportive liberal or the critical Marxist view. Liberalism and Marxism, as reviewed in part 1, are both materialistic theories. They are rationally based, objectivist theories and their substantive concern with property, either from a favorable or an unfavorable point of view, is epistemologically identical. The perspective of a skeptically based idealist theory, or, specifically, the perspective of a theory that is based on different subjective, psychological viewpoints, offers a different version of the American government. As neither Madison's nor Beard's view of government begins with the mind, neither a liberal nor a Marxist perspective adequately describes the psychological inequities, or the material inequities, of the American government.

In part 2, I will describe the psychological and material inequities of the American political system in the context of the relativistic theory that I introduced in part 1. I will describe why I believe that the American constitutional order falls short of psychological equity, as well as why the absence of that psychological equity has been instrumental in both America's recent decline and the acceleration of its material inequities. In the final chapter of part 2, I will review a number of proposals that are designed to reverse America's political fortune. Though I shall periodically cite the work of scholars who have written on the problem of institutional integrity within the American political system, I shall suggest that a sounder theoretical grounding must underlie the structural analysis of our government than those that have thus far been provided.

Chapter Eight

THEORY AND STRUCTURE

HEGEL AND THE REALMS

In this chapter, I will describe the fundamental arrangements of the American political system in the context of a psychologically relativistic theory of politics. I will also describe the American political system in terms of the "realms" that Hegel used to connote ascendants stages of historical progress, but I will note the overuse of the synthetic cognition in Hegel's prescriptions for political progress, as well as the underuse of the synthetic cognition in both the original design and the recent evolution of America's political institutions. I will also note the absence of a philosophical perspective on America's politics and will suggest the importance of the perspective of Thomas Jefferson to any philosophical vision of American politics.

I have relied on G. W. F. Hegel more than any other philosopher for the development of a psychologically relativistic theory. I have done so primarily because of Hegel's understanding of the differentiation between the analytic and synthetic cognitive forms. But I have also relied on Hegel because of his understanding of how cognitive differentiation affects the way that things are understood; the progress of the dialectic, or the progress of the improvement of knowledge; and, finally, the progress of history.

Having acknowledged the importance of Hegel's cognitive biases as they were played out in Hegel's political prescriptions, I would point out again that a psychologically relativistic theory relies only tangentially on Hegel's political writings and far more on Hegel's earlier, metaphysical writings. If Hegel's *Logic* properly describes the cognitive differentiation, what I hope to add is a "filling in" of Hegel's omission in a way that includes the principal psychological range. The linkage of that range to the principal cognitive differentiation should encourage the development of a new perspective on the American government.

In the context of the American government, an understanding of the principal psychological range of a relativistic theory underlies the notion that any government's claim to psychological equity comes from an ability to comprehend all forms of knowledge. Only if the structures and processes of a government reflect a balance of psychological preferences, therefore, can governmental structures and processes comprehend the political issues that face a nation and deal with them in an equitable way.

Beyond Hegel's discussion of the evolving political realms, his discussion of the structures of government utilized the dialectic of his earlier writings. It also utilized his notion of how the dialectic facilitated the progress of political structures from one historical stage to another. As a result of the synthetic cognition being overwhelmingly preferred in Hegel's scheme of political progress, Hegel's history, as I have noted, moved all of a piece or as a "single, ordered whole." A relativistic theory suggests that history does not move as a single, ordered whole. The analytic cognition, along with the institutional arrangements that encourage the analytic cognition, contribute to a nation's progress, but the synthetic cognition must be represented as well. In the United States, the synthetic cognition is largely excluded from the governmental form.

In *The Philosophy of Right,* Hegel's preference for both the synthetic cognition and those structures that know the synthetic cognition best was evident in his description of the "realms."[1] Hegel listed four realms that he believed represented the historical progression of polities. The first, the Oriental, existed "without inward division." It governed an essentially theocratic community wherein "constitution and legislation are at the same time religion." As Hegel put it, "individual personality [invariably] loses its rights and perishes" in such a state.[2]

The Oriental realm was followed by the Greek realm, a state wherein a "substantial unity of [the] finite and infinite" existed. It possessed that unity, however, only in the context of what Hegel called a "mysterious background." This background flourished for the first time in the Greek state, existing among what Hegel declared to be a "free and unruffled ethical life." Such life cherished "personal individuality."[3]

The Greek realm, therefore, was a realm of at least some cognitive differentiation, wherein "ultimate decision is ascribed not to the subjectivity of explicitly independent self-consciousness but to a power standing above and outside it." Unfortunately, Hegel noted that the "satisfaction of particular needs is not yet comprised in the sphere of freedom" in the Greek realm. It was, as Hegel put it, still "relegated exclusively to slaves."[4] As a result, the "explication of differences" that Hegel sought as the key to the synthetic cognition was still incomplete. What there was of it was largely exploitive.

Hegel's third realm was the Roman realm. Here, the "differentiation," Hegel suggested, was "carried to its conclusion." The "ethical life [was thereby] sundered without end into the extremes of the private self-consciousness of persons on the one hand and abstract universality on the other." The battle between aristocracy and the "principle of free personality in democratic form" typified this realm. But, sadly, it was also a realm wherein "the whole is dissolved and the result is universal misfortune and the destruction of ethical life." For Hegel, therefore, Rome achieved differentiation, but it still denied a truly organic unity by having its heroes "die away into the unity of a Pantheon." It was this inferior kind of unity that implied unanimity; Hegel said that here "all individuals are degraded to the level of private persons equal with one another." As a result, "the only bond left to hold them together is abstract insatiable self-will."[5]

The fourth Hegelian realm, the German realm, was what Hegel thought best represented the "ethical" state, it being the end of the dialectical progression in politics. It represented the culmination of a process of idealism that in turn exemplified the final realm of the mind as it reconciled mind, or essence, with existence. Such an idealistic process unquestionably utilized the dialectic. In a clear reference to it, Hegel perceived the "Germanic realm" to be where the mind reconciled itself with its "absolute negativity." This was the point that Hegel referred to as "the absolute turning point," where the mind grasped "the principle of the unity of the divine nature and the human."[6]

Hegel concluded his description of the Germanic realm by suggesting that only there could "the reconciliation of objective truth and freedom as the truth and freedom appearing within self-consciousness and subjectivity exists" take place. Only in Germany, therefore, would "reconciliation with the fulfillment of which the principle of the north, the principle of the Germanic peoples," be possible.[7]

In its cognitive form, Hegel's description of the final realm, Germany, is at least organic, if not relativistic. It is a reconciliation of the politically subjective with the politically objective, the particular with the universal. But to achieve his reconciliations, Hegel used only the synthetic cognition, and he did so because, again, he assumed it to be a superior form of cognition. Thus, as Hegel raised the issue of the reconciliation of the particular with the universal, the individual with the ethical state, an increasing integration of the individual with the existence, or the state, was imperative. Such a position, much as the liberal position argues singularly for a separation of the individual and the state, ignores the relativistic perspective. It ignores the question of to what degree different psychologies, or different essences, wish for different degrees of reconciliation of the particular and the universal. Neither does it achieve a relativistic perspective on who prefers what kinds of political structures and processes in light of the differences in their own cognitive preferences.

PHILOSOPHY AND HISTORY IN THE AMERICAN REALM

What value is Hegel's political perspective to an analysis of the American government? Hegel knew little of the United States when he published the *Philosophy of Right,* the United States being not fifty years old and, as Seymour Martin Lipset phrased it, a "new nation," different altogether from the nations of Europe.[8] But, had he lived today, would Hegel have included the United States in his evolution of the realms? At a minimum, Hegel would have been obligated to credit the United States with one extraordinary reconciliation of the particular and the universal. In spite of occasional bouts of nativism, evidenced in statutory aberrations like the National Origins Act of 1924 (effectively repealed in 1965), the United States, perhaps more than any country in human history, has welcomed large numbers of disparate peoples into its borders. In the way that the *Philosophy of Right* describes a progression of reconciliations as a growing synthesis of all that is objectively different among political groupings, the United States is surely an advanced nation.

But what of subjective reconciliations, or reconciliations of the mind? This is what Hegel intended more directly in his discussion of the realms. Does the American Constitution, both in its written and its unwritten forms, encourage a balance of public cognitions, a balance of different *forms* of knowledge? To answer that question, the issue of to what degree the United States has tolerated ideological or intellectually based differences over its short history is probably the first issue. The fact is that the United States has never encouraged the kinds of ideologically or philosophically based differentiations that, say, the Europeans have encouraged. Louis Hartz, a noted chronicler of American liberalism, once said that the typical "ethical problem of a liberal society" like the United States has been that it has feared ideological divisions, particularly those ideological divisions that might produce a democratic majority.[9] Similarly, it has not feared "the danger of unanimity." America's political institutions reflect that fear of the ideological position, and they reflect the fear of the power of the majority that typically comes with ideological politics. Our institutions discourage that form of political differentiation that would grow out of the cognitive differentiation that is the key to Hegel's advancement of the political realm through history.

As Hartz once argued, it is the consensus-driven notion of liberal government that makes up the "self-completing mechanism [that in turn] insures the universality of the liberal idea."[10] Consensus over the fundamental duties of government, as well as consensus over the minimal governmental obligation to protect property and contract, has always been at the core of liberal unanimity. Such unanimity has ensured the extension of civil liberties to an increasing number of Americans, but it has also ensured that American political institutions can deal with only those matters of existence that result in the allocation of material rewards among objective political groupings. American political institutions have little capacity for dealing with the politics of subjective states and little capacity for dealing with philosophically based ideologies.

As a result of these prepolitical and political arrangements, the structure of the American government reflects a deep cognitive bias. In doing so, the United States probably represents one of history's grandest ironies. Although it is a country with a wondrous diversity among the objective characteristics of its people and with at least a fair record of liberal, representational access into the formal channels of its government, it is also a country that has fashioned its government to be less attuned to Hartz's sense of majorities, much less to Hegel's sense of cognitive "differences," than any democratic government. Not surprisingly, the politics of America is less theoretical, more pragmatic, less organic, and more a matter of "mechanism," to use Hartz's term, than any other democratic nation's. Americans would do well to examine why this is so as well as what impact it has had on both the recent lack of governmental efficacy and the recent increase of inequities in the American polity. The effect of political institutions on the dialectic that propels the progress of a nation's history is what a relativistic theory weighs. The design of political institutions that balance equities with any polity is also what a relativistic theory weighs. Whether that balance is well secured with the American political system is what is under examination here.

TWO VISIONS

At certain times, political tensions have existed in America that, had they been strong enough, could have inclined America's political structures and processes toward a better balance of Hegel's cognitions. Daniel Boorstin has said of the political tension that marked America's early history that certain contrasts, had they persevered, might have provided for a far better balance of America's political institutions. Principally, Boorstin cited the contrast between the visions of James Madison and Thomas Jefferson as the best examplar of that tension.[11]

For Boorstin, the Madison-Jefferson contrast was a matter of an American as opposed to a European perspective. In his *America and the Image of Europe,* Boorstin described the differences between American and European politics in a revealing way, noting that in the United States, a citizen learned his or her politics from politicians, whereas in Europe young citizens learned their politics from artists, writers, and intellectuals.[12] Boorstin cited the poet Walt Whitman as the American writer who best understood the American-European differentiation, favorably noting Whitman's assertion that the rhetoric of American politicians was at best "stark" and "pallid."[13]

But Boorstin's contrast of Madison's and Jefferson's vision is more than a matter of a division between the American and European political modes. The contrast amounts to an emphasis on either circumstantial or philosophical differences for, ultimately, the contrast reflects the acceptability of philosophy itself as a politically relevant consideration. Boorstin was much concerned with the acceptance of philosophy within the public sphere, also noting that political philosophy was potentially the greatest catalyst for political innovation. Indeed, Boorstin's quest for a philosophical reconciliation with politics mirrored Jefferson's, and he fondly quoted Jefferson's belief that the nation "did not become great by doing things in any great way; we became great because we constantly did things in new ways."[14]

Daniel Boorstin's reference to innovation is significant because it linked the American nation's political survival to its ability to do things differently. But it did more than that. Boorstin also deliberately wrote of the need for innovation within a philosophical context, suggesting that America in a larger and more-interdependent world will no longer "be as singular as we used to be." Boorstin hoped that America may "have begun to discover that . . . we might be like the world."[15] He hoped that America might begin to discover what our government needed to be, a deeper understanding of the principles of government and, particularly, a deeper understanding of those principles that are best understood through an unabashedly philosophical perspective, being increasingly necessary for America's survival.

Daniel Boorstin returned to the linkage between philosophy and government in *The Genius of American Politics*. There, he again criticized America's political culture, calling it "lopsided," and lamenting how the marvelous success and vitality of our institutions [was] equalled by the amazing poverty and inarticulateness of our theorizing about politics."[16] As a people, Boorstin argued, "we have always been more interested in the way it works than in the theory behind it."[17] As a result, "Our theory is always implicit [only] in our institutions," but nowhere else. Boorstin even offered that, in the United States, "the strange fact [is] that the more flexible we have made our Constitution, the more rigid and unexperimental we have made our political theory."[18] Though the reason for such philosophical inflexibility may have been that America was "haunted by the fear that capricious changes in theory might imperil our institutions," Boorstin agreed with Frederick Jackson Turner that America has gone too far in its being atheoretical. Quoting Turner, he said that we have even gone so far as to develop "a theory to justify the absence of an American political theory."[19]

The above is not to say that a broad ideological tension has not existed from time to time within the American polity. Henry Steele Commager typified those times as periods that contrasted what he called intellectual "classicism" and intellectual "progressivism." The American order, Commager suggested, preferred the order of classicism, with its neat and largely nonideological politics. Yet within the United States, there were a great number of what he called "disorderly practices," all of which Commager argues, made up an "almost convulsive play of forces which [at times have] threatened the equilibrium of the formal political institutions." Commager claims that America, perhaps more than any country, is confounded by the "paradox of embracing at once the fixed, the orderly, the coherent and the permanent, and at the same time [embracing] the changing and the disorderly and the pluralistic and the evanescent."[20]

In the United States, Commager has also suggested that there is a greater than normal need for "an aggregation of parts [that are] always too much separated and preserving always a tendency to division by the diversity of their laws, their manners, their opinions."[21] Commager cited Tocqueville's notion that he "shall refuse to believe in the duration of a government which is called upon to hold together forty different peoples, disseminated over a territory equal to one-half of Europe in extent, to avoid all rivalry, ambition and struggles between them and to direct their independent activity to the accomplishment of the same designs." Commager noted that in the "minds of all observers—the hopeful and the cynical alike—was the tenacity and persistence of local attachments, those local and regional attachments which did [in the Civil War] disrupt the Union."[22]

The reflections of Boorstin and Commager demonstrate that America's keenest political observers have long recognized that America's political differences were and still are confined to differences of origin and the like. They have not concerned themselves with differences of philosophy, as philosophy is generally understood, and they surely have not concerned themselves with differences of cognition as Hegel described such differences. Such groups as the American Philosophical Society have contributed to what Commager called the "concentration and unity" of the American government, but the far more important political concern in America has always been the dealing with "different interests." Such objective, group-oriented differences, as opposed to philosophical differences, have invariably restricted America's politics to matters of the "rivalship and jealousies which arise" as a result of different circumstance.[23] Commager suggests that the absence of philosophy, or the absence of reconciliation between different subjective states, may eventually cripple the American nation. Predictably, Commager concluded his review of the American polity with foreboding, repeating Hamilton's famous utterance, "A nation without a national government is an awful thing."[24]

STRUCTURE AND CHANGE IN THE AMERICAN REALM

In view of what Boorstin, Commager, Hartz, and others have said of the limited role of philosophy in American politics, the impact of philosophy on the historical progress of the American polity, as well as on the equity of the system, must be limited as well. It was Boorstin, this time in *The Americans—The National Experience,* who spoke specifically to what the notion of change has meant within the American existence. After a review of the American constitutional order, Boorstin concluded that although America was born of many illusions, "none was more seductive than that the American way of government could remain unchanged." Boorstin recognized that Americans have been taught to believe that their public structures could, as he put it, be "imprisoned in one generation's conscious purposes."[25]

Daniel Boorstin surely understood America's fear of structural change within its political institutions. He claimed that as a result of that fear, the American experience had now "far outrun English [or European] theory." Philosophically, America was without rudders, having learned only that as it moved through history it should go about only such things as the "dividing and diffusing [of] 'sovereignty' in novel ways."[26] But ingenuity in the dispersion of objective political differences over time is still only an ingenuity in dealing with external circumstance. Circumstance, of course, is not merely objective, but its objectivity means that what ingenuity brings to it is still doggedly atheoretical.

One passage in the *National Experience* on the relationship between political philosophy, the American antiphilosophical bias, and the potential for change in the American constitutional order, bears special mention here. Boorstin at one point placed the American political perspective, along with its contrast to the European perspective, into a broad historical context and argued that although the United States had enjoyed only the briefest of histories, it was in America that "space played the role of time." What Boorstin meant was that though "American history had been brief" and though its brevity might someday be detrimental to political stability, in America "geography somehow made up the difference." In an ironic twist, therefore, it was "the great American emptiness [and its] varied local governments, economies and traditions [that] were separated from one another by wilderness and rivers and mountains" that gave the nation the stability that saved it in its early days. The grand distances created differences "elsewhere created by centuries," Boorstin argued and these distances, along with the differentiated circumstances or existences that they represented, had thus far diffused the nation's political tensions.[27]

Boorstin, as usual, is correct about America. The political tensions that America has experienced so far have invariably been tensions over geography, race, notions of class, and the like. But if Hegel was as correct about history in general as Boorstin has been about American history to date, the dialectical notion of history means that the *objective* kinds of political differences that America has thus far exclusively experienced cannot engender necessary political change. These differences are not the kind of differences of the human mind that bring forth the dialectical contradiction that in turn pushes history. If Boorstin was correct in suggesting that the United States would no longer be able to have its structures "imprisoned in one generation's conscious purposes" because "we might [now] be like the world," then America may not be able to deal with its recent decline.

Let us not forget that even the existential differences that Boorstin described did, in one case, tear the Union. The great regional differences of the United States were there from the beginning, as Boorstin notes in his quotation of James Madison's early despair for the Union in a 1781 letter to Thomas Jefferson. In the context of Virginia's cession of Western lands to the national government, Madison wrote that the "present Union will but little survive the present War." Madison then advised Jefferson that the Virginia House of Burgesses "ought to be as fully impressed with the necessity of the Union during the war as of its probable dissolution after it."[28]

Like Hamilton, Madison too feared that a country without a national government would be an awful thing. But the threat to the Union was not only geographical. Similarly, the inequity that the two great regions felt so strongly about was not the only political inequity. It was the way that the United States has not dealt with another whole set of "differences," roughly the "explication of differences" that Hegel described in the *Logic,* that has now threatened America's future.

THOMAS JEFFERSON'S COMPETING VIEW

Thomas Jefferson, from whom a wholly different justification for the American government emerged, was the most philosophically inclined of the Framers. In the broadest sense, Jefferson's view of the new government reflected his private philosophical search for a reconciliation, or a perfection, of the natural orders with the imperfections of the temporal world. But if Jefferson's philosophical perspective was influential in America's early years, that influence was largely realized through that marvelous early American intellectual grouping known as the American Philosophical Society. Jefferson inherited the presidency of the society from Benjamin Franklin and the company of Paine, Rittenhouse, Rush, Priestly, and so many other creative and daring thinkers. It offered Jefferson what Commager called an "alliance of philosophy and conduct" for in the society, Jefferson could claim that "philosophers were not only kings, they were master craftsmen."[29]

Unlike those who supported the dominant antitheoretical perspective of the new American government, Jefferson made no apology for either philosophy itself or for his own philosophical bearing on the government. Jefferson once said, "The pragmatic spirit may save us some of the unhappiness and doubt which came from seeing the inadequacies of our own thought." But he argued that that same pragmatism can never "free us from seeing the inadequacies" of our thought.[30]

Through Jefferson, America's politics might have become far more philosophical than it has. Specifically, America's political bearing might even have included Jefferson's extraordinary understanding of human differences. Jefferson knew of such differences in a way that is not so different from what a relativistic theory requires. Jefferson once even placed subjective differences before objective differences in public consideration, arguing, "Political difference is inseparable from the different constitutions of the human mind."[31] It was an extraordinary vision for an eighteenth-century American philosopher.

Jefferson elaborated only briefly on his notion of the differences of the mind. But he did say, "The varieties in the structure of action of the human mind, as in those of the body, are the work of our Creator, against which it cannot be a religious duty to exert the standard of uniformity."[32] Jefferson, much like Hegel in his discussion of the third realm, was more wary of human unanimity than he was of human difference. Jefferson was not principally concerned with the differences between people's geography, ethnicity, or other existences. Jefferson's differences were differences of the mind.

Unfortunately, Thomas Jefferson's vision of how America's politics might incorporate the "different constitutions of the human mind" never became a vision of either the Constitution's Framers or of the nation as a whole. I will discuss how the Framers imposed their aphilosophical perspective on the constitutional design of the United States government, but, before I do so, one final reflection on Thomas Jefferson is relevant for the context of a relativistic perspective. It goes to the core of relativism, for it deals with the progress of history as Jefferson believed history evolved.

The well-known Jeffersonian position concerning the lack of intergenerational obligation to the constitutional order quite pointedly gave the constitutional order the voluntary sanction of each generation only. Jefferson once suggested that a generation as brief as nineteen years marked the longest constitutional tenure. Boorstin has called the Jeffersonian vision of history "futuristic," but it was futuristic only in the sense that Jefferson was concerned with the *movement* of history. He still did not consider history to be either "utopian or futuristic" in its final design.[33] Jefferson emphasized the dynamic rather than the universal in history, arguing at one point, "We may consider each generation as a distinct nation with a right, by the will of its majority, to bind themselves." Each generation, accordingly, did not have the right "to bind the succeeding generation."[34]

In the above statement, Jefferson significantly melded the notion of each generations' prerogatives with the notion of an ideologically based, majoritarian political perspective. It is not an accidental linkage, for Jefferson knew of the differences within the collective human mind as well as how those differences related to the politics of any people. Further, Jefferson linked those differences directly to the progress of history, revealing his understanding of how certain minds were the catalyst of historical change. The Jeffersonian position, unlike that of Madison, was at root an idealist epistemological vision. Mind preceded object for Jefferson, and his vision presaged the importance of psychological differentiation. It was not far from Shklar's position on Hegel's differences among people" in a "common environment." It was also not far from Hegel's position on the dialectic and the progress of understanding and history.

The element of psychological differentiation was central to Jefferson's reasoning within the context of history's progress, and the writings of Jefferson's principal biographer, Dumas Malone, have pointed out that Jefferson's political vision was at root a theoretical position. It was a position of both a "harmonizer" of different interests, at the same time that it was a position of a "mobilizer" of political alliances.[35] Malone stressed that Jefferson believed in the sanctity of political opposition in the new Republic. As Malone pointed out, the real issue in the matter of something like the Alien and Sedition Acts for Jefferson was the importance of institutionalizing robust and outspoken political dissent at the outset of the Republic. In the context of the political conflict over Jefferson's Kentucky Resolution on Nullification, Malone argues convincingly that the entire purpose of the resolution was "to start a wave of protest against the denial of the right of political opposition."[36] Jefferson did not expect or prefer political unanimity in America, and thus, quite unlike so many of the Framers, he championed fundamental, philosophically based, disagreement as essential to a healthy political system.

With Jefferson in Paris during the Constitutional Convention, the political perspective of the Philadelphia Convention was left to the antiphilosophical Madison. Madison's view directly affected the governmental design of the Republic, and most of the leading works on the American Constitution, including the plethora of bicentennial works that have crowded the bookshelves in recent years, have lauded the Philadelphia Convention delegates as they molded their antimajoritarian government. Yet for all of the Framers' labors, and for all of their courageous surmounting of the circumstantial disagreements that made their summer's work heroic, it is undeniable that no "different constitutions of the human mind" ever divided them. The Framers agreed, implicit though their agreement might have been, that the differences that they would address and the government that they would design would be differences of circumstance alone. Their own differences, though much trumpeted in the traditional writings on the convention, excluded differences of essence, much less differences among philosophical perspectives or, again, differences of the human mind. The American Constitutional order still reflects that two-hundred-year-old exclusion.

THE CONSTITUTION IN THE AMERICAN REALM

The American antiphilosophical bias had an impact on the structure of the American government from the beginning. The organization of the

United States government is vastly different from that of any other government, Boorstin's warning concerning the precarious nature of America's governmental uniqueness speaking directly to a vision of government that insisted on an inordinate dispersion of its public institutions.

The incentive toward structural dispersion in the Constitutional Convention was indeed overwhelming. The two most significant dispersions, the separation of powers and the maintenance of a full-blown federalism, were supported and approved with the use of powerful arguments. These arguments were powerful, however, only in the context of a strongly felt need for the preservation of private interests from what a strengthened central government might do to them. The particular would clearly dominate the universal here, and arguments for such domination were well articulated in documents like the no. 10 *Federalist*. These arguments still rivet the notion of weak, nonmajoritarian government into the national conscience.

In the no. 47 *Federalist*, Madison's first essay on the separation of powers, the plea for public acceptance was also a plea for the protection of private interests from any majoritarian tyranny.[37] As it was the "accumulation of all powers legislative, executive and judiciary in the same hands" that "may justly be pronounced the very definition of tyranny," Madison's constitutional strategy spread the potential loci of such a tyranny as widely as possible.[38] This was the strategy that he borrowed from the writings of Montesquieu, Madison quoting Montesquieu's fear that "the *same* monarch or senate should *enact* tyrannical laws, to *execute* then in a tyrannical manner" (emphasis his).[39]

But Madison's concern was not limited to threats on property. He was concerned with whatever else a new, postmonarchical sovereign, or a majority of free people, might visit on the government. Epistemologically, of course, it was a materialist vision, for Madison was concerned solely with objectives, properties in the broadest sense. It is now well-recognized that Montesquieu (and subsequently Madison) misunderstood the British Constitution. In interviewing Bolingbroke and the out-party malcontents, Montesquieu had no hint of how Walpole was solidifying British cabinet government. Montesquieu did not realize that the evolving executive and legislature in Britain were fused, not dispersed. Critics of the American separation of powers routinely note the difference between seventeenth-century forms of separation, or the separation between the crown and the civil government, and the eighteenth-century forms of separation between a republican executive and legislature. America's Constitution, however, reflects the full measure of Montesquieu's misunderstanding.

MADISON AND COGNITION

The Jeffersonian and the Madisonian view, or the European and the American view, of the relationship of philosophy to government still best represents the two perspectives on the American government and the role of philosophy in that government. The cognitive biases of these views are clear and, with regard to the cognitive form of Madison's perspective, the language of the no. 51 *Federalist* is perhaps even better attuned to a cognitive analysis than either the no. 10 or the no. 47. In describing the federal branches of government in no. 51, Madison spoke openly of his hope that the "several constituent parts," as a matter of "their mutual relations," would be able to keep "each other in their proper places." Keeping "each other in their proper places" is revealing language, affirming that "that separate and distinct exercise of the different powers of government" would be what would permit each department to have "a will of its own."[40]

Madison's affirmation is evident again when he concludes "that the members of each [department] should have as little agency as possible in the appointment of the members of the others."[41] Madison's (and the convention's) eighteenth-century executive-legislative separation impacted directly on the quality of America's political procedures. The presidential veto and its override, the appointment and confirmation process, the treaty ratification process, and so many other interbranch constitutional relationships import arms-length interactions between distinctly separated governmental institutions. As modern organizational theory would look on it, the separation of institutions and powers necessarily import the overwhelming necessity for dyadic, contractual forms of governmental interaction.

Beyond the forms of its interactions, however, the dispersed structure of the American government also affects the balance of the fundamental demarcation of majority rule versus minority rights which Boorstin, Hartz, and so many other American scholars have written about.[42] The balance of majority rule and minority rights recalls Louis Hartz's descriptions of political unanimity and political difference, for as Madison's "differences" were never more than differences of things like the ownership and nonownership of property, they were the kind of differences that prompted Madison to argue that if "a majority be united by a common interest, the rights of the minority will be insecure."[43] Madison's position in no. 51 directly follows from the no. 10 *Federalist* because the majority-minority problem for Madison was best resolved by structural dispersion.

Although Madison depended on the separation of the powers of the federal government and the incorporation of the federal, state-sovereign form, Madison argued that "by comprehending in society so many separate descriptions of citizens, as will render an unjust combination of a majority of the whole, very improbable, if not impractible," the very size of the Republic would also help minimize the intrusion of the majority into minority rights. When Madison wrote of the "separate descriptions of citizens," he was worrying over how "oppressive combinations of a majority will be facilitated." His "best security under the republican form, for the rights of every class of citizens" spoke solely to the political threat that might grow out of majorities of citizens without properly working through a majority-facilitating governmental form.[44]

From a relativistic perspective, the psychology of the American political arrangement is obvious. Homogeneous in its jurisdictions, America's political institutions were arranged by the Framers so that office holders, much like the citizens who elected them, could not deal with each other in an aggregated, majoritarian way. The interactions of the American government, overwhelmingly contractual in their form, import the government's proclivity for understanding the issues that it chooses to face in the form of those who come to it individually. Those who contract with the government, who come to the government in the analytic cognitive form, therefore best access the government. The implications for political change when a government's cognitions are overwhelmingly analytic are precisely what Hegel spoke to. The implications for political equity are what a relativistic theory ultimately must speak to. It must speak to that equity more fully than Hegel or anyone has done so far, I think, for as any government biases how it will hear its people, so too it biases how it will govern them.

THE POLITICAL PARTY

The one institution that might have provided at least a measure of philosophical warp for the strongly atheoretical woof of the American government was and is also the institution that might have provided a measure of the synthetic cognition to balance the analytic cognition. This institution, of course, is the political party.

The distinctions among different kinds of political parties that Maurice Duverger described in *Political Parties* are still as good a place as any to begin to differentiate among political parties that are capable of a philosophical vision and those that are not. Duverger suggested that it is a "community of political doctrine" that usually constitutes "the essential impulse in the formation of parliamentary groups," but he also urged that, on closer examination, political doctrine was rarely the originator of political parties. Duverger understood that more often something like "geographical proximity or the desire to defend one's own profession" was what "seems to have given the first impulse" to the growth of a political alliance.[45] Parties such as those that Duverger described were thus largely interest-oriented, as we would call them today. They were not philosophical and they represented, largely, only those who shared similar objective circumstances.

Duverger also noted, however, that parties not based on "geographical proximity" or "profession" were also possible. Such parties dealt openly with "doctrine," as Duverger put it, and did not appear in the early period of party formation. In describing the 1789 arrival of France's provincial representatives to the Estates General, for example, Duverger noted that the provincials originally "felt rather bewildered" in their new Parisian setting. "Quite naturally," Duverger reports, representatives of the same region tended to meet together so as to "escape from the feeling of isolation which assailed them." Accordingly, they made "preparations for the defence of their local interests." Eventually, however, different kinds of political groupings formed in the wake of the Revolution and, over the years, local groupings like the Breton Club evolved into largely ideological collections and groupings like the early Jacobins.[46] Such groupings invited people of like mind to their meetings regardless of the participants' professional or geographic origin. As Duverger said, by the time of France's Constituent Assembly of 1848, groups that were organized as parties met "in the same place because they [had] ideas in common."[47] The nature of these parties, of course, was far more philosophical. They began to reflect differences in a way that Jefferson (and Hegel) would have understood.

Duverger's writings provide a convenient perspective on the American party experience generally and the impact of Madison on America's parties in particular. It is more than coincidence that Duverger's largely evolutionary model for the development of philosophical parties distinguished between factions and parties in a way that is instructive for a psychologically relativistic theory. After defining a *faction* as an as yet unfulfilled representative institution, placing it "in all hereditary or co-opted assemblies whether it be the Senate of classical Rome or the Diet of Poland," Duverger pointed out that such factions only became parties when they merged with "parliamentary groups." "Between the two," he argued, there was "the difference which exists between the inorganic and the organic."[48] His words were well chosen, for the inorganic, or factional party, is only an interest party. In form as well as in substance, it never provides more than a representation of a circumstance. Philosophically based parties, of course, do more.

Duverger's use of the term *faction* is a certain flag of recognition for the most casual reader of the *Federalist*. It puts the matter of citizen aggregation, or majoritarianism, squarely outside of the structural arrangement that America's eighteenth-century separation of powers dictated. The antimajoritarianism of the Federalist position, along with its protection of property, cut in a different direction from what an organized or an "organic" (to use Duverger's term) association of interests might have represented. The traditional rejection of factions, as Madison used the term in the no. 10 *Federalist,* was a rejection of what for Madison could only bring "tyranny" to the Republic: a real, philosophically based political party.

Madison's fear of what might bring tyranny to the American Republic was explicitly only a fear of any collaboration of objective interests, not a collaboration of ideas in some abstract sense. But the argument existed at two levels. One concerned whatever might threaten such private liberties as property. The other restricted, if implicitly, any public recognition of a sense of fundamental or philosophical differences as they might have existed in the new Republic. Madison's famed quotation on factions, his depiction of the "violence of faction" as the source of those "complaints" that come from "friends of public and private faith, and of public and personal liberty," meant that philosophically based differentiations within the populace were never to be encouraged by parties.[49]

It is altogether consistent that Madison subsequently altered his position on parties after the convention. Shortly after the new government began, a Madison who was perhaps more under the influence of Jefferson accepted the inevitability of limited, though still largely interest-oriented, political parties. Regardless of Madison's partial conversion, however, political parties as something more than a pallid collection of interests have flowered only occasionally in America's political history. They did not exist at all until the third administration of the Republic, that of Thomas Jefferson. As Daniel Boorstin has pointed out, Jefferson recognized that the political party should be the principal unifier of a nation. If the "tendencies of American political life were centrifugal," what Boorstin called America's "novel and precarious arrangement" would have to be united in some institutional way.[50] If "effective political unifying of the nation was left to the political parties," it was Jefferson, in his alliance with the Clintons of New York and in his gathering of support for the Louisiana Purchase and his other political harmonizings, who first utilized the political party in an avowedly majoritarian way.[51]

But in terms of the synthetic cognition's role in historical change, as Hegel and the dialectic required the synthetic cognition to engineer historical change and in terms of how political equity in a relativistic theory defines cognitive balance, the political party that might have brought the synthetic cognition to America has never existed. The American political party, like the American government as a whole, has been overwhelmingly biased toward the objective, contractually processed, circumstantial interest from the beginning. The party has not been an institution that has balanced the analytic cognition of America's constitutional structures with the synthetic cognition that other political parties often foster.

TOCQUEVILLE: THE PREPOLITICAL CONTEXT

It is argued by many that no foreign observer understood the prepolitical condition of the American political system better than did the noted French visitor, Alexis de Tocqueville. Recall that Tocqueville's and his friend Beaumont's travels in this country, at virtually the same time as

Hegel's last writings incidentally, fell at the very moment of modernity. Much in response to that modernity, as one of Tocqueville's biographers J. P. Mayer put it, Tocqueville was perhaps the "first thinker to lay down the principles of the era of mass democracy."[52]

The great ambivalence in Tocqueville's writings centers around the Frenchman's perspective on the evolution of democracy generally and, in particular, the mode of that evolution in the American state. Democracy, according to Tocqueville, had "its own merits and defects, its own advantages and evils."[53] But, as Tocqueville was the first to examine the American order from the perspective of a continental philosopher, he was also the first to be genuinely overwhelmed with the equality of the American social as well as political order. He noted that America's social equality carried a cost along with its benefits, believing still that an aristocracy's culture, its manners, and its "spiritual qualities" were all wanting in this country.

Beyond their balancing of democracy and aristocracy, Tocqueville's writings are significant for their view of political history. Tocqueville professed no theory of history as such, placing it largely within the hand of providence in an almost Kantian way. He nonetheless believed in the progress of history. His sense of political history surely saw democracy as the result of that progress, once saying that the "occurrences of national existence have everywhere turned to the advantage of democracy."[54] The new democratic age would probably no longer permit the social and political inequalities that aristocracy condoned.

Although Tocqueville had little use for Hegel and for Hegel's descriptions of history, he shared the perspective of Hegel's later writings on how democracy's dangers increased the threat of social atomization. As Seymour Drescher put it, Tocqueville feared for a nation that was made up of only "individual egoism without strength." Any nation that embodied only a "weak equality without collective power" would find it difficult to survive.[55]

Tocqueville had his remedies for what he called "individual egoism." He placed some stock in religion and the church's almost Platonically utopian role in provoking private virtue, but he also placed his stock in modern commerce. There, curiously, both "potential stability and individual freedom" might cement a nation.[56] Most of all, Tocqueville counted on the rise of what he called the "voluntary association" as it represented modern commerce or whatever else might bind a liberal nation together. The voluntary association, that civic or business grouping of modern, atomized society, Tocqueville hoped, could contribute the cohesion that he admired so much and that came so easily to the European aristocracy. This was an institution that America's individualistic democracy sorely needed.

According to Tocqueville, the voluntary association could contribute to political cohesion because it could both "protect the individual from encroachments by the state" and "provide continuity in space and time."[57] Again, with emphasis on the social bonding that all societies require, Tocqueville noted that the American voluntary association typically forced men to "surrender their own will to that of all the rest." This surrender resulted, at least supposedly, in making each citizen's "exertions subordinate to the common impulse." He hoped that associations would function as "large free schools, where all the members of the community go to learn the general theory of association."[58]

Though too much can be made of the point, it is clear that Tocqueville, impressed with the social equality of the American order, held onto a European sense of the need for social cohesion within the United States. He feared for the inadequate prepolitical aggregation of the North American nation and, though he commented but little on the actual structure of the American political system, he warned America about its precarious structural integrity. He feared for the social dispersions of American society and, like Daniel Boorstin's worries concerning the ability of America to maintain its unique political arrangements, his worries presage Boorstin's fears of 140 years hence.

From a relativistic perspective, Tocqueville's fears are the fears of those both in America and in Europe who were wary of the emerging atomized, liberal state. Like Hegel's last writing, Tocqueville's concern for the diffused state of American society suggested the dominance of the essentially transactional form of bonding among citizens as the principal social adhesive. The cognitions that such a prepolitical arrangement imply are obvious, they being cognitively analytic, with all that this bias foretells about historical progress and the likelihood of political equity in the American political system.

THE LAST MATERIALIST PERSPECTIVE

Boorstin's writings are sound updatings of the Olympian accountings of Tocqueville on the new American nation of the early 1830s. Lesser but still worthy writings anchor modernity's vision of America as it existed just before the postmaterial age. The writings of Theodore Lowi and Grant McConnell were probably the best mid-twentieth century critiques of the American political system, these critiques arguing that America, in Lowi's terms, had finally reached "the end of liberalism."[59]

By the 1960s, the American liberal state had indeed changed a good deal from what it was in Tocqueville's time. From the still-lingering property requirements for the exercise of the franchise, by 1964 property could no longer prevent anyone from dining, sleeping, or recreating wherever those services were offered to the public. From the demise of whatever of mercantilism still fettered an emerging free enterprise in the 1830s, the same 1964 legislative stroke that opened public accommodations to all prevented the denial of employment on the basis of race, religion, or creed. The grand liberal and Lockean agenda of inclusion, at least from a de jure if not a de facto perspective, had moved forward a great deal.

In their attempts to render the same cosmic accounting for America that Tocqueville had attempted over a century earlier, Lowi and McConnell's writings centered as much as did Tocqueville's around prepolitical and informal constitutional arrangements. Consequently, what McConnell and Lowi described is notable, if for no other reason than that it differed so much from what Marxist criticisms of the American political system, those that were updating the criticisms of Beard essentially, were arguing. Perhaps in response to writers of a Marxist or neo-Marxist bent who criticized the inequities that they felt resulted from centralized, elitist political structures (see C. Wright Mills' *The Power Elite*), Lowi's and McConell's critiques cited the fragmented or centrifugal nature of America's political arrangements as the handmaiden of inequity.[60] Lowi captured the most easily remembered phrase of the argument, and his depiction of a governmental "iron triangle" has become a staple of American governmental criticism.

America's iron triangle, for Lowi, was simple in design. It was a linkage between what Tocqueville had called a voluntary association but what was by the 1960s called an interest group; the congressional committee and subcommittee allies that shepherded favorable legislation for the interest group; and the appropriate executive agencies that oversaw the results of what interest groups and committee's began. Lowi's second most celebrated phrase, the "captive agency," incidentally, depicted the outright loss of the public perspective within bureaucratic jurisdictions. Any agency, once captured, not only worked more for those outside the agency than for the government, but a convenient three-way reciprocity between campaign contributions, support for the agency in congressional budgets, and bureaucratic fealty to those who initiated the triangle blew the captive agency around its triangular markers.[61]

Lowi and McConnell concluded from their descriptions of private cooptation that a *centrifugal* as opposed to a *centripetal* political arrangement induced distribution inequity. For Lowi and McConnell, structural *de*centralization was what permitted the best-financed and best-organized interests to capture the government.

Though the above descriptions of America's structural incentives to inequity were inventive, their linkage of structural centrifugality to inequality being essentially correct, their emphasis was still on the quest of any interest for material favor in the first instance. Their argument, epistemologically, was therefore materialistic as well. It was not idealistic for it did not attempt to account for the psychological preference, or the preference for cognitive form, of those who interacted with the American governmental structure. It did not predict the postmaterial revisions of the American government that have occurred in the last twenty-five years nor did it predict how those revisions have accelerated America's distributional inequity. Only an idealistically based, psychologically relativistic perspective, a perspective that reveals the cognitive bias of America's centrifugal structures as well as America's informal prepolitical and political arrangements, permits an accurate understanding of America's political inequities. These arrangements should be understood in a framework that goes beyond the "end of liberalism."

The psychologically relativistic perspective, particularly in the context of its differences from either liberalism or Marxism, is different because it interjects the issue of the *psychological preference for different forms of government* into the distributional consideration. This is what the postmaterial perspective offers, and this is what is both substantively and epistemologically significant about postmaterialism. True postmaterialism, again, is epistemologically idealistic.

In short, Hegel's fears were warranted concerning liberalism's predisposition to divide the particular from the universal and the subjective from the objective. His fears of liberal governmental arrangements were, appropriately, the fears of one who anticipated the loss of the synthetic cognition within those governments. Hegel, as I have said, was strongly biased toward the synthetic cognition, but granting that bias and granting Hegel's nonrecognition of differences over to what degree the politically particular should become part of the politically universal, or to what degree the subjective should become a part of the objective, a relativistic theory encourages the consideration of these differences. The materialistic epistemological frameworks of Lowi or McConnell on the liberal side, or Charles Beard, C. Wright Mills, or others on the Marxist side of the traditional political argument, do not provide such a consideration.

Most important, as the institutional arrangements of the American government reflect a psychological bias, and as that psychological bias has accelerated with the structural changes that have taken place in the American government over the past twenty-five years, these same biases now increasingly prevent the government from understanding political issues in other than the analytic cognitive form. Only a political theory that is grounded in a conscious attempt at a balancing of the *forms of understanding,* as Hegel and even to some degree Kant defined such forms of understanding, can prescribe for public institutions that are politically efficacious and, most importantly, politically equitable.

Chapter Nine

THE AMERICAN LEGAL SYSTEM

LIBERALISM AND THE COMMON LAW

If there is a psychological bias to the American political system, so too there is a psychological bias to the American legal system. In this chapter, I will briefly introduce what I think a relativistic theory's standard of equity will be in the context of the American legal system. As with the previous chapter's discussion of America's political institutions, this discussion of America's legal institutions reflects the role of the dialectic in the progress of the American legal system and the role of the dialectic in the achievement of psychological, and material, equity through the law.

The grand triad of America's constitutional allocation prescribes that the legislature makes the laws, the executive executes the laws, and the judiciary interprets the laws. The textbook division is misleading at best, for reasons other than the traditional paeans to the overlapping nature of America's institutional prerogatives, because in the United States, even more than in most common law countries, the role of the judiciary in the making of law is substantial. The idea that law is made in the courts is always controversial. But English and English-derivative courts have always made law and they will continue to do so. The cognitive nature of the American judiciary's law-making process is significant for a relativistic theory.

In my discussion of liberal democratic theory I suggested that there is an absence of a law giver in the common law. This absence, along with the common law's "bottom to top" legal reasoning, directly affected the jurisdictional separation between law and government in common-law systems. In the common law's native England, the private nature of the common law affected that always ill-defined but still important line that nations draw between their governmental and legal jurisdictions. The private nature of the English law was the principal reason for why England carved its government-law demarcation substantially more toward the law than did the continental, civil-law jurisdictions. The law was more trusted when it was distanced from a crown.

The limited government notions of John Locke, of course, fit well into England's government-law demarcation. That same limited government, common law foundation was the Framers' legacy from Edward Coke and John Locke. In the United States, the government-law demarcation is even farther on the side of the law than it is in England. The abolition of primogeniture and entail in Virginia was emblematic of a falling away of encumbrances on real property titles and was emblematic as well of the great faith in private law, and particularly private contract, that the new nation had. The extensions of Locke's notion of liberal and limited government that the Framers adopted was well in keeping with a reliance on the legal jurisdiction.

HAMILTON AND THE AMERICAN LAW

In the elementary grades, the now obviously sexist canard that the United States had a government of law and not of men was a blackboard staple for years. Such an understanding, of course, necessitates a scrutiny of private as well as public law if one seeks the American legal balance. The primary locus of discussion concerning the boundaries of government and law in the United States has centered on the supremacy of judge-made over governmentally legislated law. The original fodder for that position is stored in Hamilton's no. 78 *Federalist*, Hamilton arguing there that "The complete independence of the courts of justice is peculiarly essential in a limited constitution."[1]

Although the argument never fully dies,[2] it is the predominant view that not only the independence of the courts as an institution, but the very supremacy of adjudicated law as a body of appropriate behavioral mandate, is what sanctifies the doctrine of judicial review. This position, ratified by John Marshall's opinion in *Marbury v. Madison* (1803), was Lockean at heart, reaffirming that no government could overstep the boundaries of protected, private jurisdictions. The protection of property, along with the protection of free, alienable property that comes through contract, enjoyed and would continue to enjoy as secure a judicial protection in the United States as it had in England.

But the no. 78 *Federalist* deals with a good deal more than Hamilton's judicial supremacy. An examination of Hamilton's reasoning suggests that his rationale for supremacy was illustrative of his larger position on the foundations of government. What is crucial to an understanding of the American constitutional and legal order is that Hamilton's no. 78 is founded on more than the *substance* of liberal, property-based protections. Even more central to Hamilton's reasoning is his adoption of the *form* of the private law, particularly the law of contract, to the public law.

Specifically, Hamilton's language in no. 78 discussed the balance of legislative and constitutional jurisdiction. It concluded, "No legislative act therefore contrary to the constitution can be valid." Hamilton's rationale depended on the notion that holding to the contrary, that is, placing legislation above the Constitution, means that a "deputy is greater than his principal." Continuing, Hamilton said that to deny the supremacy of the Constitution over the legislative act is to claim that "the servant is above the master." The Constitution "ought to be preferred to the statute," according to Hamilton, because "the intention of the people [ought to be preferred] to the intention of their agents."[3] The form of Hamilton's reasoning is that of the contractual relationship.

Also, the form of Hamilton's reasoning in no. 78 is the form of private, not public, law. A lawyer, Hamilton found the law of principal and agent, a corner of the private law directly adjacent to contract, to be most useful to the judicial review argument. But beyond his definitions of *principal, deputy, master,* and *servant,* the remainder of Hamilton's argument is no less revealing. It too relies on private, common-law reasoning in the resolution of disputes. Hamilton states at one point that if two public statutes conflict, they should be reconciled by using the underlying principle that "reason and law conspire that this should be done." If one statute is to be given priority, then the hard choice as to which is to be preferred must be made as a matter of "the nature and reason of the thing."[4] This reasoning comes from nothing more complicated than the English belief in what had undergirded the common law for centuries. In contract law such reasoning was represented by what was called "the meeting of the minds."

Hamilton's use of common law reasoning continued into the no. 80

Federalist. There, Hamilton suggested that a resolution of disputes among states could be accomplished only at a national level, this being so because "No man ought certainly to be a judge in his own cause."[5] The rationale of that argument comes directly from the celebrated Dr. Bonham's Case (1610), wherein the surgeon Bonham was released from the judgment of those who benefited from their finding of Bonham's unfitness to practice. The case is a model of early seventeenth-century common-law principle, well in keeping with how Edward Coke, fifty years before Locke, thought of reason and the law.

A further example of private, common-law reasoning comes from the latter portion of Hamilton's no. 80, where Hamilton sought to defend reason, as well as the independent judiciary that would proffer it. He noted that the Framers properly included both law and equity in Article 3 of the Constitution, and found it necessary to defend the inclusion of equity there. He pointed out that there is "hardly a subject of litigation between individuals" that does not include matters for the equity jurisdiction.[6] Importantly, his reference to "what are called hard bargains" is curiously anticipatory of a relativistic understanding. It is only a little different from what Hermann and Kogan wrote about concerning the authoritarian's dominance in contract. "Hard bargains," as Hamilton put it, were "contracts, in which though there may have been no direct fraud or deceit . . . [there] was still some undue and unconscionable advantage taken."[7] He suggested that in the law of private contract, such bargains showed no meeting of the minds.

From the perspective of a psychologically relativistic theory of politics, it should not be surprising that Hamilton's argument for the political protection of private rights embodies the cognitive form of the private law. Neither should it be surprising that such private law, as it embraces contract and assumes a meeting of minds in the interpretation of contracts, includes the qualitatively similar variable that all contracts require. The meeting of the minds of common law contract is but an objective meeting, a confluence of the value of a price and a product on which each participant to the contract settles. It is not an equality of each mind's psychological adaptability to the contractual form. It is not a *subjective* meeting of the minds.

Of course, Hamilton's rendition of the economic bias of the hard bargain, or the nonmeeting of the minds that results from it, reveals no psychological sense of how different minds perceive the form of a contract. The cognitive bias of the contractual form has never been an issue in the jurisprudence of either the public or the private law. But private law, which became a part of the American experience as it evolved from Coke, Locke, and even William Blackstone, reflects a cognitive form as much as it ever did. It still overwhelmingly reflects the analytic cognition.

The relativistic perspective can contribute to an understanding of psychological equity within those legal arrangements that reflect the contractual form. A psychologically relativistic perspective can also describe how the psychological character of the contractual form affects government.

With attention to the courts, Hamilton spoke laudably of the accepted rule of legal construction that requires a judge to reconcile conflicting interpretations in the adjudication of a contract. To Hamilton, it was clear that such rules of construction were "not derived from any positive [that is, governmental] law." They were, rather, "adopted by themselves, as consonant to truth and property."[8] Hamilton meant that it was within the domain of the courts either to search for a meeting of the minds or, alternatively, to impose an equitable resolution on the conflict over what the parties to a contract more than likely meant when they contracted. This resolution, however, only considered the objective intentions of the contractors, not their subjective preferences for the contractual form.

The traditional solution of common law contractual disputes, as with all adjudications within the common law, is never accomplished without an assumption concerning the similarity of minds. But it is difficult to find how such traditional common-law interpretation can include a determination of psychological price as Greenstein defined it. If all minds are held to be equally compatible to the similar variable, contractual form of cognition, no psychological price can be found to exist because the contractual form is assumed to be equally commodious to all. As a result, just as with governmental structures and processes that are biased toward the analytic cognition, so too a legal system that is biased toward the analytic cognition favors some psychologies over others.

A relativistic theory requires a weighing of the cognitive preferences of all. It requires an understanding of the preferences of different kinds of minds for different forms of doing things. In its attempt to define psychologically relevant distinctions among approaches to the law, in much the same way that I have attempted to define psychologically relevant distinctions among different structures of government, a relativistic theory weighs the allocation of psychological price within any nation's legal arrangements. To do that, at least in part, it must determine the balance of the subjective states of mind that come to the legal bargain.

The position of Hamilton, with its acceptance of the possibility of such economically based inequities as those that occur through the hard bargain, still does not describe the psychological dissimilarities, and thus the psychological inequities, that occur in the contractual setting. The legal assumption concerning the similarity of minds, and its implicit negation of the "explication of differences" that Hegel described, effectively proscribes any consideration of psychological price in a legal context. But a psychologically relativistic theory requires that the cognitive form of the law be as subjected to the standard of psychological equity as anything else. This standard of psychological equity comes only from an understanding of the relativity of minds. Within the American constitutional order, the essentially private and contractual form of both private and public law is not psychologically neutral.

KARL LLEWELLYN AND LEGAL REALISM

James Madison and Thomas Jefferson provide apt contrasts on both eighteenth-century political philosophy and preferences for governmental arrangement. There is, however, no good analogue to that contrast on the matter of the equity of America's legal arrangements. No jurisprudential position in particular satisfies Jefferson's notion of the "different constitutions of the human mind" within the context of the law. There is, however, a jurisprudential perspective that offers a psychologically relevant rebuttal to the presumed objectivity of the law, particularly of contract law and the common law of which it is a part.

Until the early twentieth century, the traditional English and American view of legal interpretation was that law was discovered, not made. The crux of that view was that the law was rational and that a single, objectively based rule was the correct rule for each adjudicated case. The jurisprudential perspective that challenged this prescription was known as legal realism. Karl Llewellyn defined legal realism in the American context and it was his definition of legal realism that challenged the common law's assumptions concerning objectivity and discoverability.

For Llewellyn, the law was always something more than a matter of what he called "rules of remedies." Llewellyn's view, lodged significantly within its German, historical-school context, held that "[r]emedies seem to . . . have a purpose, [or] to be protections of something else."[9] Because remedies had a purpose, Llewellyn went on to suggest that the perspective of legal realism provided more than what the "often archaic remedy-law" provided. Being a realist about the law's true function could offer both "a new synthesis" about the law as well as "a base for law reform."[10]

Although it is only delineated in a preliminary way, Llewellyn's prescription for the law reflected the specific role of the mind in the determination of the law. Llewellyn, in keeping with the German tradition, put the mind before the object, although, to be sure, he addressed only those legal biases that grew out of a decision maker's objective, existential as opposed to subjective or psychological, condition. "Right eternally suggests its connotation of inherent 'rightness'—social, political, economic and especially moral," he said, and he went on to suggest that it "takes more careful self-analysis than most have been interested in giving to the *non-legal* 'right' " than common law decision making had done.[11]

Llewellyn was suggesting that an ostensibly rational following of the "accepted rules" of judicial behavior "may not be a very accurate description of the judge's actual behavior."[12] He contended that "such accuracy of description is rare" and he contended as well that rather than enforce an "elimination of the subjective value-judgment" in the law, interpreters of judicial decision making should concentrate on "an illumination by objective data of the bias and bearing of a subjective value-judgment."[13] If the biases Llewellyn wrote of were social, economic, and not psychological biases, his epistemology solidly placed the interpreter before the interpreted, the mind before the object. His perspective was thus idealist, and though it was not one of a psychologically relativistic idealism, it nonetheless signaled the introduction of an idealist perspective to twentieth-century American jurisprudence. Most important, it signaled the coming of the mind to the law as it questioned the rule of law as something discovered and not made. When Llewellyn claimed that the most central differences of constitutional interpretation came not from "patterns of doing" but from "patterns of thinking of emotion-attitudes," his challenge marked what for its time was the most profound questioning of legal interpretation's rational mask.

Though Karl Llewellyn borrowed from the idealist perspective in his reflections on jurisprudence, he was soon followed by others who recognized the significance of the idealistic perspective in the determination of legal equity more fully. Shortly after Llewellyn, Lon Fuller, for example, argued that legal decision making should never be looked on as a mechanistic, value-neutral enterprise. Fuller argued that legal decisions were the result of "attitudes of the mind to which actions merely give external expression." Further, Fuller contended that the incorporation of more than "those facts of the case which are visible through the prism of legal theory" were necessary to equitable legal rulings. Debunking the objectivity of law as has Llewellyn, Fuller claimed that a "judge's decision represents a reaction to a whole situation, including many facts which from the standpoint of legal theory are irrelevant."[14]

It is crucial to an understanding of relativism's role in legal decision making to acknowledge that Fuller's sense of the importance of the differentiation among attitudes corresponds to Llewellyn's argument that "no institution consists of *like* ways among all the persons concerned" (emphasis his). Indeed, as Llewellyn put it, "it is the unlikeness plus the complementary crossplay of the organized ways which is the most convenient criterion for marking off an 'institution' from a mere 'way' or simple culture-trait."[15] Though Llewellyn's statement refers only to the biases of entire, that is, undifferentiated political interests or groupings, his incorporation of human purposiveness is still anticipatory of a relativistic perspective on the law.

LLEWELLYN AND LEGAL CHANGE

Just as important as Karl Llewellyn's sense of mind-directed judicial purposiveness was his sensitivity to how imposed meaning engendered legal change. Llewellyn spoke to the issue of legal change with specific reference to alterations in the American Constitution. At one point, he wrote boldly that "the working Constitution is amended whenever the basic ways of government are changed." Arguing that the process of amendment occurs "without alteration of the language of the document," Llewellyn noted that a kind of constitutional amendment occurs when the "relevant specialists alone," as he called the significant governmental actors, "change the manner of government in vital aspects."[16]

As these actors do what they do, according to Llewellyn, they "widen it [the Constitution] startingly, [and] ring out old pieces of the Constitution as bells ring out an Old Year." Continuing, Llewellyn pointed out that in an informal, amendatory way, significant political actors have frequently "remade the pattern of government as we have passed from a dominantly agricultural into a dominantly industrial and on into a dominantly financial economy." With an extraordinary prescience concerning the current difficulties of the American political system, Llewellyn noted that the people who have pressured the government for structural change contributed to it as they "tinkered, twisted, [and] invented, on the governmental side." He suggested that these are the people who will continue to change the government "either to further shifts in economic institutions or to catch up with such shifts."[17]

Llewellyn's sense of how unwritten constitutional shifts were products not of "legislation" but of "executive or administrative practice" is significant for an analysis of the structural and procedural changes that take place in any government. His observations are especially relevant for any consideration of the dynamics of government organizations for Llewellyn is correct in saying that this dynamic in the public sector is propelled by significant interests that "build the wherewithal to elect or control executives or legislators."[18] In a postmaterial age, in the context of an idealistic perspective, that wherewithal is frequently psychologically and not economically driven.

Karl Llewellyn, in speaking of the engine of change in American constitutional history, charged that engine with "some adjustment of the emergent new to the persistent old."[19] Referring directly again to those who "remade the pattern of government" as the stages of history passed, Llewellyn properly argued that formal amendment was "in the main unnecessary." The process of change was more often informal, he said, formal amendment being "rarely resorted to" as a source of Constitutional change.[20] In sum, the position of Karl Llewellyn on constitutional change, growing out of his jurisprudential legal realism, took a large step toward understanding the structural generators of legal renewal. But Llewellyn's patterns of legal change, analogous to Grant McConnell's and Theodore Lowi's descriptions of structural political alteration in their own way, are both psychologically as well as institutionally biased.

In an epistemologically idealist, and particularly a relativistically based, theory of the law, the psychological balance within the cognitive forms of the law is central. In keeping with the idealistic hierarchy that begets equity in a postmaterial political system, this balance is essential for building the kinds of legal institutions that can grant equity within everyday considerations of the law. It is essential in the first instance, however, to achieve psychological balance in the structure of legal institutions, as well as in the structure of the decisions that those institutions make.

The idea that the law may not always render justice is hardly original to a relativistic theory. The English acknowledged the possibility of legal injustice when they created the equity jurisdiction to balance the legal jurisdiction in the fifteenth century. Hamilton candidly acknowledged the possibility of injustice in America's courts when he embraced the equity jurisdiction's inclusion in the Constitution's third article and warned of the "hard bargain" in *Federalist* no. 80. A relativistic perspective only furthers what are now well-accepted understandings of legal equity. What a psychologically relativistic perspective adds is that a legal standard of equity must now achieve a balance of the legal structure and process as we understand each of these legal elements in a psychologically balanced context.

Any standard of legal equity, of course, must also reflect on how the law engages the dialectic and how it encourages or impedes the progress of legal understanding in new legal situations. Postmaterial societies must now be ready for a relativistic assaying of such understanding and to bear up to the new standard, any postmaterial legal system must consciously engage both qualitatively similar and qualitatively dissimilar variables in the law and a balancing of their influence. In the final analysis, it must consciously balance the analytic and the synthetic cognitions as they exist in the law and as they each move the law forward through its dialectical stages.

INTENT AND PURPOSE

The above discussion of law and cognition in the American context has briefly defined the standard of psychological equity for the law. It has also defined how that standard of equity affects both legal equity and the historical and political progress that comes from legal change. A nascent psychological relativity in the law is well represented, for example, within an argument such as the classical debate between those who search for the *intent* of the law as opposed to those who search for the law's *purpose*. A similar, psychologically relativistic contrast exists between those who have been shown to prefer *strict* construction of legal documents as opposed to those who prefer *broad* rules of construction. The broad perspective more likely includes nonlegal considerations in the legal equation. Matters such as the relative conditions of the contestants to a legal ruling are the stuff of purpose and broad construction. They are thus an example of the synthetic cognition.

The debate over intent or purpose, or strict or broad construction, is as joined today as it has ever been. It is available in mainstream textbooks, Lief Carter's *Reason in Law* being representative, although Carter declined to expand on the psychological dimension of his jurisprudential argument there.[21] Recognizing the linkage of a purposive view of legal interpretation with a quest for a progress in the law that ostensibly ensures better standards of justice, Carter argues that the just development of common-law precedent is dependent on purposive rather than intentional interpretations. Carter highlights the importance of the ends of the law as these ends conflict with the immediate environment of either a precedent case or a statute. Carter, for example, cites the perspective of both Oliver Wendell Holmes and Benjamin Cardozo on the limitations to common-law precedent, quoting Holmes as saying that "if the grounds upon which it was laid down have vanished long since," then precedent should not rule.[22] Cardozo, in a similar vein, argued, "Few rules in our time are so well established that they may not be called upon any day to justify their existence as means adapted to an end. If they do not function, they are diseased."[23]

Beyond case interpretation, however, Lief Carter also argues for purpose over intent in the interpretation of statutes. In a way that would fully include both psychological relativity and its relationship to legal progress, Carter embraces the nonlegal, qualitatively dissimilar variable, arguing for the availability of the widest possible range of sources for the judicial decision maker. Carter, for example, admires the judge who searches for the purpose of statutes by looking "much further, into dictionaries, canons, verbal contexts and competing social policies as well as history itself."[24] Within the arena of constitutional interpretation, Carter suggests that "it is perfectly proper for [courts] to apply policy decisions in terms of their purpose as best [they] can determine it."[25]

In Lief Carter's justifications for purposive statutory and constitutional interpretation, the public-policy implications of moving beyond original intent, with its linkage of legal adjudication to no more than the immediate circumstances of the law, implies the inclusion of more than those circumstances in the process of adjudication. It implies the usage of cognitively dissimilar considerations, or the considerations of the synthetic cognition.

The debate over legal interpretation, of course, goes well beyond the textbooks. It fills the everyday political dialogue, with the recent, somewhat-less-than-profound debate between a recent attorney general, Edwin Meese III, and Supreme Court Associate Justice William J. Brennan, Jr., for example, serving as a representative outcropping. Meese, who publicly deplored so much of what the Supreme Court Chief Justice Earl Warren had done to extend Bill of Rights protections, argued that judges should engage in a form of legal reasoning that was not "tainted by ideological predilection."[26] Such a pristine vision, Meese contended, could be accomplished only by reference to the Framers' original intent. Brennan, noting that "the days when common law property relationships dominated litigation and legal practice are past," argued, "The modern activist state is the concomitant of the complexity of modern society."[27] The cognitive preference of each position is clear.

THE SYNTHETIC COGNITION AND JUDICIAL ACTIVISM

Beyond arguments over the law's methodology like that between Justice Brennan and former Attorney General Meese, one more dichotomy of thinking about the law is illustrative of what a relativistic theory requires for legal balance. The argument over judicial activism versus judicial restraint has been with American jurisprudence at least since the time of Chief Justice Marshall's tortuous reasoning in the case of *Marbury v. Madison*. The debate over judical activism, a first cousin of the intent-purpose debate, is different in at least one respect. The difference is that judicial activism may borrow, and has borrowed, from either a synthetic or an analytic cognition as each promotes a desired political objective.

A contemporary writer who argued most eloquently for limits on judical activism is the late Alexander Bickel, Bickel's *Least Dangerous Branch* borrowing its title from Hamilton's somewhat disingenuous depiction of courts in no. 78 *Federalist*. Bickel did not repudiate the availability of interpretive devices within common-law adjudication outright, but he strongly leaned toward Learned Hand's now famous admonition against turning the Supreme Court into a "third legislative chamber."[28]

Bickel addressed the issue of judical review in the flush of the Warren Court's Bill of Rights expansions. He did so clearly fearing that the benchmark of legal interpretation would be pulled away from the common-law calculus of legal rationalism. Because of that fear, Bickel championed what he called the "passive virtues" of nonexpansive adjudication.[29] The restrictive definitions that he gave to those jurisdictional doorways of legal standing, judical ripeness, and a variety of other helpmates to judicial self-discipline marked Bickel's antidote to a Warren-like activism.

From a relativistic perspective, the legal activism that Bickel challenged was virtually all of the synthetic cognition. But earlier courts, particularly in the late nineteenth century with the contrivance known as "substantive due process," and in the early days of the New Deal before the "switch in time saved nine," were examples of analytically driven periods of activism. They were each designed to counter the expansive nature of legislatively directed change. The Warren Court's extension of the federal jurisdiction in regard to the states, and indeed Warren's expansion of the public jurisdiction in regard to the private jurisdiction, were without question further aggregations of the political realm as Hegel would have described it. Predictably, they rested on purposive readings of the Constitution's deeper meanings, not its intent. Much as with the acceptance of Louis D. Brandeis's introduction of sociological variables in *Muller v. Oregon,* they rested, within substantive cases like *Brown v. The Board of Education* (school integration) and procedural cases like *Baker v. Carr* (reapportionment), on patently nonlegal considerations.[30] They were, without question, cognitively synthetic rulings.

The best examples of judicial inclusion of the dissimilar, or synthetic variable, in significant Supreme Court rulings come from controversies that had a deeply private impact. One, *Griswold v. Connecticut,* held that Connecticut's law against the dissemination of birth-control information violated constitutional protections. There, Justice William O. Douglas's majority opinion disavowed any intention to "sit as a super-legislature to determine the wisdom, need, and propriety of laws," but still argued that the Bill of Rights was laden with "penumbras formed by emendations," all of which anticipated the expansion of personal liberties through the years. Justice Arthur Goldberg, in his concurring opinion in *Griswold*, went even farther and created something that he called "the right of marital privacy" out of a combination of expressly protected rights. Goldberg contended that although "that right [privacy] is not mentioned explicitly in the Constitution," it was nonetheless "supported both by numerous decisions of this Court" and "by the language and history of the Ninth Amendment."[31]

To an extent that had not been seen before, Justice Goldberg incorporated a fully historical, purposive reading of the Constitution into an opinion that was as cognitively synthetic as any the Court has yet seen. Indeed, it incorporated what Lief Carter would have called "history itself," just as it incorporated a variety of other variables, as Goldberg thought such variables to be necessary in the search for legal equity. In their judicial notice of what were previously nonlegal questions, the Douglas and Goldberg opinions each engaged in something far different from a literal reading of the Constitution. They were both highly synthetic in their cognitive form.

Psychological balance as it may exist in any legal context (but particularly as it exists in a common-law context, with its emphasis on the rule of precedent) thus goes well beyond any finding of a balance among either the objective circumstances of psychologically undifferentiated individuals or objective groups. The standard of psychological balance requires that the *form* of what is included into a consideration of legal reality be balanced between similar and dissimilar variables, or between analytic and synthetic cognitions. The contractual form, the form of the common law and the form of the private law that is the underpinning of the American legal system, is a cognitively analytic form.

The reliance of American (and English) jurisprudence on the contractual form shows that that form, all things equal, is cognitively unbalanced in its adjudging of whether contracting parties might or might not have sustained a subjective identity and not only an objective meeting of the minds. The unconsidered use of the contractual form implies an automaticity of a meeting of the minds when outright fraud or coercion is not present. It excludes any recognition of the psychology of the contractual form itself.

Is it any wonder that the cognitive *form* of the judge-made law that has typified judical activism (at least in this century) has directly responded to the form of what the larger political or social issue originally represented in its avowedly political context? The legal considerations of *Brown* and *Baker* are cognitively synthetic, because both in the form of the precedent that they rely on and in the reconciliation of new standards into the legal fabric, the new, qualitatively dissimilar cognition was already included in the consideration of the political issue that framed the legal dispute.

Supreme Court scholars like Henry Abraham typically define judicial activism in terms of the resultant policy implications of the changing law. Abraham, for example, lists justifications like "personal commitments to policy goals," "pragmatism," or what Oliver Wendell Holmes once called the "felt necessities of the time" as justifiable catalysts to judicial activism.[32] What Abraham and traditional legal scholars point to, however, is nothing more than a balance among the *resultant* claims of petitioners as their cases are decided among legal claimants. A psychologically relativistic perspective on judicial decision making requires that a deeper balance be struck. It is a balance that requires far more of the law, asking for nothing less than that a balance among the cognitive *forms* of the legal argument be present. It also requires that something that extends Karl Llewellyn's idealistic notion of legal realism, or the notions of legal meaning as they are imposed in an idealistic sense on the law rather than as they are drawn from an ostensibly objective law, must be paramount in any legal determination. What a psychologically relativistic theory means for the law, in short, is that legal equity originates in what are psychological, not economic or social, preferences.

A cognitively relativistic perspective on the law, in keeping with the idealistic hierarchy of a relativistic theory, simply does not begin with specific preferences for substantive choices within the judicial arena. Neither does it begin with a consideration of the material or resultant distributions that judicial decisions typically bring. The primary issue from a relativistic perspective is the issue of the cognitive *form* of the law. This form, as with the form of the political arrangements of any national polity, must be adjudged according to a balance of what the law really is. In an historical framework, it must be weighed in terms of its contribution to a dialectical form of change of the law's very structure. Only then can it be weighed in terms of its contribution to resultant justice. Hegel's synthetic cognition and its relationship to the dialectic, from a legal as well as from a political or even a metaphysical perspective, applies to the historical progress of the law as much as it does to any other progress.

Chapter Ten

THREE CONSTITUTIONAL CRISES

CRISIS AND COGNITION

In this chapter, I argue that the balance between the analytic and the synthetic cognitions in the American government and legal system that I have described has had a noticeable impact on the three major constitutional crises that America has faced. Each of these three constitutional crises, I suggest, was characterized by two identifiably different perspectives on the solution to a public difficulty as all three offered a conflict between analytically and synthetically grounded resolutions for the difficulty.

Each of the constitutional crises that I will describe occurred, of course, before the postmaterial age. From the perspective of a relativistic theory, therefore, each crisis evidenced less of the impact of the idealistic hierarchy of psychological balance, structural and procedural balance, and material or resultant equity that I have described. The political issue that ignited each crisis embraced equities among groups, regions, or classes without reference to psychological differentiation. For that reason, although the three crises illustrate cognitive differentiations, they still largely reflect the objective political motives of each position's advocates. Nonetheless, each crisis illustrates, I think, that the cognitive balance of the structures and processes of the American government was of significance in determining whether the resolution of the crisis was successful or unsuccessful. From a Hegelian perspective, each crisis illustrated how the progress of history, even before the postmaterial age, was affected by the ability or the inability of America's public institutions to know the synthetic cognition and achieve a dialectical, and equitable, resolution of the crisis. Though the synthetic cognition and the dialectical form were not achieved through a deliberate cognitive balancing of structures and processes, the ability or inability of the American political system to achieve the synthetic cognition's natural understanding was instrumental in whether or not the system surmounted the constitutional difficulty.

The American constitutional order has survived its three most challenging crises, but sadly, the record reveals that these crises were amicably resolved in but two instances. The crisis of the early constitutional or national period, as well as the crisis of the Great Depression, found America's political institutions capable of a synthetic resolution. The country, as a result, moved through the crisis reasonably well, meeting Hegel's standard for the dialectical progress of history. In the period leading up to America's Civil War, however, America's political institutions, and America's legal institutions both failed to either know the nature of the crisis or transcend it.

A relativistic perspective on the arrangement of competing political groups or classes begins with an identification of the cognitive *form* of the argument. An understanding of the *form* of the political argument in the three constitutional crises, as that argument is placed within the Hegelian standard for the progress of understanding and history, is therefore the primary focus of this chapter. Even before the postmaterial age, the cognitive balance of the structures and processes of the American government was important in the resolution (or nonresolution) of America's most serious crises. Though the participants were surely not conscious of the psychology of that balance, it existed nonetheless.

THE NATIONAL PERIOD

The American Constitution is a brief document. Those who favorably note its mere 4,300 words properly suggest that it purposely wrought only the barest outline for the new national government. Americans know, however, that public acceptance for even this undetailed document was not easily granted. Its immediately appended Bill of Rights was the price for the capitulation of the Constitution's opponents and, appropriately, the Bill of Rights incorporated a liberal notion of what the rights of a free people should be. The incorporation of those rights into the American Constitution began the most extensive inclusion of a citizenry into the affairs of a nation that political history yet knew.

America's first constitutional crisis tested the very structural integrity of the new nation's government. The country's perilous geographical positioning between the still-ominous British, Spanish, French, and native North Americans mirrored an equally perilous financial positioning between foreign, national, and state debts, a chaotic collection of financial institutions, and an as yet undeveloped national economy. Whether one individual contributed substantially to the successful postconstitutional development of the United States has been much argued. Yet Andrew Hacker's suggestion (in opposition to that of Clinton Rossiter, Russell Kirk, and Louis Hartz, among others) that the still-young Secretary of the Treasury Alexander Hamilton did more than anyone to sink this nation's pilings beneath a very stormy sea still carries great credence.[1]

The postconstitutional role of Hamilton, who was "devoted to his country and desirous of seeing it endure," has perhaps been more debated than has the role of any of the Framers.[2] Kirk saw him as a mercantilist, Hartz as an elitist, and Rossiter, with perhaps the unkindest cut, scored Hamilton's "schemes" for the centralization of governmental power.[3] The charges carry their obligatory grain of truth but are unfair nonetheless. Hamilton was a mercantilist, an elitist and, after a fashion, a centrist. Yet he favored these identifications only until such time as the weak and scattered nation of four million could fend for itself in a very difficult world. Hamilton was thus expedient to a fault, but his writings hid neither that expediency nor his motive for it.

The Report on Public Credit. After the *Federalist,* Hamilton wrote three principal works concerning the perils of the new American republic. They dealt with the assumption of the public debt, the creation of a national system of banking, and the invigoration of a postagricultural economy. Curiously, one of Hamilton's postconstitutional political opponents was his *Federalist* coauthor, James Madison. Madison, when under Jefferson's influence, developed a view of the Constitution that grew more limited by the day. Hamilton, on the contrary, wanted constitutional government to begin, not end, with the written document. His vision of a vigorous government assumed a Constitution in full flower.

In his plea for debt assumption, for example, Hamilton argued for the benefits that he assumed a newly debt-free nation could enjoy.

Hamilton felt a resolution of the public debt was essential, arguing, "The credit of the nation should be well established." Failure to pay off the debt would mean that the new nation might find itself *"borrowing and buying dear"* (emphasis his).[4] For Hamilton, the accumulation of the Revolutionary War debt had been nothing less than the "price of liberty." But to reassure its creditors, the federal government now needed to pay that debt in full. And to pay it, the federal government needed to be "clothed with powers competent to calling forth the resources of the community."[5] Today's ingenious euphemisms for taxation are no match for Hamilton's.

In the first of the three Treasury documents that Hamilton wrote, the intrepid New Yorker called for full exploitation of the nation's natural largesse. In doing so, however, he managed a marvelous duplicity between a political end and what he wanted citizens to believe were his preferred means. Hamilton surely knew that much of the war's indebtedness was no longer held by the bond's original purchasers. He also knew that the subsequent sales of the war bonds had been at well below the unredeemed instruments' par value. The possibility of outright nonredemption or, at the least, the possibility of redemption at a subpar price, accounted for that reduced value. Just as clearly, the likelihood of subpar redemption or outright nonredemption was, of course, what had led the sellers, mostly Southerners, to offer their paper so cheaply.

The structure of Hamilton's argument on redemption in the *Report on Public Credit* is a clear example of a cognitively synthetic perspective. Hamilton argued for redemption at par value, but to achieve that end (to assure a price that was different from a market price), Hamilton surely concocted a "scheme." But Hamilton's scheme purported, at first glance, to embrace, not reject, the market price for redemption. It purported to follow the traditional *contractual* form of Hamilton's *Federalist* writings, while in fact it argued for paying par value to current bond holders, regardless of the bond's market value.

Hamilton's position on debt assumption, in the context of a bitter debate over the redemption price, was nothing short of remarkable. Hamilton contended that it would be "inconsistent with justice" to do otherwise than redeem the notes at par. To not redeem them would constitute "a breach of contract; a violation of the rights of a fair purchaser." Hamilton, pleading for an understanding wherein "[e]very buyer . . . stands exactly in the place of the seller," used this standard in arguing that the *"intent* in making the security assignable, is, that the proprietor may be able to make use of his property, by selling it for as much as it *may be worth in the market.* Further, the buyer may be *safe* in the purchase" (emphasis his).[6] The contractual form of value determination, along the lines of Nozick and not Rawls, even included the alleged meeting of the minds of the buyer and seller.

At first glance, no noncontractual factor, no cognitively dissimilar factor, was a part of Hamilton's determination of a national bond's redemption value. A closer look at Hamilton's position, however, reveals that his reification of the "safe purchaser" was at best a non sequitur. The bonds had already been purchased "for as much as they may be worth in the market," but that price was well below par. Also, the bonds were hardly purchased in good faith, Hamilton's reference to the buyer's standing "exactly in the place of the seller" conveniently neglecting that the bonds were bought precisely because the buyers believed they had governmental leverage to have them fully redeemed.[7] The plea of the buyers for par payment was looked on by many, particularly the earlier sellers of course, as little short of fraud. Though Hamilton's argument appears to have the form of contract to it, it is a clear plea for an extraneous consideration, a government subsidy.

The above review is appropriate for a relativistic understanding of Hamilton because whether there was to be full redemption of the war's indebtedness or not, or whether Hamilton was motivated by the interests of his financial friends, as some have charged, or by doing what he thought best for the country, is not important to it. A relativistic analysis, in focusing on the cognitive *form* of the Hamilton position on the debt, reveals that though Hamilton tried to mask his argument for redemption in contractual terminology, he was, again, advocating the introduction of a wholly noncontractual concern into the equation. Hamilton's insistence on the cognitively dissimilar variable of "national respectability" is surely of the synthetic form and, therefore, Hamilton's position in favor of full public debt assumption, or in favor of an assumption that was beneficial because "[t]rade is extended by it . . . [a]griculture and manufactures are also promoted by it . . . [and] [t]he interests of money will be lowered by it" is also of the synthetic form.[8]

The National Bank. The next treatise of America's first secretary of the treasury mirrored Hamilton's writings on the debt. No early American political issue was joined with the vigor of the argument over the National Bank. Some of the dispute was sectional, with Southerners, who had been sensitized to say the least by the redemption controversy, taking the antimercantile position on the government's link to banking interests. But the sectional divide was frequently overridden in this controversy by the dispute between propertied and unpropertied Americans. As a result, the longevity of a dispute that led to the acceptance of the first National Bank in 1791, the nonrenewal of the Bank in 1811, the chartering of a second National Bank in 1816, and the tumultuous, Jackson-inspired nonrenewal of that second Bank's charter in 1836, was exceeded only by the slavery debate in nineteenth-century American political controversy.

In the matter of the National Bank, Hamilton once again advocated governmental action. This time, however, his natural opponent Jefferson was more fully on the field against him than he had been during the debt conflict. Hamilton's argument was nearly identical in its form to his position on the debt. There were real economic opportunities for the nation, Hamilton claimed, specifically citing capital augmentation, the circulation of capital, the facilitation of the payment of taxes, and monetary liquidity as among the benefits that would flow from a national financial structure.[9] Hamilton's avoidance of the Smithian notions of purely private capital accumulation and investment, his willingness to use the government for capital accumulation, was as synthetic in its cognitive form as was his argument on the debt.

The issue of the National Bank was one of more than statutory preference, a more direct interpretation of the Constitution coming into play. The debate over the bank, initiated by Hamilton's report to the House of Representatives in December of 1790, exemplified much of the debate over constitutional construction that I have reviewed. Before the courts were involved, however, the political joust fell along the early division of the Washington cabinet. Secretary of State Jefferson and, more meekly, Attorney General Edmund Randolph were on one side of the debate. Hamilton at Treasury and Henry Knox at War were on the other. Washington, a Federalist far less than a mediator in so many early cabinet disputes, had received the opinions of Hamilton's adversaries on the constitutionality of the bank when he gave Hamilton "an opportunity of examining and answering the objections contained in the enclosed papers."[10] Hamilton was delighted to do so.

Beginning his defense of a bank with a discussion of what national sovereignty ought to mean in America, Hamilton deplored what he called a *"political society* without *sovereignty,* or . . . a *people governed, without government"* (emphasis his). Hamilton depicted the Constitution as the *"supreme law of the land,"* and it was this designation of supremacy that permitted Hamilton to turn to things that were thus properly "incident" to that sovereign power (emphasis his). Hamilton's reasoning was not arcane. He spoke simply about things that were rightfully "intrusted to the management of the government," denying the inference that "Congress can in no case exercise any power not included in those enumerated in the Constitution." With these strokes, he was off to the notion of implied constitutional powers, not stopping until he had engrossed a third class of powers that he said may be properly denominated *"resulting powers"* (emphasis his).[11]

To bolster the implicit and resultant powers of the Constitution, Hamilton relied on what are now well-understood expansions of the constitutional letter. The necessary and proper clause, he argued, permitted actions that were *"needful, requisite, incidental, useful* or *conducive to"* the demands of any political crisis (emphasis his). Continuing, he suggested that the Constitutional Convention had meant "to give a liberal latitude" to the specified powers, as they were not simple handmaidens to "restrictive operation". They surely should not be subject to an interpretation that placed the words *"absolutely* or *indispensably"* before "necessary and proper" (emphasis his).[12]

Inevitably, Hamilton turned his argument to the benefits of an expansive interpretation of constitutional language. He suggested it was within the inherent power of any government to create institutions that nurtured the government's interest even if it was only the *"incidental* and *auxiliary* power of the government, not some *"independent* or *substantive"* power that permitted the American government to create a facilitative corporation.[13] In short, Hamilton found that a "natural and obvious relation between the institution of a bank and the objects of several of the enumerated powers" fully embodied his interpretation of the government's constitutional powers.[14]

From a relativistic perspective, the extensions of governmental power that are found in Hamilton's broad and expansive interpretations of constitutional prerogative were as clearly the product of a synthetic cognition as were Hamilton's arguments for funding the public debt.

The inclusion of a more relaxed standard for governmental necessity and, perhaps most important, the inclusion of the bank into the improvement of the nation's economy, placed qualitatively dissimilar variables firmly into the constitutional equation for Hamilton.

Predictably, Hamilton's argument is in clear contrast to Jefferson's rejoinder. The Virginian's February 1791 position paper to President Washington specifically cautioned against taking "a single [constitutional] step beyond the boundaries thus specially drawn around the powers of Congress."[15] Jefferson, of course, was taking the strict-constructionist view and, in doing so, he rejected the notion that Congress was empowered "to do whatever would be for the good of the United States." Jefferson believed that the Constitution meant to "lace them [the congressional powers] up straitly within the enumerated powers" and therefore the power to tax, to borrow, and to regulate commerce, all expressly given to the Congress, could be accomplished "without a bank" and without what was only "convenient" and not "necessary."[16] Cognitively, such restrictive interpretations as Jefferson's are manifestly within the analytic mode. They embrace only the qualitatively similar variable of the direct intent of the Constitution and they surely contrast with the cognitive form, not merely the substance, of Hamilton's broad construction position.

The Report on Manufactures. Almost immediately after delivering himself of his debt redemption and National Bank positions, Hamilton launched into his third and final early Republic writing. Andrew Hacker, in his response to those who had preceded him in describing Hamilton, vigorously defended Hamilton from the mercantilist charge[17] by maintaining that "Hamilton is the complete libertarian," one who is "devoted to a 'system of perfect liberty.'" Hacker found Hamilton to be persuaded by the need for governmental promotion of manufactures only because of the requirements of an "imperfect world." "Only because of this," according to Hacker, was Hamilton an "interventionist" and thus Hamilton, in the matter of manufactures, was no less expedient than he had been on the debt or the bank, even if Hacker is correct that Hamilton was at heart "a libertarian, then, and not a mercantilist."[18]

In his expedient mercantilism, nonetheless, Hamilton openly courted the direct intervention of government in the generation of the nation's wealth. Hamilton recognized that with the advent of the industrial revolution in England, the feeble American economy bucked its own political inertia and swam upstream as well against the deep-seated American biases in favor of an agricultural society that were fueled by his adversary Jefferson. In the early pages of *The Report on Manufactures,* therefore, Hamilton sought to placate those troubled by his apparent abandonment of a national ethic, even arguing that manufactures complemented and enhanced agricultural productivity.[19]

Hamilton's thrust in the *Manufactures,* expectedly, pointed toward an improved international competitiveness for the United States. Hamilton contended that America's belated entry into industrialization, along with America's labor shortage and its need for increased immigration, all weighed against America's international economic competitiveness. Further, in the submission of his December 1791 *Report,* Hamilton argued strongly against those who contended that the promotion of manufactures would "give a monopoly of advantages to particular classes, at the expense of the rest of the community."[20] Those who could become industrialists, he argued, should be encouraged to do so without undue concern for profits.

Perhaps most important as a further example of Hamilton's embellishments on "perfect liberty," however, was Hamilton's response to those who argued for laissez-faire strategies of economic growth. "If the system of perfect liberty to industry and commerce . . . were the prevailing system of nations," Hamilton conceded that "the arguments which dissuade a country . . . from the zealous pursuit of manufactures, would doubtless have great force." With the working out of concepts like comparative advantage, each country would "have the full benefit of its peculiar advantages to compensate for its deficiencies or disadvantages."[21] But Hamilton was as much a realist in the matter of international trade as he was in the matter of domestic manufactures. Expediency reigned here too for Hamilton, this time in his argument that "the system which has been mentioned [the free-trade position of comparative advantage] is far from characterizing the general policy of nations."[22] If the global competitive playing field, as a current expression has it, was in fact uneven, then America's finger on the scale would be as appropriate as any other nation's. The cognitive form of that argument, once more, is clearly synthetic.

Hamilton and Psychology. Though I wish to say little more about Hamilton's early positions, I cannot resist referring to what, for nearly two hundred years ago, was a remarkably introspective psychological reference in Hamilton's writings. After his discussion of the public debt, capital enhancement, and the financial benefits that debt funding and a new bank might bring to America's manufactures, Hamilton paused for what can only be described as an apology. Uncharacteristically for a man of considerable pride, the offering that Hamilton made to his reader apparently resulted from what he called the "Due allowance" he felt he should make for the possibility of error in his advocacy. This allowance was preceded by Hamilton's reflection, it should be noted, that "[r]easonings on a subject comprehending ideas so abstract and complex, so little reducible to a precise calculation, as those which enter into the question just discussed" are fraught "with a danger of running into fallacies."[23] It is a revealing observation, and it is the only reference in Hamilton's national triad of writings that speaks directly to the quality or the rhetorical form of his own argument. Hamilton and Hegel were surely far from each other in many ways. But if only for a moment, Hamilton, like Hegel, seemed to understand that "precise calculation" was inappropriate to speculative analysis as well as to new and active governmental policy.

Hamilton's apology bolsters the argument of those like Hacker who have contended that Hamilton's natural political bent was probably far different from the cognitive bent of his mercantilism. Precise calculations may well have been the stuff of Hamilton's psychology. Yet as expediency won out for Hamilton, he saw that the "perfect liberty" or the free-market calculus of cognitively similar variables simply could not produce the result that he wanted for the country.

Hamilton's writings on the debt, the bank, and manufactures later served, not surprisingly, as the basis for the arguments that Supreme Court Chief Justice John Marshall made in his opinions in several landmark Supreme Court cases. In *McCulloch v. Maryland*'s concern with the constitutionality of the National Bank, for example, Marshall's argument that "there is no phrase in the instrument [the Constitution] which . . . excludes incidental or implied powers," along with his insistence that the necessary and proper clause should be "understood as employing any means calculated to produce the end," mirror Hamilton's earlier language on the subject almost precisely.[24] Similarly, in *Gibbons v. Ogden*'s expansion of the commerce clause, Marshall asked rhetorically whether the commerce power should only be interpreted by a "narrow construction, which would cripple the government and render it unequal to the objects for which it is declared to be instituted?"[25] Marshall affirmed broad, penumbral extensions of express constitutional language in *Gibbons* by preferring the cognition that extended the Constitution into a judicial ratification of mercantilism. This cognition was clearly synthetic.

Like Hamilton, John Marshall's positions in several landmark constitutional cases may have been contrary to his natural psychological bent. Marshall's sense of what the young government needed, however, included the synthetic form of understanding as the flooring for constitutional expediency. The Chief Justice's references to an "effective government," his concern for the "happiness and prosperity of the nation," and his fear of those things "which would cripple the government, and render it unequal to the objects for which it is declared to be instituted," all demonstrated Marshall's judicial preference for the broader purposes, not the narrow intent, of the new Constitution.[26]

From a relativistic perspective, the analysis of America's early national period is not complicated. The "explication of differences" in the synthetic cognition was illustrated so well within the Hamilton-Jefferson contrast that the structural and procedural accommodations of the new American government were able to differentiate between opposing political options and aggregate the political majorities that effectuated public policy. The second National Bank was approved by an initially unsympathetic Congress in 1816, largely because the financial trauma attendant to the War of 1812 made a Hamilton-like argument for national financial stabilization irrefutable. The previous minority position, the position of a badly faltering Federalist party, won converts and carried the roll one more time.

The important lesson from a relativistic perspective is that America's young institutions were able to adapt to the synthetic cognition. Those whose political positions fostered the synthetic cognition, perhaps regardless of their own psychologies, were able to forge a majoritarian position around the synthetic *form* of understanding. Significantly, the political institutions of the day, particularly the presidency, the Congress, and to some extent the parties, at least did not impede the creation of that majoritarian position. In short, though Hamilton had fallen in his duel with Aaron Burr, his form of knowing about something like the National Bank and how that bank might assure financial stability for the nation, like his form of understanding many of America's early difficulties, was effectively realized.

THE CIVIL WAR

America's second constitutional crisis presented an altogether different circumstance to the still-young nation. First, the political events that led to the American Civil War were more complex and more obscure than those of the national period. Second, the structures of the American political system, as well as the sorting out of the nation's majority and minority wills through the day's parties, worked very differently indeed from how they worked in the national period.

America's Civil War was a conflict of the two grand sections of the country, and the stubborn differences between two cultures, economies, politics, and what to this day is still called "a way of life" in one of the sections. The flint of the controversy, however, was a straightforward matter. Slavery existed in some states and it did not in others. It was the conflict between those who saw this single institution from very different perspectives that ignited the uncontrollable blaze.

Political controversy between the North and South was not new to the American political debate. Indeed, it had antedated the debate over the financial considerations of the national period by several years. The argument over how slaves would be counted for representation within the House of Representatives elevated Philadelphia's summer warmth still further until the so-called three-fifths compromise was reached. The agreement to have slaves count as three-fifths of a citizen ranks second only to Roger Sherman's large state-small state compromise in saving the Constitutional convention.

But in the rush of other matters, North-South tensions remained largely dormant for the first forty or so years of the new republic's history. Some Southerners, most notably the Pinckneys of South Carolina, but other wealthy and federalist supporters as well, strongly endorsed both a vigorous national government and the Hamiltonian hard-money financial policies of that government's early years. Though it is always difficult to draw a line through history and mark the beginnings of conflict from there, the protective-tariff legislation of 1828 surely drew a line in the sand between Northern and Southern interests that was never crossed lightheartedly again. The tariff issue, of course, was never as flinty as the slavery issue. But it is noteworthy if for no other reason than that it served as the place of entry into the public debate for someone who gave great credence to the Southern view, John C. Calhoun.

Calhoun and the Concurrent Majority. Calhoun, a South Carolinian like the Pinckneys, was of very different stock from his low-country, aristocratic predecessors in the South. Scotch-Irish and Calvinist, not English and Anglican, he represented that anti-Bourbon South that made its living from smaller chunks of more uneven soil than the state's lowland plantations enjoyed. Calhoun was a Southern prodigy, traveling to Yale for his bachelor's degree and returning to practice law in his native Abbeville. Elected to the House of Representatives at twenty-eight, he later served as James Monroe's secretary of war and is still the only vice president to have served different presidents.[27]

Calhoun's 1832 resignation from the Andrew Jackson vice presidency marked his final break with a national identity. Calhoun had presaged his departure for a goodly time after the first tariff's passage, most notably in his *Exposition and Protest.* Though that document was immediately enacted as a resolution by the South Carolina legislature, it was not until his later-life *Disquisition* that Calhoun devised broad arguments for both the nullification of federal authority, as well as for the justifiable secession from the federal government of unhappy states.[28]

From a relativistic perspective, Calhoun's writings are stark indeed. At the outset, Calhoun's position, the Southern position, was based on what Hegel would have found to be an identity much like Kant's equation. At a moral level, the Southern argument rested on the notion that a paternalistic system of slavery was no less destructive of human dignity than what Southerners called the "wage slavery" of Northern manufactures. The form of that argument, its insistence on an equivalency, clearly denied the "explication of differences" of a synthetic cognition.

Significantly, what Calhoun argued for was a "giving to each interest, or portion [of the country] the power of self-protection." Self-protection should be granted, according to Calhoun, so that "all strife and struggle between them [the different interests or portions] is prevented."[29] He preferred the isolation of self-protection to any government that "periodically stakes all its honors and emoluments as prizes to be contended for."[30] His device for effectuating such self-protection was to grant each section a constitutional "negative power," including the "preventing or arresting [of] the action of the government" that could be realized by "veto, interposition, nullification, check, or balance of power."[31]

Calhoun's misnomer for the vehicle of nullification is well known. He called it the "concurrent majority," but it is the cognitive form of the concept and its justification that made the argument what it was. Madison's no. 10 *Federalist* had argued the danger of majorities, and the reinforcement of that view in its new guise by Calhoun was hardly out of the American political character. But Madison had also argued that there were two methods of controlling majorities, the first "removing its causes" and the second "controling [*sic*] its effects." Madison thoroughly eschewed the former option, finding that its substrategies of "destroying the liberty which is essential to its [factions] existence" and not recognizing that "[a]s long as the reason of man continues fallible . . . different opinions will be formed," were both unconscionable. Indeed, Madison found the first remedy "worse than the disease" and the second wholly "impracticable."[32] Madison thus foreclosed any attempt at reducing the "causes" of majorities. The controlling of the effects of factions was thus what no. 10 was about, and most of the rest of the *Federalist* described the checks and balances of the American constitutional order that Madison argued would do just that.

Although concerned with majorities and their potential for tyranny, Calhoun's arguments nevertheless went well beyond Madison. In contrast to Madison, Calhoun opted for Madison's first alternative, or for the removal of the "causes" of majorities. Though not specifically advocating the repression of "different opinions," Calhoun suggested that differences that could lead to the development of a majority never confront the general government. Instead of advocating the outright suppression of different views, Calhoun got to where he wanted with a philosophical identity. He granted all regionally embossed political views an automatic equality by saying, in effect, "If we shall agree on one thing, we shall agree that our positions are equally valid for each of us." We shall do this, in Calhoun's own words, in the name of "self-protection."[33]

Of course Calhoun's concurrent majority is not a majority at all. But apart from its not being a majority, it is a rejection of differentiation among political perspectives and a negation of what makes up the dialectical oppositions that mark any historical contradiction. Politically, it encourages the rejection of a majoritarian position, and it rejects the value of those institutions (such as a political party) that might bring about a majoritarian position like that of the Federalists in the matter of the second National Bank. Calhoun specifically railed against the idea that "[w]hen once formed, the community will be divided into two great parties—a major and a minor—between which there will be incessant struggles on the one side to retain and on the other to obtain the majority."[34]

Importantly, Calhoun rejected the majoritarian form of political resolution precisely because he found such resolution, as in the case of the "fiscal action" of the government, "impossible to equalize."[35] The qualitative identity, or the tautology of his political position, not only denied the dialectic but imported the analytic cognition. Under the political guises of the need for self-protection, or the need for "two federations" as the historian Arthur Bestor once defined it, slavery and nonslavery needed to be qualitatively equivalent for Calhoun. One may have been a five and one may have been a seven but they were both nothing more than numbers.

The Complicity of Structure. Though John C. Calhoun was the spokesman for nullification, interposition or, "be it called by what term it may," as Calhoun once phrased it, he of course did not initiate the political incentive to qualitative similarity that exists in the American constitutional order.[36] The fact is that as a result of the compromises of the convention, the Framers' original design for the American government permitted, and even encouraged, the possibility of something like the concurrent majority position. Substantively, with the three-fifths compromise, the structure and processes of the American constitutional order enshrined the political equivalency between slavery and nonslavery from the beginning of the Republic. That equivalency also reflected, and reinforced, the proclivity for unanimity and against a majority in the resolution of America's political problems.

This proclivity was reinforced frequently, first thirty years later with the Missouri Compromise. That compromise, of course, was designed specifically to avoid the slavery issue's further agitation of the nation, proclaiming that slave states and nonslave states would be admitted into the union in equal numbers. Equal numbers, of course, meant equal representation in the United States Senate, where the voting was, and still is, by state.

It is almost a truism that America's political structure encouraged Calhoun's argument of equivalency and the prolongation of the North-South conflict. Beyond the three-fifths compromise on slavery, the American political structure reflected the rejection of Madison's plan that had provided for two population-based legislative houses, the second elected by the first. Such a plan would have proscribed state-based representation, and as a result, the enforced equivalency of the two sides of such a difficult political issue as the issue of slavery may well have been faced, and resolved, much sooner.

The New Jersey Plan, submitted by the small states, provided for but one house and state-by-state representation in it. The plan would have facilitated the maintenance of political equivalency, but the Connecticut Compromise, which ensured bicameralism, also ensured equivalency, if only in the upper house. Roger Sherman's "Solomon," by permitting equivalency, meant that when America's great sections began their battle over slavery, the structure of the government favored an understanding of the issue in the analytic, not the synthetic, form. America's political obfuscation of its principal difference lay deeply in its political structure and the development of a majority position among those who differed was thus constitutionally proscribed. The Missouri Compromise, and the later compromises over slavery, fit neatly into the Constitution's cognitive preference but forestalled any solution of the slavery issue. The national government that Calhoun feared and that the South would eventually attempt to abandon took advantage, in the short run, of an institutionalized form that favored Calhoun's concurrent majority to any real majority.

Lincoln's House Divided. Robert E. Johannsen, in his book on the Lincoln-Douglas debates, delights in Abraham Lincoln's comparison of himself with Stephen Douglas, the man whom Lincoln debated in seven Illinois towns in 1858 during their race for the U.S. Senate. Lincoln, Johannsen reports, said about Douglas that "we were both ambitious," but that "[w]ith *me,* the race of ambition has been a failure—a flat failure; with *him* it has been one of splendid success" (emphasis his).[37] The contrast was valid from the perspective of one who had served but briefly in the Illinois legislature and but one term in the federal House of Representatives.

Before the Lincoln-Douglas debates began, Lincoln made a postnomination acceptance speech before the Republican state conventioneers at Springfield. In the first paragraph of that speech, the full magnitude of the contrast between the Northern position and the Calhoun and Southern, not the Douglas position, was cast in marvelous relief. There, in his

Old Testament recollection that "[a] house divided against itself cannot stand," as well as in his prediction that "I believe this government cannot endure permanently half slave and half free," Abraham Lincoln attempted to restructure the form of the North-South debate over slavery.[38] In doing so, Lincoln brought the cognitive forms of the slavery argument into vivid contrast, for what he said, quite simply though powerfully, was that he hoped that the Union would not be dissolved so many years after constitutional ratification. What he said was that he expected the Union to soon "cease to be divided" over the slavery issue, but it would cease to be divided, he also said, because one side would win the struggle over slavery and one side would lose.

From a relativistic perspective, Lincoln's argument, in contrast to Calhoun's, rests first on the notion that slavery and nonslavery were not equivalent or identical. As a result of the nonequivalency of the two positions, or as a result of Lincoln's explication of "a difference" between slavery and nonslavery, the two could never be equated or reconciled. The contrast between Lincoln's and Calhoun's positions could not be more dramatic, for if the fives and sevens of Calhoun's position were not available for an analytic cognition, as they were not for Lincoln, then the alternatives must not only be different from each other. One must be better. One alternative on the issue of slavery must finally become the path of history.

Though fully aware of history's direction with regard to slavery around the world, Lincoln in his "house divided" speech curiously depicted America's alternatives as something in which "[e]ither the opponents of slavery will arrest the further spread of it, and place it where the public mind shall rest in the belief that it is the course of ultimate extinction," or "its advocates will push it forward, till it shall become alike lawful in all the States, old as well as new-North as well as South." No dialectical argument was ever better stated. In the words that immediately preceded Lincoln's "house divided" sentence there is a nice anticipation of the metaphor of the divided house. They read: "In my opinion, it [the turmoil] will not cease, until a crisis shall have been reached and passed."[39] Of course, the pre-Civil War debate did present the country with its greatest crisis. But the dialectical form of Lincoln's position on that crisis, particularly in contrast to Calhoun's position, implied a progress toward resolution.

The Civil War and the American Constitutional Order. Few among those who have written on the American Civil War have stressed the role of the American constitutional order in the conflict. Not many writers have chosen to believe that the greatest of all American conflicts had a great deal to do with how the American political system was structured from the outset. But the historian Arthur Bestor has been an exception, Bestor claiming that the Civil War is in fact best understood as a "Constitutional catastrophe." Bestor's view of the causes of the Civil War even includes an open chiding of those who, in more traditional analyses, have only gone so far as to acknowledge that "the complex interactions of law, institutions and interests" were significant, while still insisting "that the legal and Constitutional framework within which basic disputes over power and wealth occur are not important elements in shaping this course."[40]

Bestor's structural analysis of the Civil War begins by arguing that "the very form that the conflict finally took was determined by the preexisting form of the constitutional system." Bestor says that the "way that the opposing forces were arrayed against each other in war" was simply "a consequence of the way the Constitution had operated to array them in peace." This arrangement, Bestor suggests, was the manifestation of a "compact among the sovereign states," and it was what made the "dissolution of the compact [into] a conceivable thing." The American Constitution for the South, as Bestor points out, was never more than a compact. The contractual nature of the relationship among the American states, as well as the embodiment of that contractual relationship in the Senate's representation of the states, was for Bestor America's deepest structural flaw. As a result of that flaw, the South could argue for nothing less than the guaranteed independence of what Bestor called "two federations" of states, even though both federations were "shaped by the same constitutional tradition."[41]

Bestor's epistemological position, like Lincoln's and in contrast to Calhoun's, revolves around the inevitability of history. How Lincoln would have brought history about was something Bestor labeled as the "containment" of slavery, pointing out that Lincoln considered the Framers to have intended just that result. Lincoln said, "I believe if we could arrest the spread [of slavery] and place it where Washington and Jefferson and Madison placed it, it would be in the course of ultimate extinction."[42] Bestor, like Lincoln, saw history's movement as inevitable, and the form of that movement, for Bestor, was unabashedly as dialectical as was Lincoln's prescription. The cognitive form of such a position is, of course, synthetic.

Dred Scott. The record of the adjudicated law of pre-Civil War America, sadly, is much the same as the record of America's political institutions, the *Dred Scott* case virtually ending hope for a peaceful mitigation of sectional conflict. Scott, a slave taken from his native Missouri to Illinois and given his freedom, was declared a slave again on his return. In 1857, Chief Justice Taney of the United States Supreme Court declared that the state of Missouri could in fact reenslave Scott because Scott's leaving, according to Taney, did not activate what for Taney were nonexistent federal protections of Scott's liberties.[43]

Dred Scott was a case of some legal complexity. It dealt, in part, with the jurisdictional question of whether Scott had standing to sue for his freedom because of what he took for granted was his federal citizenship. The resolution of that issue, however, relied on a determination of the far more simple question of how the Constitution defined a federal citizen, if it defined it at all. Taney's ruling on citizenship held that Scott, and all of the "subordinate and inferior class of beings" of which he was a part, could not claim citizenship. As a result, Scott could not ask for the court's protection.[44] Taney's ruling declined to move beyond the barest language of the Constitution, if it went that far. It ignored the simple fact, for instance, that black citizens had been federal (and state) citizens at the time of the Constitution.

Beyond the narrowness of its interpretation of liberties, however, the key to *Dred Scott* lies with Taney's declaration of national governmental impotence. Specifically, *Dred Scott* neutralized what was left of the Missouri Compromise spirit by declaring that the federal Congress never had the power to allocate where slavery and nonslavery could exist in the first place. The case forbade any incipient congressional action that "prohibited a citizen from holding and owning property of this kind [a slave] in the territory of the United States north of the [Mason-Dixon] line."[45] It did so by giving states the exclusive right to define such property. In the context of the constitutional issues brought forth by *Dred Scott,* the case's references to "delegated and restricted powers," the "union of states," and "the dominion of the United States," all evidence contractual understandings of the American union.[46] Taney's opinion mimicks Calhoun's *Disquisition* not only in the approval of the state's rights position and the restriction of federal power to its "trustee" relationship toward the territories, but also in the form of Calhoun's argument with regard to a contractual Federal structure. From a relativistic perspective, the nature of Taney's (and Calhoun's) contractual form of argument, along with its nonevolutionary, nonhistorical sense of what the Union was, is undeniably analytic. In Taney, the absence of a sense of the progress of understanding and history emanated from the absence of a sense of a qualitative differentiation between slavery and nonslavery and a qualitative differentiation between the states and the nation. As Lincoln's "house divided" vision was decidedly dialectical, Taney's decision in *Dred Scott* was most decidedly not. Taney's pre-Civil War Supreme Court declined to utilize the synthetic cognition, the cognition of historical progress. In doing so, *Dred Scott* surely contributed to what Arthur Bestor rightly called a "Constitutional catastrophe."

THE GREAT DEPRESSION

Between the constitutional catastrophe of the Civil War and the current constitutional crisis, the American political system met, and survived, one additional challenge. The Great Depression of the 1930s was sparked by the stock market crash of October 1929 but it was enflamed by a series of national and international miscalculations that deepened the most severe economic crisis America had yet faced. That the Great Depression presented a political along with an economic crisis is manifest not only from the appeal that a variety of antidemocratic political personalities enjoyed in the decade of the 1930s, but from the degree of that order's alteration that resulted from the crisis. The crash occurred while the Republican president Herbert Hoover's administration was still in its first year. The brilliant engineer, who had been so influential in both the Harding and Coolidge administrations, never lost confidence that the depression was reversible. Throughout his final three years as president, Hoover frequently reassured America that it had passed the worse of the depression.

To be fair, Hoover's formula for returning the nation to prosperity rested on long held assumptions. In some ways, it involved the federal government as an overseer of the nation's economy in a way that the nation had never before seen. But in others, the federal government's method for such oversight was scrupulously designed not to threaten the traditional insularity of private business. Politically, Hoover's strategy was decidedly nonconfrontational. As he thought the depression to be but a crisis within the business community, Hoover easily concluded that business needed encouragement, not interference, from the federal government. From a cognitive perspective, the Hoover strategy was similarly unexceptional. The political and legal underpinnings for what was by then a highly industrialized American economy were still those of private contract and property. Nothing that Hoover and the Republicans of the early 1930s put forth as depression remedies threatened those institutions.

The historian Arthur Link described Hoover as a man whose personality had a "rigid, unyielding mental quality" to it. Link thought it difficult for Hoover, as a matter of that personality, "to adopt to new circumstances."[47] For industry, Hoover urged that full production be maintained, an entreaty that carried with the business community for a short time only. The business instinct for pulling back during hard times won out over Hoover's entreaties and beyond those entreaties, Hoover would not, or could not, go.

Unsuccessful as were Hoover's cures for the depression, he steadfastly held onto his perspective throughout the ordeal. Even when vigorous congressional opposition confronted him after a midterm election drubbing in 1930, Hoover continued to oppose governmental initiatives that either intervened in the economy or lent direct assistance to an increasingly distraught citizenry. He repeatedly rejected plans for expanded public works, his successful veto of the Muscle Shoals project illustrating his resistance to public enterprise.[48] The Reconstruction Finance Corporation, finally passed in Hoover's last year as president, was the riskiest of the dying administration's attempts at recovery. Even it, however, merely provided loans to banks and other capital markets so that they would be inspired to stimulate the economy. As Arthur Link put it, Hoover considered federal involvement in the economy to be " 'impractical,' 'dangerous' and 'damaging to our whole conception of governmental relations.' "[49]

The First New Deal. The election of 1932 brought someone of a very different psychology to the presidency. Franklin Delano Roosevelt, as described by Arthur Link, was a "radiant and warm personality." He was one who felt that "he could 'get through' to any person" in an intimate setting. Link also found Roosevelt to have "a capacity for . . . thinking in broad terms," often preferring "intuition to reason in solving difficult problems."[50]

The first days of the Roosevelt administration won approval from all for the former New York governor. Roosevelt's hastily devised bank moratorium had, after all, saved nearly everyone, including the bankers. It also ensured that the business community, at least for a while, could look on Roosevelt as an accompanying if not a "warm" friend. As Arthur Schlesinger, Jr., said, Roosevelt achieved banking stability because "I've just had every assurance of cooperation from the bankers."[51] Roosevelt even received early commendation from noted conservatives of the day like William Randolph Hearst and Hamilton Fish.

In those early days of the Roosevelt administration, the president's most significant innovation was the National Industrial Recovery Act (NRA). The NRA, the Blue Eagle in business windows, created a litany of codes designed to spur competition. These codes, however, dealt largely with the stabilization of prices, as well as what were hoped to be adequate restraints on productivity. Not so different from the Hoover program, the Roosevelt finger on the scales of private business's arrangements was still a light one. From a relativistic perspective, the National Recovery Codes did not inject much of anything new into the political dialogue. What government might do directly to affect public welfare, or what government might do to affect the private calculus of contract and property, were not yet part of a Roosevelt plan. The codes, in seeking to cloak business with an *appearance* of normality, encouraged companies to fix prices and production levels much as they had done before antitrust laws came along. They placed little burden on America's industry and some found larger businesses to be delighted with what often nicely squeezed smaller competitors.

The Second New Deal. But Franklin Roosevelt's Second New Deal was altogether different from the first. It was different, in part, because important political actors were considerably less cooperative than they had been only a year or two earlier. It was also different because new actors had begun to appear on the national political scene. Many brought a harsher message to the depression dialogue and the frayed temper of frustrated Americans often spilled into support for a frightening collection of political extremists. The "soak the rich" rhetoric of Dr. Francis E. Townsend, along with the nativist rantings of Father Charles E. Coughlin, for example, were eclipsed only by the demagogic enticements of Louisiana's Kingfish, Senator Huey P. Long.[52]

But along with new and strident political actors, the original players and their shift of perspective on the depression also made Roosevelt's Second New Deal very different from the first. Casting off the brief *mea culpa* that had been their public stance since the stock market crash, America's business community after 1936 increasingly found it convenient to place the blame for the nation's economic debacle on "that man in the White House." Sensing that Roosevelt was vulnerable after a first term of unrelieved depression and also sensing, correctly, that Roosevelt's bid for their cooperation in the early New Deal days was merely expedient, America's business elite turned on him soon after his reelection. Its attacks were followed, sometimes with even greater intensity, by Roosevelt's early supporters in the press. Hearst, for one, freely labeled the president's program as socialistic, if not worse.[53]

But even more important to a relativistic analysis than the perspectives of either the extremists or the no-longer-contrite business community was the change in Roosevelt's own policies. After the early period of attempting what Arthur Schlesinger called "the conception of overhead industrial planning," Roosevelt, in his second term, undertook an "aggressive radicalization" of the country's politics.[54] This radicalization, which Schlesinger claims "sprang from disenchantment with the experience of business," revealed a sharp change from what had preceded it.[55]

Roosevelt's second term was far different from his first term in that he repaved the path out of depression as an essentially adversarial road. Whereas Hoover and the first-term Roosevelt had neither encouraged nor incorporated fundamentally different political perspectives among the recovery players, by his second term Roosevelt was willing to make political enemies in the quest for recovery, to elaborate publicly on his differences with his political enemies, and to fight vigorously for his position. The position Roosevelt chose is well known. As Schlesinger has phrased it, Roosevelt became "the natural leader of all Americans who felt themselves excluded by the business tradition."[56] Roosevelt became "more and more the instrument of the politics of coalition and ideology,"[57] and he was less and less the seeker of nonmajoritarian consensus.

Roosevelt's adversarial politics, his politics of coalition and ideology, grew into the New Deal realignment of American politics that was successful for nearly forty years. But this realignment was still one of a repositioning of objective, largely demographic groupings. The repositioning began before Roosevelt's first term with Alfred E. Smith, the Catholic Democratic presidential candidate of 1928, Smith appealing to a novel collection of American voters in his unsuccessful presidential campaign. Trying to strengthen the Northern wing of the party after the horrendous 1924 Democratic Convention's North-South split, he appealed candidly to "ethnic minorities, women, Negroes, even intellectuals" in a campaign that nonetheless eventually succumbed to Hoover and the Republicans.[58] Four years later, Roosevelt added some patches to Smith's quilt, and by holding onto the conservative South with his plans for rural electrification and other public works, Roosevelt cemented Smith's Northern, liberal coalition at the same time that it coopted the extremists and isolated business and its allies. When even more successful in the 1936 presidential election, the New Deal coalition signaled the end of the nonideological politics that Schlesinger called "national planning through national unity."[59] That election ushered in the "coalition of non-business groups" and promptly reignited the stimulus to more radical depression-fighting proposals such as the Social Security Act, the Holding Company Act, the Banking Act, the Wagner Act, and the Guffey Coal Act.[60] From a relativistic perspective, the political differences that Roosevelt sharpened in the first New Deal coalition were not significant. They were objective, differences of existence, and not differences of essence or understanding as idealist thinkers such as Hegel would have understood them. But what Roosevelt crystallized into the Second New Deal was a far clearer definition of the differences between groups who preferred one ideology to another. He, like Hamilton and Lincoln before him, gave an essentially dialectical form to the American political argument as he incorporated new, cognitively dissimilar variables into the American political debate.

The Fair Labor Standards Act, with its minimum wage, maximum hours, and child labor standards, for example, greatly affected the contractual freedom of American business. The Social Security Act directly interjected the government into the private calculus of personal retirement and pensioning. Perhaps most important, the National Labor Relations Act (the Wagner Act) directly affected the contract between a laborer and an employer by protecting the bargaining of many workers with only one entrepreneur. In short, Roosevelt's legislative victories interjected a variety of noncontractual, qualitatively different considerations into America's political and economic arena, and the cognition that included those considerations was invariably synthetic.

The Judicial Synonym. Not surprisingly, the judicial decisions that at first negated and then ratified Franklin Roosevelt's New Deal reflected the cognitive relativity of America's third constitutional crisis every bit as much as did the political initiatives. Four Supreme Court cases, two of which held New Deal legislation to violate the Constitution and two others, decided only shortly thereafter which reversed field and interpreted the Constitution in an expansive way, reveal the contrast.

The early New Deal-destroying cases still ring in the liturgy of American constitutional history. They deal primarily with the commerce clause, but they include discussions of both federal and state authority as well as limitations on personal liberties. The first case, *Schechter Poultry Corporation v. The United States,* interprets the NRA codes in a way that virtually destroyed the Blue Eagle.[61] Specifically, *Schecter* deals with those codes that governed live-chicken processing, particularly the slaughter of kosher chickens. The opinion in *Schecter,* written by Chief Justice Charles Evans Hughes, rests principally on the notion that the codes violated two constitutional precepts. The first was the separation of powers. The second was the limit to the federal government's power over interstate commerce.

In writing of the separation of powers, Justice Hughes first attacked the congressionally sanctioned codes as a vague and overreaching delegation of legislative power to the executive branch. Hughes specifically deplored the delegation of the legislative prerogative to the executive branch that permitted bureaucratic code writers to "roam at will"[62] and in doing so, Hughes pointed out that the standard of what constituted unfair competition in the common law restricted itself to what lies "outside the ordinary course of business." If it was not "tainted by fraud, or coercion, or conduct otherwise prohibited by law," it must be legitimate for business.[63] For Hughes, power granted to the executive branch that defined unfair competition beyond that standard violated the separation of legislative and executive powers.

With regard to the interstate commerce clause, Hughes acted similarly. Drawing a line between direct and indirect effects on interstate commerce, and drawing another line between "commerce 'among the several States' " and "the internal concerns of a [singular] State," Hughes declared that "neither the slaughtering [of chickens] nor the sales by defendants were transactions in interstate commerce."[64] Again, Hughes found the NRA codes to violate the bounds of federal power.

In the following year, Justice George Sutherland's majority opinion in *Carter v. Carter Coal* mirrored the reasoning of *Schecter* and provided an even grander lecture on the virtue of intentional over purposive constitutional interpretation.[65] There, Sutherland declared the Guffey Coal Act unconstitutional and argued, "Plainly, the incidents leading up to and culminating in the mining of coal do not constitute" interstate commerce.[66] Citing *Schecter*, he concluded that "none of these essential antecedents of production constitutes a transaction in or forms any part of interstate commerce."[67] Sutherland clearly opted for jurisprudential intent over purpose, declaring that "the fixed balance intended by the Constitution" required that "the powers of the general government be not so extended as to embrace any [powers] not within the express terms of the several grants or the implications necessary to be drawn therefrom."[68] Consistent with his preference for strict constitutional interpretation, Sutherland closed by condemning the Coal Act because it "undertakes an intolerable and unconstitutional interference with personal liberty and private property."[69]

The cognitive form of the arguments within *Schecter* and *Carter* are both obvious and important. Their reliance on the analytic cognition in protecting the form of the private contract is analytic both in its reasoning and in the substance of what they protect. But shortly after 1936, the Supreme Court developed an altogether different way of thinking about things. In a ratification of the New Deal agenda, the case of *West Coast Hotel v. Parish* validated the State of Washington's minimum-wage law against a challenge to the law's invasion of the due process protections of the federal Constitution.[70] The opinion was written by Chief Justice Hughes but directly contradicted his position of only one year earlier. Hughes's language also directly responded to his brother Sutherland in *Carter,* with its distinction between liberty and contract, and claimed, "The Constitution does not speak of freedom of contract." Hughes argued that it speaks merely "of liberty and prohibits the deprivation of liberty without due process of law."[71]

Hughes's conversion to the faith of constitutional expansionism, however, did not stop with his contract delimiting conversion. The Chief Justice who came within California's electoral votes of being president twenty years earlier went on to write that "the Constitution does not recognize an absolute and uncontrollable liberty." Engaging in a review of the nature of contract that begins with the notion that "freedom of contract is a qualified and not an absolute right," Hughes distinguished such liberty from contract once again, asserting that "the guaranty of liberty does not withdraw from legislative supervision that wide department of activity which consists of the making of contracts." Hughes held that legislative supervision could concern things that a legislature finds to be "in the public interest," particularly with regard to contracts "between employer and employee."[72]

If the *West Coast Hotel* case is significant beyond its portent of a reversal of New Deal cases, its discussion of contracts is revealing as well for a Chief Justice who in citing the 1898 case of *Holden v. Hardy* argued that contracts between employers and employees "do not stand upon an equality" with the proprietors "lay[ing] down the rules and the laborers . . . constrained to obey them."[73] The legislature, according to Hughes, should be able to interfere with such contracts, and to further his position he cited the case of *Muller v. Oregon,* mentioned earlier, wherein the now-famous "Brandeis Brief" brought a variety of nonlegal circumstances into judicial consideration.[74] Though these considerations were surely objective, or nonpsychological in their nature, they nonetheless extended the standard for the fairness of a contract beyond fraud, coercion, and the like.

The most prominent case marking the Supreme Court's acceptance of the New Deal was the case of *NLRB v. Jones and Laughlin Steel.*[75] It was Hughes, this time addressing the most sacrosanct of constitutional interpretations, who wrote the majority opinion once more. The National Labor Relations Board, the administrative arm of the Wagner Act and the enforcer of a union's right to organize and bargain collectively, had been challenged by a major steel company. In a dramatic rending of the previously sacrosanct interstate commerce demarcation between manufacturing and commerce, Hughes freely borrowed language from the NLRB Act to argue that the "term 'affecting commerce' means in commerce, or burdening or obstructing commerce or having led or tending to lead to a labor dispute burdening or obstructing commerce or the free flow of commerce." In his own words, Hughes concluded, "Acts having that effect . . . are within the reach of the congressional power."[76]

Of course, Hughes broadened the entire definition of interstate commerce by declaring the above activities to be part of a "stream" or "flow" of commerce. He offered "of what avail is it to protect the facility of transportation, if interstate commerce is throttled with respect to the commodities to be transported?"[77]

In sum, each of the four cases cited here placed the issues of governmental jurisdiction and the interpretation of private contract directly under the Supreme Court's scrutiny. In doing so, each of these cases also raised the issue of whether the extraneous, qualitatively dissimilar cognitive variable should receive judicial consideration. The two anti-New Deal cases not only strictly defined the jurisdictional boundaries of both the legislative and executive branches and the federal and state jurisdictions, but also clearly limited the interpretation of common-law contracts. They thus permitted consideration of nothing that was extraneous to the narrowest legal calculus. In contrast, the two cases that confirmed New Deal initiatives permitted a blurring of the jurisdictional lines between state and federal governments, as well as a blurring of the traditional legislative and executive jurisdictions. Most important, however, these cases permitted an interpretation of a contract to go forward in the context of nonlegal, noncontractual considerations. The exclusion or the inclusion of the cognitively dissimilar variable within the interpretation of the private contract is apparent within *West Coast Hotel* and *Jones and Laughlin Steel.* Consideration of the cognitively dissimilar variable in these cases is clearly illustrative of a cognitively synthetic preference.

With this review of four legal rulings, I suggest that the road that leads from Justice Hughes's rejection of noncontractual concerns to Hughes's only slightly later inclusion of such matters within the consideration of a contract case, is central to a relativistic analysis of America's courts. The court's consideration of equity, its consideration of the unequal bargaining power of a contractual setting apart from fraud or coercion, provides the step toward the broader definition of economic equity that the New Deal cases took. Just as Chief Justice Hughes and the Supreme Court that eventually acknowledged the danger of the Great Depression to the American political system realized the importance of that step, so too, from a cognitive perspective, that step invariably acknowledged the importance of the synthetic cognition in its deliberations.

Chapter Eleven

AMERICA'S FOURTH CONSTITUTIONAL CRISIS

This chapter will apply the standard of a relativistic theory of politics to America's current constitutional crisis. It will rely on a postmaterial, idealistic framework in describing recent changes, and the psychology of those recent changes, in America's politics. The epistemologically post-material framework, which describes the mind's role in the progression of America's politics, will include the full, cognitively driven range of political perspectives that I have described. The psychologies of the relevant political actors who have brought about this crisis are more relevant than the psychologies of such actors in previous crises because we are now in a postmaterial age.

Is America in crisis? Much has been written recently on the subject of what most call an American decline. Robert Reich and Lester Thurow, among others, have chronicled the global retreat of the American economy.[1] Paul Kennedy has described a national decline that he attributes to the overextension of the American military.[2]

But decline is not crisis. The recountings of a constitutional crisis come from a different set of writers than those mentioned above. Using terms like *gridlock, fragmentation, balkanization,* and the like, political scientists James MacGregor Burns, James L. Sundquist, Charles M. Hardin, and others now argue that the American political system is incapable of making comprehensive decisions about America's most important political issues.[3] No policy that takes the multitude of increasingly dire political circumstances into simultaneous account, they say, can emerge from our tangled government. In his book on constitutional reform, Charles Hardin, for example, claimed that the "heritage of Washington,

Jefferson and Lincoln—so long miraculously intact—was crumbling to dust."[4]

I will review Hardin's and other writers' positions on America's current constitutional crisis shortly. But before I do, I will attempt to identify the specific impact that contemporary politicians' psychologies have had over the past few years on American's government. I will argue that America's fourth constitutional crisis is in great part the result of recent, psychologically biased inputs in America's institutional arrangements and that the current crisis evidences a Toynbee-like life-cycle crisis in America's government.

THE POSTMATERIAL DYNAMIC

That psychologically driven changes have accounted for much of America's life-cycle crisis is evidenced by two kinds of data. The first is historical, not structural, noting the resolution of a number of traditional, nonpostmaterial issues within America's political arena. Several writers have suggested that America has passed through its traditional liberal democratic agenda for although stubborn, informal barriers to political participation still exist, America's citizenry is included, at least formally, in this country's political process. The political inclusion of women and the eventual, if long delayed, inclusion of America's African-American minority through a variety of statutory and judicial innovations have marked important steps in that inclusion while the Warren Court extensions of the Bill of Rights to the states have bolstered the rights of individuals in many areas. To be sure, the liberal agenda is hardly complete: The Equal Rights Amendment failed to pass, and informal discouragements to minority and feminine political participation and economic equity still appear all too frequently in America. Nevertheless, the traditional Lockean guideposts of formal citizen inclusion within the polity and legal protection of individual rights have been largely fulfilled.

The near completion of the liberal agenda is, of course, one indicator of the arrival of the postmaterial age. But a second set of indicators exists, including the character of the recent revisions of the unwritten constitutional arrangements of the American government. The legal realist Karl Llewellyn's understanding of constitutional change is relevant here, Llewellyn claiming, much as we saw before, that "the working constitution is amended whenever the basic ways of government are changed."[5] Llewellyn, arguing that the "working" constitution can be significantly altered "without alteration of the language of the [original] document," accurately pinpointed who it was that affected such changes. The "relevant specialists alone" were the ones who "tinkered, twisted [and] invented" constitutions in the past.[6] In America, they have done so again.

Like so many others who have written on constitutional change, Llewellyn optimistically assumed that tinkerings with the unwritten Constitution would be adaptive rather than maladaptive. He cited what he considered to be the utility of remaking "the pattern of government as we have passed from a dominantly agricultural into a dominantly industrial and on into a dominantly financial economy."[7] Recent "tinkerings" with the American constitutional order, however, suggest that such constitutional adjustments may not have been adaptive.

Beyond the issue of governmental efficacy, the impact of the structural alterations of the American government on the equity of the American political system is also important. Marxist theory's inability to distinguish among members of a class prevented Marxism from embracing a relativistic theory, and liberalism's undifferentiated individualism left it incapable of relativity as well. Political equity in America today, judged within a postmaterial or idealist epistemological framework, must measure the arrangement of America's governmental institutions and how those institutions deal with America's current political issues.

Ronald Inglehart's research on postmaterialism, even with James Savage's inclusion of the ideological range, did not describe the linkage of relative psychological orientations to the issue of equity. These postmaterial writings did not speak to Fred Greenstein's concern over different psychologies' preferences for different organizational structures and processes or to Greenstein's observation on how differentiated psychologies alter the structures they work in. The idealistic hierarchy that I described in chapter 6, however, suggests that a relativistic, postmaterial perspective can create a standard for the determination of psychological equity within political structures. By doing more than describing the political nature of "such 'post-materialist' goals as belonging and self-expression," as Ingelhart said, a relativistic theory can supply a standard by which the psychological bearing of any government's institutions is judged in terms of relative preferences for different political structures.[8]

Max Weber, Anthony Downs, Howard Aldrich, and others writing on institutional change identified the inequitable ascendance of analytic cognition over the synthetic cognition during the life cycle of institutions. Downs's "rigidity cycle," and Aldrich's "boundary personnel" dominances, recall, were not psychologically neutral. As the political import of such nonneutral life-cycle change within America's institutions is included in a relativistic theory, the *equity* of life-cycle changes in America's political structures must be similarly measured.

The dynamic of a flexibly constructed general government, the dynamic of America's separation of powers, the dynamic of the American Congress, and the dynamic of America's political parties and electoral financing have each contributed, I believe, to America's life-cycle crisis. No doubt, structural changes in the internal arrangement of the executive branch, the arrangement of political jurisdictions within America's metropolitan areas, and a number of other recent political changes have also contributed to America's life-cycle crisis, but I think that America's institutional flexibility, its separation of powers, its internal congressional arrangements, and the current condition of its political parties and campaign financing best typify the life cycle. I will focus on them here.

AMERICA'S FLEXIBLE ARRANGEMENTS

The central tension of Alexis DeTocqueville's *Democracy in America* was between the appeals of aristocracy and the appeals of democracy. Tocqueville understood the importance of the decline of America's untitled aristocracy. He specifically noted its passage from public life by saying that once "the democratic party got the upper hand," the aristocracy knew that they could no longer "occupy in public a position equivalent to what they [held] in private." As a result, the aristocracy "abandoned the former and [gave] themselves up to the latter."[9]

Tocqueville described the impact that the withdrawal of America's aristocracy from public life had on the arrangement of America's political structures. Tocqueville knew well how dispersed the arrangement of political structures was in the United States, and besides reporting, "Nothing is more striking to a European traveler . . . than the absence of what we term the government, or the administration," he also observed that the United States had now diminished "the influence of [political] authority" by "distributing the exercise of its powers among various hands."[10] The withdrawal of America's aristocracy from public life meant more for Tocqueville than the structural dispersal that seemed to him to come inevitably with democracy. It also meant that the American democracy, even if it was "well distributed," might be as subject to tyranny as traditional monarchical and aristocratic systems typically were. Tocqueville, at the beginning of his discussion of America's government, pointedly said, "I do not regard the American Constitution as the best, or as the only one, that a democratic people may establish."[11]

Much of the focus of Tocqueville's disapprobation grew out of more than America's structural dispersion. It grew as well out of the volatility of democratic systems generally and the American system in particular. Some of that volatility was substantive: Whereas aristocracies, according to Tocqueville, were "possessed of a self-control that protects them from the errors of temporary excitement," democracies, he felt, were prone to make laws that were "defective or incomplete." Democratic governments "sometimes attack[ed] vested rights, or sanction[ed] others" in doing so. Also, democratic lawmaking was prone to an excessive "frequency."[12]

But Tocqueville's deepest fears for the American Republic concerned the structural volatility of the system. As he put it, the "bustle and activity" of a country wherein "the whole community [was] engaged in the task" of improving the society created "a kind of tumult; a confused clamor." With "a thousand simultaneous voices" asking something from the government, those voices would invariably demand "the satisfaction of their social wants,"[13] no matter what might be the cost to the general political system. But such was democracy. The American political system encouraged the participation of its citizens, particularly through that "vast number" of voluntary associations for which Tocqueville is so well known. Those associations complemented America's propensity to look "upon the social authority with an eye of mistrust and anxiety."[14] Though it might still succeed as a nineteenth-century democracy, thought Tocqueville, America's political volatility would be troublesome as the years passed.

Tocqueville's worry over America's political volatility is important from a relativistic perspective. Apart from the dispersion of formal political authority, America's vast number of associations for Tocqueville, in keeping with his observation that these "associations know as well as the nation at large that they do not represent the majority," contrasted sharply with the small number of European political interests. European associations, Tocqueville said, invariably "affect[ed] to represent the majority." But Tocqueville sensed that America's organizations might never attempt to make up a majority, and the very multiplicity of America's voluntary associations might thus be dysfunctional. Like so many others, however, Tocqueville assumed that the changes such volatility encouraged in the American political arrangement would be as adaptive as they were maladaptive.[15] This position is similar to Llewellyn's and others, but it may not be justified.

Nearly a hundred years after Tocqueville's American tour, Howard McBain also discussed the flexibility of the American system. McBain coined the term "living constitution" to describe the flexibility of America's political institutions. A constitutional order that was "developed by the growth of custom, by the practices of political parties, by the action or inaction of Congress or the President, and especially by judicial interpretation," according to McBain, would assure America's political vitality.[16]

In arguing such a position, McBain cited Lord Bryce's position that the essential difference between the British and American constitutions was not between written and unwritten constitutions. The difference, Bryce said, was between "the ease or difficulty with which constitutions may be temporarily or permanently altered."[17] McBain, refuting the general wisdom that the British Constitution, because it was unwritten, was more flexible than the American Constitution, suggested that in spite of what may seem to be the "peculiarly rigid" process of formal amendment, America's Constitution could be "altered and enlarged by several different methods."[18] In fact, he argued that it could be altered more easily and more dramatically than the British Constitution, and that it had frequently been so altered by "the customs or coventions of the American constitution, by which this or that provision has been added, expanded, contracted, perverted, or even wholly nullified."[19]

McBain concluded that the unwritten American Constitution has frequently been changed by nothing more than an "act of Congress or by the action of one or the other house of Congress." He pointed out that "legislative interpretation [and] legislative development of the Constitution comes first," but that there was a "huge development of our Constitution" that came about only by "judicial interpretation." Mc-

Bain contended that the "courts have merely followed where Congress has led," but this is true, he said, mostly in areas of legislation like those concerning the commerce clause.[20] No matter the area, however, Mc-Bain recognized that it was the courts which had "the last word upon the subject." Their "declaration of meaning [was] final."[21]

Other prominent constitutional scholars have echoed the writings of McBain. Edward S. Corwin, for example, has argued for the necessity of political input into the Constitution by saying that the Constitution's "elaboration was an event of the greatest historical interest." Corwin went so far as to argue that it was best to regard the Constitution "as a living statute, palpitating with the purpose of the hour." With such flexibility, the Constitution was "reenacted with every waking breath of the American people."[22]

C. Herman Pritchett, another student of the American Constitution, also took the side of constitutional flexibility. After suggesting that "America's history is the American Constitution," he argued that the best way to understand the Constitution was "through the history of American Constitutional crises and practices."[23] The need for "adapting the Constitution to changing conditions is the device of Constitutional interpretation," he said.[24] Citing a variety of such interpretations, including the development of the party system and the development of congressional committees, Pritchett argued that what he called the "experiential approach" to the study of the Constitution ensured that "decisions on constitutional allowability are made with full recognition of the need for the adjustments and expansions inevitable in a dynamic society." Pritchett concluded that America's constitutional system must perform "the vital function of giving order and structure to the inevitable processes of change."[25]

All of these reflections on America's constitutional flexibility are reminiscent of Karl Llewellyn's view of the structural alteration of all governmental constitutions. In their acceptance of informal but important change, McBain, Corwin, Pritchett, and Llewellyn all assumed that such revision would more than likely be adaptive, not maladaptive. In the American context, they all assumed that constitutional alteration would improve the efficiency of the American government, as well as improve the equity of the system. Implicitly, if not explicitly, the above writers assumed that the "looseness" of the formal American constitutional order was invariably functional.

In his argument, Howard McBain quoted the eminent Supreme Court Justice Oliver Wendell Holmes, Jr.'s notion that a word "is the skin of living thought." McBain claimed, "As applied to a living constitution the expression is peculiarly apt," because "living skin is elastic, expansile, and is constantly being renewed." [26] Like Corwin, Pritchett, and others who have written since, McBain considered only that constitutional change could adapt to political crises, not contribute to them. None considered that America's "relevant specialists," rather than react to public needs, could alter the political system in their own favor and not in the interest of the citizenry. Epistemologically, their positions were all materialistic, the political issues of the day ostensibly dictating an adaptive change of the Constitution. But the life-cycle lesson is not materialistic epistemologically. It is idealistic; it sees the specialists as those whose minds are most adept at the governmental "tinkering" that favors their way of doing business. If the life-cycle dynamics that all structures undergo, as Downs, Aldrich, and other organizational theorists have described them and as Toynbee, Sorokin, and other historians have also described them, have accounted for structural change and the emerging dominance of one psychology over another within America's political institutions, then these changes may also account for the inefficiencies and the inequities of the American political system. A relativistic theory examines whether structural inefficiencies such as those now referred to as "gridlock" in the American government in fact describe deeper causes for the inefficiencies *and* inequities of the American political system. Both inefficiency and inequity are seen better from the perspective of psychological imbalance and the idealistic hierarchy of equity, I think, than they are from any other perspective.

THE AMERICAN SEPARATION OF POWERS

As the separation of powers between the federal executive and the federal legislature is the key structural element in the American political system, let us first determine whether that element has in fact contributed to the balkanization of our government. In responding to his own query over "whether *any* set of leaders . . . can make the present constitutional structure function," and, as a part of his argument that the American separation of powers creates "difficulties faced only in the United States," James L. Sundquist reminds us that for the American government to act effectively, "three independent centers of power must be brought into agreement."[27]

Sundquist fully recognizes that these power centers have not been in agreement lately, arguing that the presidency, the Senate, and the House of Representatives are now more frequently at each other's political throats than ever. They are at each other's throats principally because they "are elected at different times and are responsible to different constituencies," Sundquist suggesting that such discordance in the "dilemma" of the American government predictably leads "to governmental stalemate and deadlock, to indecision and inaction in the fact of urgent problems."[28]

Sundquist's perception of an increase in the distance between the executive and legislative branches is well supported. Figures collected by the Committee on the Constitutional System (CCS), for example, point out that less than 25 percent of the years before World War II saw a "divided government" wherein one or both of the houses of the Congress was controlled by the nonpresidential party. Since 1956, however, that division has occurred over 60 percent of the time and, since 1968, the figure has risen to over 80 percent. Recent years have also witnessed an increasing division in voting patterns for the presidency and for Congress. Whereas in 1900 only 4 percent of congressional districts voted for a representative of the party other than its presidential choice, that figure rose to 44 percent by 1984. Wholly separate patterns of voting for House seats as distinguished from the presidency are illustrated as well by the congressional incumbency rate. In the past five elections, the reelection rate for members of Congress has grown to fully 92 percent, while in 1986 and in 1988, incumbents who contested their seats won 98 percent of their races.[29]

If the record of legislative competitiveness in the American government has gone sour in the last years by any traditional democratic standard, a relativistic standard provides an even more damning indictment. What is the cognitive form of the interaction between an entrenched office holder and a constituency and how does that form of interaction divide the already separated powers of the American government still further? The answer to those questions, quite simply, is that the electorally secure office holder is one who has developed a form of interaction with his or her constituents that is dyadic and contractual. The relationship is much like the descriptions of Kelley and Thibault, for every elected legislator in America has now developed well-established avenues of contract-like support that assure continued sustenance as the reward for service.

Perhaps the best evidence of the psychology of those changes in congressional representation comes from research on the reasons for why the dramatic increase in legislative incumbency has occurred. John Ferejohn, who analyzed a collection of data concerning the increased incumbency of members of Congress, has argued for what he calls a "behavioral change" theory of the Congress.[30] Ferejohn notes initially that increasing voter support for incumbents has had almost nothing to do with political party; he suggests that changes in voting preferences occur substantially among "partisan identifiers rather than among Independents." Ferejohn further contends that new voting patterns have resulted from "changes in behavior within [rather than across] the various party identification categories,"[31] arguing that "Voters are different than they used to be," and that the "change in electoral behavior is rooted in an increased unwillingness of voters to utilize party identification as a voting cue." Ferejohn concludes that "voters seem to be shifting away from the use of party affiliation as a decision rule and toward increased utilization of incumbency."[32] The dyadic interaction between the incumbent officeholder and the constituent needs support from both sides, and the constituent seems as willing to provide it, Ferejohn suggests, as the officeholder is willing to receive it.

Clearly, the institution of the Congress, as well as the overall government, has undergone a good part of its balkanization because of the assured incumbency of the American legislator. Though most of what is now written on the difficulties of the Congress concerns internal changes in the institution, the cooperation between the legislative and executive arms of the government is primarily affected by the way that each of the federal branches interacts with the citizenry. For the Congress particularly, these arrangements have changed markedly over the past thirty-five years, and the readiness of the Congress to cooperate with the executive has suffered for it. Sundquist is right about the separation of powers, but the assured incumbency of the legislator who is elected so separately from the executive and the legislature's other house has added to the difficulty more than has the original separation of powers.

America's political deadlock has at last become the focus of a handful of scholars like Sundquist, but it is unfortunate that their discussions concerning the government deal almost exclusively with the government's efficiency. Sundquist's declaration that "so much of governmental failure in the United States is due to partisan squabbling and deadlock between the branches" is an accurate, but still traditional, depiction of the problem.[33]

From a relativistic perspective, more is going on with gridlock than mere governmental inefficiency. The equity of the American political system is affected as well, and of all the writers on the subject of the American political gridlock, perhaps James MacGregor Burns, who has written on the structural separation of the American political system for years, comes closest to understanding the inequity of the American system's recent changes. Though Burns assumes no philosophical stance, he writes of the American political system in terms of both its intellectual origins and the need for a sound intellectual understanding of the current governmental crisis. There is more than a hint of psychology in Burns's writing too. For example, Burns favorably cites Richard Hofstadter's definition of political leadership for its approval of "the critical, creative and contemplative side of mind." Burns also cites Hofstadter's notion of the enormous difference between mere "intelligence" that "seeks to grasp, manipulate, re-order [and] adjust," as opposed to "intellect" that "examines, ponders, wonders, theorizes, criticizes [and] imagines."[34]

Burns's writings on American politics reveal a good sense of the differentiation among minds. Burns is the creator of an interesting dichotomy of leadership that is also, at least implicitly, psychological. In fact, his distinction between "transformational" and "transactional" leadership comes closer to portraying what Jefferson meant when he spoke of the "different constitutions of the human mind" than any current terminology on America's political leadership. Burns's description of the different forms of leadership is also propitious for its placing of leadership directly into the context of how the United States might surmount its separation of powers gridlock. The transformational mind, with its ability "to shape and reshape institutions and structures," Burns argues, can "achieve broad human purposes and moral aspirations."[35]

Noting that "there arise occasions in a nation's history when government must take a strong lead and direction . . . in order to bring about concerted and energetic social change," Burns clearly assigns the transformational and not the transactional mind to the task of recreating America's structures in what a relativistic perspective would define as an adaptive rather than a maladaptive way. It is only the transformational mind, according to Burns, that naturally transcends "immediate events and day-to-day routines."[36] The transactional mind, Burns argues, thrives "on bargaining, accommodating, manipulating and compromising within a given system."[37] But, though Burns's descriptions draw from an implicitly psychological form, Burns, too, does not couch his petitions for reform within a relativistic framework. His call to "[w]omen, blacks, Hispanics, peace activists" and others is still principally a call to objective, psychologically undifferentiated groups. His, for all of its insight, is still a liberally based political plea.

THE CONGRESS

The above quotations are from Burns's *Power to Lead,* a book that lamented the crisis of the American political system. Like Sundquist, Burns properly highlighted the growing tensions along the American separation of powers as a principal deterrent to sound government. Evidence exists, however, beyond what is implicit in Burns's and Sundquist's observations, that identifies the psychological role in the declining efficiency and the equity of the American political system. A good deal of that evidence assays the recent changes in the internal workings of the United States Congress.

The House of Representatives, the popular assembly in the American Constitution, is a very different body now from its original form. The strong mid-nineteenth-century speakership of Henry Clay, along with the speakerships of Thomas Brackett Reed at the end of the nineteenth century and Joseph Cannon at the start of the twentieth, have never been duplicated in the past half century. But the House's stripping of Speaker Cannon's much abused powers in 1910–11 was very different from the structural reforms that have marked the post-World War II era. The first, the Legislative Reform Act of 1946 appears, curiously, to be a centripetal structural reform. In its jurisdictional consolidation of a disorganized cacophony of committees, it did abolish unused congressional panels and merged others into more rationalized jurisdictions. But it also, if less obviously, provided for centrifugal changes in the Congress, leaving a hint of what was to come in succeeding congressional revisions. It restricted the number of committees on which any member could serve, and most important, it began the still-snowballing increase in the staffing of congressional committees. This increase provided each member of Congress with the wherewithal to negotiate effectively with both the committee leadership and the constituency. Though the plea of post-War reformers was one of government efficiency, not "democraticization," the act actually initiated the centrifugal rearrangement of Congress.

The motive behind the next wave of reformist pressure in Congress grew out of the civil rights period of the 1960s. These reforms, directed at legislative roadblocks to employment, public accommodations, and voting legislation, among others, included the formation of the House Democratic Study Group. The Study Group hoped to fashion a far-reaching social agenda for America and generate a set of procedural improvements for the House at the same time.[38] But the specific reforms of that civil rights period did three significant things, all of which further dispersed constitutional power. First, they ended seniority's automaticity; second, they permitted easier circumvention of the Rules Committee (for so many years the legislative chokepoint of the civil rights recalcitrant, Judge Howard Smith of Virginia); and third, they encouraged the use of such vehicles as the "twenty-one day" rule, with its opportunity for committee circumvention in the House.[39]

The next burst of congressional reform culminated in the Legislative Reform Act of 1970. This act signaled the coming of a variety of structural reorganizations that were not completed until the middle of the decade. Virtually all of these reforms were centrifugal in nature, with the quest for centrifugality being more openly advocated. The opening of committee hearings to the public, the approving of the minority's right to call witnesses, the further restricting of the number of committees that a member could serve on, and the further increasing of congressional staff ostensibly "democratized" the Congress.

One of the early commentators on such congressional democratization, Leroy Rieselbach, has written that though "there is likely to be conflict between responsibility and responsiveness" in any democratic legislature, by the late 1970s, after the democratizing reforms, America's congressional legislators clearly gave their "prime attention to their districts" and not to general legislation.[40] The weakening of the role of political parties in Congress, along with the internal "fragmentation and decentralization" of the Congress's internal procedures, convinced Rieselbach that legislators from the 1970s on needed "to vote their districts rather than the party line if tension between the two occurs."[41]

Rieselbach was but one of many writers on the Congress who recognized that the post-Watergate, post-Viet Nam and post-Nixon, that is, post-impoundment, period of the early and mid 1970s made it necessary that the Congress, as Rieselbach put it, "appear in a considerably better light" to an angry public.[42] Rieselbach further noted that Congress's "openness, decentralization and bargaining style of decision making" were considered to be "admirable features" in the public mind. But such mid 1970s House reforms as the "subcommittee bill of rights," which prohibited anyone from serving on more than two subcommittees and which enjoined committee chairs to respect subcommittee jurisdictions and empowered subcommittees to write their own rules and hire their own staffs, only furthered congressional fragmentation.[43] Soon after, the Senate adopted many of the House's "openness" and democratization standards, permitting the public into "mark up" sessions in the Senate after 1975 and conference committee sessions that same year. The Senate's novel permitting of all committee members to appoint individuals for the committee staff "democratized" the "world's most deliberative body" even more.[44]

By the close of the 1970s, Congress' internal structures and processes were more organizationally centrifugal than they ever had been. The civil rights reforms of the 1960s, followed by the "democratization" reforms of the 1970s, have prompted congressional scholars like Walter J. Oleszek to coin terms like "subgovernments" and "multiple decision points" to explain the obstructive congressional relationship with "pressure groups, executive agencies and scores of other interested participants."[45]

From a relativistic perspective, why did such centrifugal reforms take place within the United States Congress? Oleszek and other traditional writers point to real-world conditions that undoubtedly did impinge on the congressional members' ability to achieve legislative coherence. The jet airplane, television, and the development of computer-assisted communication devices such as mergemail and the fax machine certainly make each congressional member more accessible than ever to a constituent.

But though material, technological explanations have contributed to the congressional dispersion, the case for these factors' causing the entirety of the dispersion is simply not convincing. If power "has been dispersed further throughout Congress's components-committees, subcommittees, caucuses, party committees, the leadership and informal groups" than it ever has been, as Oleszek has said, something else has contributed to the centrifugal excess.[46] As Oleszek has noted, a different generation came to the Congress during the years of change, and he properly points out, "More than three-fourths of the seats in each chamber changed hands" in that period.[47] This generation, particularly the post-Watergate "Class of 1974," contributed mightily to the destructuring of the United States Congress.

Besides Oleszek's sense of generational change, evidence that the new congressional generation reflected something other than the realities of modern technology comes from a host of recent studies that have examined the growing disquiet about Congress among its members. A survey conducted by the Center for Responsive Politics, for example, found that many members now routinely express frustration with the Congress;[48] these studies also show that frustration has had a direct impact on the increase in retirements from the legislature. Steven Franzitch, noting as early as 1978 that the Congress was beginning to suffer an "increased frequency of retirements," argued that these retirements were not merely the result of the traditional causes of age, disability, and electoral vulnerability.[49] They were, Frantzich found, more often the result of a "general dissatisfaction" with "the increasing pressures from citizens" and interest groups. The "inefficiency and futility of the whole process" that came from such pressure was increasingly cited as a retirement cause by those who left the Congress.[50]

But did these dissatisfactions fall evenly on all legislative psychologies? A number of studies give a clear sense of a psychological differentiation between those who left the Congress and those who did not. These studies show that some legislators clearly enjoyed the fragmented, individualized politics of the new Congress; others did not. Supporting the center's and Frantzich's conclusions, direct evidence exists of the emerging psychological dominance of some psychologies over others within the Congress. For example, a number of recent studies of the Congress have spoken to the marked differentiation in preferences for Congress's new openness. A *Congressional Quarterly* (*CQ*) report highlights differences in how Senators have reacted to the Senate's internal changes,[51] arguing that though works on an earlier Senate, such as those by William S. White and Donald Matthews, may have painted an overly glossy picture of the Senate "as a close-knit place," the chamber of that day contrasts with the place where some Senators now pay for what *CQ* calls a "day-to-day Senate life [that] has been changing in a way that makes true community very difficult to achieve."[52]

The loss of community and the abhorrence of that loss by some but not all Senators is what CQ found to be so important. It noted, for example, that many of "[t]oday's Senators sometimes have to go to extraordinary lengths to establish the personal relations that were once part of everyday life." Joseph R. Biden, Jr., Democrat of Delaware, has pointed out, "Ten years ago you didn't have people calling each other sons of bitches and vowing to get each other."[53] Senator Dale Bumpers, Democrat of Arkansas, remembered that the Senate was once a place where "[t]here not only was a social camaraderie" but "[t]here was [a sense of] teamwork." Bumpers went on to say that "occasionally [Senators] could vote to accommodate a friend in ways that would be politically lethal now." Similarly, David Durenberger, Republican of Minnesota, noted that with regard to senatorial reciprocity, "If you sacrifice one day for the collective will, you do it knowing that somebody else will refuse to do the same thing the next day."[54] David Boren, Democrat of Oklahoma, summed it up by saying that "you have this increasing fragmentation and you add to that rules which allow the individual to exploit that fragmentation and you've got problems."[55]

But, again, all Senators do not mourn the lost community of the old Senate. Some Senators, in contrast to Biden, Durenberger, and the others, happily flaunt the Senate's traditional, deferential norms. Howard Metzenbaum, Democrat of Ohio, for example, has said that though he recognizes that the old Senate "custom [was] to go along to get along, I don't do that." Metzenbaum has taken the position, "If I'm not the most popular guy in the Senate—well, I can live with that."[56] Metzenbaum's perspective is echoed by Senator Jake Garn, Republican of Utah, who has openly defended his style of finding "some tactic to keep a bill off the floor," no matter how obstreperous. He has said, candidly, "I don't particularly have loyalty to tradition." His fellow Utah Republican, Orrin G. Hatch, openly boasts that his use of the filibuster is "the only way the majority of the people, who are represented by a minority of the Senate, can be heard."[57]

Apart from the admitted importance of technological changes, therefore, it is clear that changes in the Senate, and the Congress as a whole, are at least in part the result of and at the same time more commodious to the psychology of some Senators and members of the House than they are to others. Changes in the Congress's formal processes, along with subtle but real changes in the informal norms of the Congress, have been favorable to some psychologies and not to others. Though direct evidence of the dominance of one psychology over another will always be blended with evidence of technological change, the Downs and Aldrich perspective on organizational balkanization, taken from an idealistic perspective wherein the choice for organizational forms stems principally from the members of an organization, places the struggle among psychologies at the root of Congress's structural revisions.

What a relativistic perspective concludes from all of the above, of course, is not only that the Congress is a far less efficient organization than it was years ago. The new congressional arrangements that have resulted from the recent dynamic of the Congress, like the dynamic of all life-cycle organizational changes, is neither psychologically, nor politically, neutral. Greenstein's psychological price is as relevant to the United States Congress as it is to any other organizational setting, and this price now firmly places the issue of psychological equity into the equation. Senators or House members who might have wished a) to have their chamber observe civil interpersonal norms and b) deal with aggregated, cognitively synthetic issues rather than the contractual form of constituency and interest group service, represent a different psychology from those who do not. If what has happened to the politics of the Congress during the last years, as Oleszek puts it, is that "broader issues are [now] divided into smaller sub-issues," and if the preferred form of dealing with subissues, with all their similar quality cognitions, has affected the informal structuring of the Congress, it has done so as one psychology has clearly triumphed over another in the Congress.[58]

POLITICAL PARTIES AND CAMPAIGN FINANCE

Much like the Congress, America's political parties have experienced enormous recent alteration. Party scholar William Crotty reminds us that contempt for the political party as a political institution is as old as the Republic. He quotes the nineteenth-century British observer of American politics, James Bryce, who concluded that America's contempt for parties, as with Duverger's notion of factions, has meant that "neither party has any principles, [nor] any distinctive tenets," beyond the "getting or keeping" of patronage.[59]

But political parties are a part of the American political fabric nonetheless. Late-nineteenth-century party reform, responding to the excesses of the Gilded Age, was carried forward into the twentieth century's progressive-era reforms in an attempt to give credibility to America's parties. These attempts to reconstitute political parties and clean up the corruption of party machines evidenced themselves in the "good government" response to corruption. But that response was overwhelmingly restrictive of parties. The circumvention of party organizations, and the surpassing of "barriers to honest and effective government," as Crotty put it, is still evident in such devices as non-partisan elections, the direct primary, and professionally managed local government.[60] Inventions like the initiative, the referendum, and recall have severely limited the role of the political party.

For all of its scope, however, the early twentieth-century wave of party reform did not attempt significant changes in any party's internal structures. It took a second, midcentury wave of party reform, beginning with the outcry over the 1968 Democratic Convention riot in Chicago, to bring about party change. Nelson Polsby, in his work on party reform, has argued that though dependence on traditional party leadership had already waned with the primary-led nomination victory of John F. Kennedy (and even earlier to a degree in the unsuccessful primary-led run of Estes Kefauver in 1956), the intensity of the Chicago conflict and the perception that Hubert H. Humphrey's nomination was engineered by Chicago's powerful mayor Richard J. Daley incited the most dramatic internal party changes in America's political history. The reforms that followed Chicago, originally encased in the proposals of the Democratic McGovern-Fraser Commission, banned such traditional party decision processes as the closed party caucus and the delegate primary. For a time, they even virtually eliminated the participation of federal and state officeholders, as well as party regulars, from national conventions. Restrictions on unpledged delegates at the national convention also furthered organizational party dismemberment.

The new processes of Democratic Convention delegate selection, of course, have severely hampered the nominating campaigns' role as a vehicle for issue aggregation and platform construction. The open party caucus and the candidate primary, wherein delegates were bound to presidential aspirants, sparked the incentive for presidential candidates to appeal to local and state interest. Fixed representation for minorities, young people, and women, along with specific prohibitions on ex-officio party or officeholder delegates and a prohibition on the unit rule within state delegations, further dispersed the Democratic presidential nominating process. The increase in the number of primaries that followed on the passage of the reform rules further diluted the influence of party regulars. Issue aggregation in the Duverger sense has become far more difficult under the Democratic party's latter-day processes.

Nelson Polsby concluded his review of the above changes in the Democratic party rules by saying that the behavior of aspiring candidates for the presidency has also changed substantially as a result of the reforms. "Candidates must [now] behave differently in a presidential nominating process that is dominated by primary elections rather than in one in which primaries played a smaller part," he said.[61] This is so because the party as an institution is simply far less important in a primary-dominated system than it has ever been.

Reminiscent of Madison's view of the political party, Polsby finally noted that the reduction of party importance has brought a clear reversion to the politics of faction rather than the politics of coalition building within the Democratic party. Reminiscent of Duverger as well, Polsby noted that coalitions or "alliances among groups organized for the purpose of achieving goals common to their constituent parts" are much more difficult to garner now.[62] "Interest groups" and "pressure groups," which do not typically engage in either "ideological justifications for party programs" or "organizational linkages between leaders and followers," now dominate Democratic party politics.[63]

The increasingly dyadic and transactional nature of the party processes that reward factions or interest groups over party aggregation is clear from Polsby's language. When he says, "Where party organizations are strong, coalition-building flourishes: where they are weak, the politics of factional rivalry prevails," the form of the ostensibly reformed processes could not be clearer.[64] It is contractual and dyadic, and the cognition of such processes is analytic.

To be sure, the more extreme products of the reform movement have been ameliorated somewhat in recent years. The Mikulski, Winograd, and Hunt commissions in the Democratic party reintroduced party regulars to the nominating process, and they strengthened the role of the national party as an arbiter of party disputes.[65] But lately, new reforms, passed by the 1988 Democratic Convention, partially reversed even these adjustments by assigning candidate allegiances to 40 percent of the superdelegates (officeholders, principally) and bifurcating the Democratic National Committee's vice chairship.

The Democratic party, and to a lesser degree even the Republican party which expanded its own number of primaries, are very different structures today from what they were twenty years ago. As a result of their centrifugal modifications or as a result of their centrifugal rigidifications, a reversal of Duverger's natural progression by which factions supposedly turn into philosophical parties, has now occurred. As the form of a nation's party structure relates profoundly to the form of the issues with which it can deal, just as the form of the separation of powers or the form of the internal structures of the United States Congress relates to how issues are dealt with there, the psychological bias of both America's original and now much-revised party structures is clear.

Though no one has written on the relationship of party structure to the issue of psychological equity, one writer has related the question of political equity to the structure of political parties. E. E. Schattschneider foretells a standard of psychological equity in parties in his *Party Government,* which argued for the necessity of comprehensive, ideologically based parties in order to assure political equity. In a later work, *The Semi-Sovereign People,* Schattschneider went even farther and argued that a party's introduction of new, as yet unconsidered, issues to any government was an absolutely essential element of political equity. As he put it in reference to the issues that a political system may or may not consider, *"scope and bias* are aspects of the same tendency in government" (emphasis his).[66]

Just as a narrow scope of issue consideration, for Schattschneider, portended a bias for issues that found the government more accessible to issues that were more readily defined, a broader scope permitted less accessible and less definable issues to be considered as well. Without addressing the psychology of it, Schattschneider understood that political parties must be intermediaries in the negotiation between private individuals and public entities. They must also be aggregators of the full agenda of public concerns. Not only should parties, therefore, expand the scope of government but, in Schattschneider's words, it is "the function of public authority to *modify private power relations by enlarging the* [political] *conflict"* (emphasis his).[67] Schattschneider's belief that *"the end product of party politics is inevitably different from that of pressure politics"* (emphasis his) foretells an analysis of parties that includes the broadest range of public issue consideration.[68]

From a relativistic perspective, the bringing of the aberrant, qualitatively heterogenous consideration into the public calculus is what the expansion of the political agenda is all about. Schattschneider's bias is more than material; it reflects, if unconsciously, the psychological equity that exists or does not exist within reformed parties that are now so dyadic and transactional in their processes and so analytic in their cognitions. The cognitive form of doing the public's business through weakened political parties and strengthened pressure groups is not neutral in its psychological character. This character, in an idealistic framework, affects all who work in the public interest as well as the public interest itself.

Before closing, I should note that significant changes have also taken place recently in the area of national election campaign financing. So-called reform has altered the campaign financing process in America, and it has done so far more dramatically than even its proponents ever envisioned. In 1968, W. Clement Stone, a wealthy Chicago insurance executive, contributed $2 million to Richard Nixon's presidential campaign. He went on to contribute more than $2 million in 1972, and the general reform spirit that was sweeping the Congress and the Democratic party easily carried itself over to a push for changes in how national campaigns should be financed. Under Democratic leadership, the Congress included election finance reform in the early 1970s revisions of America's campaign laws. The provision of the 1971 Federal Election Campaign Act, which had provided for public financing of presidential campaigns, along with the 1974 campaign finance law amendments to the 1971 act that were inspired by Watergate, limited what individuals, political committees and, most damagingly, political parties could contribute to federal campaigns.[69] Shortly after the 1974 amendments, a Supreme Court ruling declared all limits on a candidate's personal spending, independent spending, and total campaign expenditures to be violative of First Amendment freedom of speech. It left the contribution field more open than ever to that new political contribution creation, the political action committee (PAC).

As the Supreme Court case uncapped the limits of what could be spent in presidential, senatorial, and congressional campaigns, it contributed, if perhaps unwittingly, to a major alteration of how national campaigns were conducted. This alteration is psychologically significant, since the issue of the amount of money necessary to run a federal campaign is significant from the standpoint of even traditional democratic standards. The cost of federal campaigns has exploded, and the Federal Election Commission has reported, for example, that 1988 expenditures reached $201 million for thirty-four Senate races and $256 million for 435 House races.[70]

But important as the money is, the quantity of the modern contribution is not the key problem in American campaign financing. More important than the dollar figure for any national campaign is the extraordinary dispersion, and the private nature, of campaign funding sources. Over four thousand private PACs have long outstripped the political party, or even profligate contributors such as Mr. Stone, as the principal campaign-financing source. Common Cause figures show that by the 1986 Senate elections, total PAC contributions had grown more than eightfold for Senate members in the preceding decade and nearly fourfold for House members.[71] PAC contributions to Senate incumbents were 2.3 times what they were to Senate challengers and eight times what they were to challengers in races for the House.[72] That imbalance of contributions in the House has surely contributed to the 92 percent return for incumbents in the past five elections.

What does the relativistic perspective bring to these reforms of campaign contributions? Most of the debate over the PACs has centered around the *amount* of the contributions. In fact, however, the long-term impact of PACs on America's political parties more seriously reflects the cognitive form of the singular PAC contribution. In distinction to the party contribution, the PAC contribution places the officeholder in a dyadic and transactional relationship to each of his or her contributors and thus the form of the PAC contribution, along with the internal congressional reforms, has turned congressional officeholding into an overwhelming dyadic and transactional form of representation.

William Crotty, Nelson Polsby, and a host of observers of American's current political difficulties have pointed out that the dispersion of political funding, and the accompanying dispersion of political allegiance that has come with that funding, have seriously affected the efficiency of the American political system. From the standpoint of the nation's governmental gridlock, too many cooks now almost certainly spoil America's governmental broth. But none of the writers on the current problems of the American government have assessed the psychological inequities or the political inequities of the party-reform or the campaign-financing period. None have described the current generation's governmental crisis as a matter of unbalanced cognitions and deep psychological biases. But this is exactly what the current pattern of party organization and campaign funding demonstrates. As with the Congress, the reform of parties and campaign financing provides clear evidence of psychological bias. The party nominating structures and the national campaign-financing processes of the American political system are far more dispersed, far more centrifugal, and far more dyadic and contractual today than they have been at any time in the history of the United States government. These structures and processes are clearly biased in favor of the analytic cognition and those who prefer it. They are also clearly biased in favor of certain material interests.

Chapter Twelve

EQUITIES AND REMEDIES

THE MATERIAL INEQUITIES OF DECLINE

I have said only a little so far of the equities of material distribution from a relativistic perspective. Be assured, however, that what I have labeled resultant or material equity is fully a part of a relativistic theory. I will speak to material equities as well as psychological equities in this chapter in the context of what I consider to be the necessary remedy for America's current political difficulty. Fair distribution, much as Aristotle prescribed for it in terms of proportional contribution and reward, must be as much a part of an idealistically based theory of politics as it is a part of materialistically based theories like liberalism and Marxism.

How is the material equity issue best assimilated into a relativistic theory? I have described the idealistic hierarchy in such a way as to suggest that a postmaterial standard of equity requires the proper ordering of psychological equity, the equities of structural and procedural arrangements, and the equitable consideration of resultant or material rewards. According to contemporary political theories, the dominant purpose of political activity is to further material interests. This view, as in the Lowi and McConnell "end of liberalism" argument, is a product of an epistemologically material perspective and considers only the objective realities of the political world, thus ignoring the political impact of different human minds.

A relativistic theory, placing the mind before the realities of the political world, insists that subjective perceptions impose meaning on reality. Descriptions of the recent alterations of America's "unwritten constitution" highlight what I believe to be an increasing psychological and material bias in America's constitutional order. With regard to the issue of equity, for example, I argue that it is more than America's structural fragmentation that has permitted political interests to pressure the governmental "access points" that benefit them. To be sure, a relativistic perspective no more denies the measure of truth in the materialist perspective than Hegel denied the importance of the world's realities. America's myriad interest groups, the modern heirs to Tocqueville's voluntary associations, access the government in part to further their material interests, but a relativistic perspective argues that such political activity is not the key to the favor that some interests have over others in a postmaterial political struggle.

What is primary, and what has accelerated in the postmaterial years in American politics, is that a *psychological* preference for a cognitively commodious *manner* of accessing the government has facilitated the inordinate success of those who have recently gained governmental favor. Favored interests now more easily access government, in other words, because of a Downs-like rigidification of America's political structures, that rigidification meaning that the cognitive form of access to the American government has been increasingly limited to dyadic and transactional access.

With regard to material distributions, how does a bias in favor of the analytic cognition disproportionately assist some interests over others? In general, a cognitive bias, or a psychological inequity as it stands at the pinnacle of the idealistic hierarchy, affects distributional equity because that bias permits well-defined interests to enjoy an advantage over less well defined interests. In a dyadic organizational structure, the cognitive simplicity of dealing with qualitatively similar variables almost invariably wins out over the cognitive complexity of dealing with the qualitatively dissimilar variables that typify the synthetic cognition.

Though no political writings have specifically spoken to the importance of relative cognitive forms of political variables, the writings of Peter Bachrach and Morton Baratz, much like E. E. Schattschneider's depictions of strong and weak parties, have described what at root is a psychological phenomenon in governmental access.[1] Decrying the emphasis that traditional political analysis gave to so-called scientific understandings, Bachrach and Baratz have questioned the favor traditionally given to such understandings over less-scientific understandings.[2] They have asked, "How can one be certain in any given situation that the 'unmeasurable elements' are inconsequential, [or] are not of decisive importance?" With specific reference to the linkage between political structures and the characterization of political issues that different political arrangements encourage, Bachrach and Baratz have recognized that "Some issues are organized into politics while others are organized out."[3]

Unfortunately, Bachrach and Baratz, like Schattschneider, have addressed only the relative accessibility of the government of certain political groupings over others. Yet their now quarter-century-old perspective, implicitly if not explicitly, linked the cognitive quality of certain issues to their chances for political favor. It at least differentiated between the quality of variables that make an issue amenable to the transactional form of political consideration in America's very transactional government.

We must now make explicit what was implicit in Bachrach and Baratz. We can do so, I think, by weighing the *cognitive quality* of all claims on the government and the cognitive preferences of the government in hearing these claims. In the order of their qualitative discreteness, the plea of the automobile industry for an import limitation of three million Japanese automobiles, say, ranks as a highly discrete, cognitively analytic plea. It is a plea that fits neatly into the dyadic form of representation and the separation of powers-enhanced nonaggregated policy of America's government. Generally speaking, most purely economic claims on the government are discrete, although the claims of labor groups for safety and health protection for workers, for example, may be somewhat less discrete than management's claims for import restrictions, tax relief, and the like.

Successively, claims for the environment, sometimes ably put by groups with specific agendas, probably rank slightly ahead of the claims of minorities, the handicapped, the young, and particularly those groups whose claims are hindered by a multiplicity of complex and highly interactive needs such as those of the inner city African-American population. Their claims are only well represented by a cognitively complex aggregation of the different services that a dyadically organized government is generally resistant to.

Perhaps the most ill-defined interest in the political arena, not unexpectedly, is the interest of what must be set aside for the future. What should not be consumed or injured today in order to assure a viable tomorrow is invariably open to a great deal of debate and speculation. Such factors as the extrapolated capability of a variety of future technologies, not to mention the differences among peoples who think that technology can or cannot keep up with the needs of tomorrow, are subject to only the most imprecise of calculations. For this reason, along with the complexity of what it is that any new age will require, the needs of the future in an area like the management of the environment are the most poorly defined of all public needs.

The fact that the American government has done an increasingly poor job of dealing with postmaterial political issues should not be a surprise in view of the above. That the federal deficit, for example, has grown so dramatically over the years in which postmaterialist pressures have reshaped the federal government is much in keeping with a cognitive theory of political structures and political issues. The dyadic relationship of all constituencies with their legislative and executive contractors has accelerated the demise of aggregated fiscal considerations along with a number of other aggregated considerations.

The ability to maintain immediate political favor, for presidents and members of the Congress alike, is enhanced in a structure that deflects blame from officeholders who now serve their constituencies in an increasingly dyadic way. Also, the success of such political initiatives as deregulation, privatization, and the loosening of adequate safety, health, and regulatory oversight procedures, as in the recent cases of the savings-and-loan industry and the housing industry, all reflect the ascendance of the analytic cognition in American governmental policy.

In sum, the cognitive quality of America's preferred political issues, with its attendant lack of willingness to confront the complexity of the truly difficult public issues, retards the equity, as well as the efficiency, of the American government. Recently, the "measurable" interests have more certainly won out over the less "measurable" interests than ever before. The increasingly dyadic, transactional set of processes that the American government offers increasingly fails the public interest. Moreover, the nature of this cognitive bias is not addressed nor can it be addressed as a political issue within a liberal, or even a Marxist, framework. Indeed, it cannot be addressed by any materialistic, objectively based theory of government. It is only through an idealistic, subjective understanding of such biases that the cognitive issue, which lies fallow in the writings of Burns, Schattschneider, Bachrach and Baratz, and others who have described the *qualitative* nature of American politics, can be understood.

Returning to the consideration of resultant or material equities, as Schattschneider and others have pointed out, the most aggregative institution in a modern political system should be the political party. It is the political party's unique ability to "know" less well defined issues, and to give simultaneous hearing to a multitude of issues that are more likely the issues that affect less well represented groups, that distinguishes it from all other political institutions. The political party can, and must, make full use of the synthetic cognition, for as Duverger defined it, the political party is the institution that aggregates the dissimilar political demands that make up a political ideology. Unfortunately, America's political parties do nothing of the kind today.

With regard to the issue of distribution, it is only through institutions that know the synthetic cognition that any political system can consider the issue of resultant or material well being at all. The distributional issue, as the leading traditional issue of politics, has only been known and will only be known in the future by a patterned as opposed to a contractual mode.

But in the hands of those, like Robert Nozick, whose cognitive preference is for the transaction, the distributional issue is never addressed. The "patterned" thinking that looks at the fairness of distribution among a number of different kinds of contributions is simply not available to the transactional form. It is only through a fair balance of patterned as opposed to transactional distributional methodologies in the government, or only through political institutions that can know both patterned and transactional methodologies, that less-discretely defined issues receive fair hearing.

In the consideration of material equities, therefore, an idealistic epistemological perspective holds that both the cognitive form of a nation's political structures, and the cognitive form of the issues that those structures address, are primary political considerations. A psychologically equitable balance of public institutions precedes consideration of the distributional gap between the advantaged and the disadvantaged in any society. No attempt to access public institutions that permits only dyadic and contractual forms of political interaction will ever adequately consider the issue.

THE COUNTERCYCLICAL PRESCRIPTION

What, then, is the specific prescription of a relativistic theory of politics within America's fourth constitutional crisis? When I discussed the issue of equitable remedies in part 1, I said I believed that the best remedy was one that adapted the Keynesian model of countercyclical adjustment to a historical and organizational life-cycle framework. In chapter 7, I outlined the epistemological contrast between John Maynard Keynes and Joseph Schumpeter, Keynes's position on the intermediary role of human interpretation in the working of economic cycles, though hardly relativistic, being at least epistemologically idealistic. In contrast, Joseph Schumpeter's reliance on technological innovation as the largely unmediated explanatory variable for cycles was epistemologically materialistic. As a consequence of his epistemological position, Keynes's remedy for the cyclical downturns of an economy included a human consciousness of the behavior that caused economic contractions. Keynes's countercyclical prescriptions for public spending, tax reduction, and the like reflected a conscious attempt to alter that behavior. Keynes's recommendations also assumed that a government could anticipate how people naturally think and behave during an economic contraction and then compensate for that thinking and behavior. Keynes's lessons are relevant for American constitutional reform, I think, with but two alterations.

First, if Keynes' countercyclical remedy is applied to political reform, it must be placed into a political context. As Keynes described economic habits of spending, saving, and investing, he prescribed for the alteration of those habits when they were unfavorable to a healthy economy. Dealing with political rather than economic activity, America's political reform must first address the cognitive issue, or how it is that institutions know any issue, in its political setting. America's countercyclical reform must therefore address the impact of the cognitive structure of its institutions on its political thinking before it prescribes for structural reform of its government.

Here, Weber is relevant too. The contrast between rational organizational structures, with their homogeneously defined institutional jurisdictions, and collegial organizational structures, with their heterogeneous institutional jurisdictions, is the Weberian analogue to Keynes's categories of economic contraction and expansion. If Downs-like alterations of at least informal governmental structures occur over time, much as Karl

Llewellyn suggested, then a conscious counterbalancing of those structural imbalances is as required for a political remedy as reduced taxation and increased public spending are required as remedies for economic depression.

A second revision of Keynes is also necessary if Keynes's countercyclical strategies are to be adapted to constitutional reform. Keynes wrote about long-cycle economic swings. He did not write about the kinds of life-cycle dynamics that Toynbee, Sorokin, Spengler, and others have written of in their depictions of history and culture. Keynes also did not write about the life cycles that Downs, Aldrich, and others used to describe the structural alterations of organizations. Nonetheless, Keynes's sense of the role of human psychologies within cycles, again in contrast to Schumpeter's nonpsychological depiction, encourages an adaptation of Keynes's long-cycle understandings to the life cycles of organizational structures.

The rules that govern long-term cycles in economics apply equally well to life cycles of any kind. A life-cycle countercyclical strategy requires that the constitutional changes that Charles Hardin and others have argued for be placed within a framework of conscious life-cycle reversal. I will not attempt to describe that strategy in detail here, but it should be obvious that it must begin with a conscious political reinvolvement of those citizens who exemplify Toynbee's definition for "experimentation" and "creativeness." I know of no time in history in which fundamental structural change of a government did not include some alteration of the personnel of that government. That the synthetic cognition comes from those of a certain psychology should be as clear to us now as it was unclear to Hegel almost two centuries ago. That those of the synthetic cognition must be made a part of both the movement for governmental reform, as well as the governmental process once that reform has taken place, should no longer be controversial. No government can either survive or govern equitably when it is dominated by those who, by their psychology, engage solely in the contractual mode.

Though Keynes dealt indirectly with psychology in noting its role in economics, he surely did not deal with *relative* psychological preferences for structural and procedural arrangements. But Keynes was passionately committed to political as well as economic equality and I would like to think that Keynes would approve of the adaptation of his countercyclical remedies to the political inequities of America today. Keynes's consciously countercyclical prescriptions, clothed within a political rather than an economic order, and clothed within a life-cycle rather than a long-cycle dressing, can undergird the efficacious and equitable revisions of America's political structures.

THE CENTRIPETAL FRAMEWORK

How then to restore cognitive balance to the American government? How does America best address its psychological imbalances in light of what has perhaps become a somewhat less democratic governmental arrangement? Do not forget that America's reverence for its constitutional form is unmatched anywhere in the world. Whether it is its brevity, its Bill of Rights, its promise of limited government, or whether it is America's absence of such institutions as an established church, a monarchy, or an aristocracy, Americans deeply identify with their primary political document. As a result of their almost universally uncritical affection, however, there are still very few critical writings on the American constitutional order. But what has been written does bear consideration.

Perhaps the most comprehensive criticism of the American Constitutional arrangement before the work of a group called the Committee on the Constitutional System came from Rexford Tugwell and a group of prominent Americans in 1960.[4] Tugwell, a respected member of the Franklin Roosevelt brain trust of the 1930s, was bold enough to suggest thirty years ago that something more comprehensive than the subconstitutional recommendations that came from groups like the two Hoover Commissions was necessary to modernize America's political system.

But Tugwell's analysis, sadly, suffered from a major flaw. Not recognizing that the American government's problems were precipitated by fragmented authority, not overaggregation, the Tugwell proposals championed such changes as the election of members of the Senate from private groups and the further dispersion of the executive branch through a variety of functionally defined vice presidencies. Such remedies for America's governmental ills, of course, were centrifugal, not centripetal. They would, had they been adopted, have only furthered the cognitive biases of America's political system.

To its credit, the proposals of a more recent assemblage that also addressed America's constitutional order properly defined the problem of the American government as one of excessive *de*centralization.[5] Though unfortunately seeing America's political problems as a matter solely of inefficiency, not inequity, CCS's suggested reforms point toward a coalescence, not a further dispersion, of America's structures as the appropriate remedy for America's political difficulties.

Several years before his efforts were directed toward the formation of CCS, one political scientist saw that the structural reform of America's government must be centripetal. In 1974, Charles M. Hardin offered a comprehensive set of proposals that spoke boldly to the fragmentation of the American government. Among those proposals, three stand out. First, recognizing the importance of conflating the terms of federal officeholders, Hardin recommended that "presidents, senators, and congressmen should all be elected on the same date for four-year terms."[6] Hardin understood that the divergence of voting patterns for the presidency and the two legislative houses had become increasingly troublesome for the country's governance.

Second, Hardin suggested that "presidential candidates should be nominated by committees of the parties composed of all House members from single-member districts, as well as all candidates for election in such districts."[7] Hardin recognized that party caucuses, as they existed in the early days of the Republic and in Madison's original Virginia Plan in which the Congress elected the president, were an incentive to an assimilated government.

Third, Hardin proposed "that part of Article I, section 6, clause 2 of the Constitution that prevents members of Congress from serving in other offices of the United States should be repealed."[8] Hardin's reach toward parliamentarianism, quite obviously, included what traditional European democracies, as well as the Confederate Constitution incidentally, had included. Hardin was the first to prescribe for structural remedies to America's political difficulties in a consciously centripetal way.

Not content with academic prescriptions, however, Charles Hardin was, more than anyone else, responsible for the founding of CCS. This group, after six years of deliberation, completed its *Report* and submitted it to officeholders, the press, and the public in January 1987. The work product of a broad collection of academics, party officials, journalists, business, labor leaders, and lawyers, CCS's *Report* suggested a variety of constitutional and subconstitutional changes. Principal among these changes were: an increased role for congressional office holders and candidates in the selection of a party's presidential candidate; eight-year terms for senators and four-year terms for House members, the terms to be concurrent; and per Hardin's early suggestion, permission for members of Congress to serve in the cabinet.[9]

At James MacGregor Burns's particular urging, the CCS *Report* also suggested that states be encouraged to provide a "team ticket" option on all national election ballots.[10] A voter under such an option could choose a presidential, House, and, if appropriate, senatorial candidate of the same party with a single pull of a lever. This suggestion, along with such subconstitutional recommendations as having congressional elections funded by the public and having a "shadow cabinet" formed by the losing presidential party, all reflect a consciously centripetal bearing on constitutional reform.

Unfortunately, however, the committee made some mistakes. It suggested, for example, consideration of the parliamentary device of governmental dissolution after a no-confidence vote as another solution to governmental gridlock. It is easy to forget that just because the parliamentary system is far more centripetal than the American presidential system, each feature of parliamentarism is not necessarily more centripetal. A fair amount of evidence suggests that the European convention of parliamentary dissolution is in fact a complementary, *centrifugal* protection against the overcentralized parliamentary form. CCS considered the dissolution option with the unexamined assumption that it would ensure structural cohesion in the U.S. government. I doubt it.

On the whole I endorse Charles Hardin's early proposals and am generally sympathetic to the direction of CCS's proposals as well. Their offerings are a guidepost, at the least, to the kinds of structural reforms that the American political system probably requires. That I was disappointed, quite frankly, with the narrow range of CCS's considerations, I am sure, reflects my sense that in the first instance the structural problems of the American government are as much a matter of *intra*institutional, *trans*institutional, or subjectively-driven factors as they are the result of interinstitutional phenomena. Philosophically, purely objective considerations ignore the importance of intersubjective balances, or imbalances, as they exist within and among objectives like whole institutions. The Newtonian paradigm is as outdated in political science as it is in physics and what has gone on subjectively within and across each of

Washington's institutions accounts for as much if not more of the governmental difficulty, I think, than does any interinstitutional difficulty.

To put it simply, there are two well-rooted reasons, not just one, for the inefficiencies and the inequities of the United States government. Only the first reason is objective, the century-old expansion of the middle class in America meaning that the numerical balance of haves to have-nots is now clearly in favor of the haves. The traditional proponent and recipient of redistributional politics has now been outnumbered by those who would lengthen the distributional pyramid and extend the government's centrifugal arrangements in doing so. That objective reality must be faced as part of any equitable analysis of the government.

But apart from this objectivist reason for the increasing inequity of the American distribution, I suggest that even should a redistributive candidate be elected president of the United States at the same time that a redistributive membership dominates the Congress, the subjective imbalances within and across the government's principal institutions, and the resultant cognitive form of the government's inattention to the distribution question, is such that redistributive policies may not be possible. I think it is fair to argue that the structures and processes of the American government are now so skewed toward the analytic cognition that even a liberal Democratic president and a liberal Democratic Congress may not be able now to reverse the increasing maldistribution of America's wealth.

Finally, I am disappointed by one more failing in CCS's recommendations. Even as objective, interinstitutional conflict was properly recognized as at least a part of the cause of government inefficiency, CCS never bothered to question the degree to which interinstitutional collusion rather than genuine conflict has generated the problem. The law of antitrust has a marvelous little concept in it called "conscious parallelism." It describes a condition wherein each of the collusive players to price fixing, market sharing, or whatever are so attuned to each other's thinking that no communication is required to achieve their mutual goal. There is a good bit of conscious parallelism in Washington today, both in what goes on between the principal constitutional institutions and in what goes on between the less than competitive political parties. The outright misrepresentation of progress on the budget deficit that members of both parties in the Congress have engaged in recently in order to give the appearance of a declining deficit is only the most patent example of party collusion in the government. That reality should have been included in CCS's discussion.

Apart from the specifics, however, my criticism of CCS rests ultimately on the notion that the study of the causes, the costs and, eventually, the remedies for America's structural difficulties will only be undertaken effectively when it is placed into an unabashedly philosophical context. Only a philosophical context will reflect the true causes, and point to the true remedies, for America's governmental difficulties. As with all Hegel-like progressions from one historical crisis to another, America's current historical crisis will require a new, far more robust, intellectual framework than any yet available.

Sadly, the writings in the area of structural reform, and the report of a group such as CCS, have thus far simply not developed such a framework. As a result, although the idea that the original, written Constitution should be reviewed and, perhaps, updated in a place or two has some merit, the far more important reality for the nation is that its governmental problems originate and still exist in places where something more than an epistemologically and institutionally objectivist perspective can effectively diagnose them. Lloyd Cutler's noting that the greatest federal deficits have occurred during the periods of what CCS invariably referred to as "divided" government evidences the kind of misunderstanding that a non-philosophical, institutionally objectivist analysis affords. The fact is that the recent, monumental tripling of the federal budget deficit began during the administration of Jimmy Carter, one of the few periods in the postwar era in which the government was all of the same party. It was also during the party-unified Carter administration that the Roosevelt-initiated redistribution of income among Americans suffered the secular reversal that continues today. Unless an appropriate, philosophically based analysis underpins the diagnosis of the ultimately political causes of the subatomic disintegration of the United States government, no efficacious, and certainly no equitable, remedy for that disintegration will be forthcoming. My heart-felt plea is for those who are concerned with the structural maladies of the government to move beyond objectivist, institutional analyses to a meaningful identification of, and a meaningful remedy for, the repair of the Llewellyn-like "tinkerings" of America's unwritten Constitution. Those tinkerings have come, after all, from the "relevant specialists" in and close to our government.

THE JUDICIAL AND THE IDEAL

Not all of the cognitive imbalances of the American government, of course, lie within and between its two avowedly political branches. If the ingenuity of, say, Chief Justice John Marshall in the National Period, or Chief Justice Charles Evans Hughes in the period of the Great Depression, borrowed generously from the deeper purposes of the American Constitution, so too the Supreme Court today must find ingenious ways to meet the current constitutional crisis. Just as Marshall's and Hughes's opinions brought the additional consideration, the synthetically cognitive consideration, into judicial notice, there are several places where the Court's inventiveness today could help the country through its present crisis. Three are more obvious to me now than any others.

First, in an appropriate case, and most propitiously in response to a new legislative initiative, the court must be willing to overturn its ruling in *Buckley v. Valleo*. It must permit the duly passed legislation of the Congress on the matter of election financing to once again become the law of the land. America's first amendment freedoms, particularly the freedom of speech, are rightly thought of as the most precious that Americans possess. But it is not inconsistent with the right of individuals to speak their mind on political issues, as well as contribute financially to those candidates whom they favor, to legislate the amount of money that is spent to assist any candidate. Striking down that portion of the election-reform legislation has only reinforced the insulated and essentially contractual relationship that candidates and officeholders have with individuals and interests. It has negated the attempt to not only limit the amount of campaign expenditure but to have American campaigns be less reinforcing of the dyadic, cognitive analytic manner of representing America's citizens once candidates have been elected.

Second, in the spirit of *Baker v. Carr* and its progeny, an active Supreme Court should now extend its rulings on the rough numerical equality of America's voting districts to the achievement of as much competitiveness in voting districts, particularly congressional districts, as is feasible. As this is written, the country faces its 1990, constitutionally prescribed decennial census. Looking beyond the intent of the Framers to the purpose of their design for a representative government, it is no stretch of the Constitution to suggest that the Framers meant for the result of any democratic election to fairly represent the will of the citizenry. But it is beyond dispute today that the primary decision rule of each state legislature's drawing of its congressional districts includes the preservation of each district's incumbent representative. When 98 percent of the incumbent members of the House of Representatives who offer for reelection are reelected, as they have been in the last two elections, it is hardly inappropriate for the Supreme Court, in the spirit of the democratic nature of the lower House as defined in Article 1, as well as in the spirit of the census with its clear linkage to fair political representation as it is also defined in Article 1, to grant standing to any claimant who challenges those 1992 congressional district lines that unduly favor the reelection of incumbents.

Third, though somewhat more difficult to achieve than the former two goals, the fragmentation of the nation's metropolitan areas, particularly the isolation of the cities from their all too insulated suburbs, cries out for the approval of those regional plans of education, transportation, health-care delivery, and other public services that are so often thwarted by the suburbs and their allies in the state legislatures. The need to broaden the occluded agendas of the often better-off and racially homogeneous suburbs so that the legitimate needs of an entire metropolitan community can no longer be thwarted by the legal fiction of suburban municipal incorporation is essential.

Charging the American Supreme Court with a judicial agenda that is responsive to the synthetic cognition is well in keeping with previous landmark rulings of the Court. The ingenuity and the courage of those like Marshall and Hughes in the past, in dramatic contrast to the antihistorical position of those like Roger Taney, were built on the conscious inclusion of the otherwise extraneous, nonlegal variable into judicial consideration. Karl Llewellyn, in keeping with the German idealist tradition, placed the mind of the judge between the facts of any case and what had until then masqueraded as the objective nature of the judicial decision. But Llewellyn's advance of an idealistically based jurisprudence only insisted on the inclusion of the economic or social reality of a case into the legitimate considerations of the case's decision. The step beyond Llewellyn extends a judge's recognition of his or her economic and social biases into a consideration of the idealistically based cognitive relativity of judicial decision making.

The next step for the idealistic and psychologically relativistic perspective in jurisprudence, therefore, is to encourage the conscious inclusion of our growing knowledge of psychological and cognitive judicial preferences into the consideration of how cases are decided. It is the next natural task for the epistemologically idealist position, in the context of the psychologically relativistic theory of politics, to reflect on the cognitive form of the issues that come before the Supreme Court in light of the proclivity of its justices to either favor or not favor that cognition. Such considerations are primary in such judicial questions as to what extent standing should be granted to groups and not just individuals under the class-action provisions of the Federal Rules of Civil Procedure, for example. They are even more appropriate in those judicial decisions that directly bear on the structure of the American government, for it is with the structural issues of the government that the structure of the judicial mind is so clearly a part of the decision.

THE PHILOSOPHICAL FRAMEWORK

Earlier, I remarked on Daniel Boorstin's reflection on the lack of a healthy balance between the essentially Jeffersonian, or philosophic, as opposed to the Madisonian, or pragmatic, perspective in America's politics. In citing that imbalance, I warmly endorsed Boorstin's criticism of the nonphilosophic nature of America's politics, as well as Boorstin's assertion that the United States can no longer consider itself a unique polity, immune from the universal rules of politics. It was Boorstin who quoted Jefferson on the importance of "the different constitutions of the human mind" and he did so within the context of his argument for a more philosophical understanding of the American political system. Knowing how different citizens prefer to think about the current constitutional crisis is consistent with Jefferson's (and Boorstin's) philosophical position. I think we must begin there if we are to rediscover the proper balances of the American government.

For reasons that I have already detailed, neither liberal nor Marxist theory, not even the updated McConnell-Lowi criticisms of traditional liberalism nor the well-worn Beard-Mills neo-Marxist perspective, can provide an understanding of the postmaterial, psychologically engendered structural imbalances that now exist throughout the American government. As liberal and Marxist thought are materialistic theories, they cannot reach deeper than an understanding of how undifferentiated groups or classes, and the corresponding objective, singular character of governmental institutions, work together. Neither theory offers an explanation of the role that differentiated psychologies have played within the recently and maladaptively altered institutions of America's constitutional order.

Apart from the philosophic merit of a relativistic theory, such a theory can engender an understanding of the true nature of meaningful reform in the American political system. The very nature of such reform is political, and it begins with an acknowledgment, indeed an affirmative declaration, that the structural issue is rooted in the very different understandings that different citizens have concerning the American government. What citizens who are interested in constitutional reform must realize is that the very argument over the American Constitution, in the context of America's fourth constitutional crisis, will be and to a large degree already has become, highly political. To some degree, particularly in the case of President Bush's proposed use of the line-item veto, it has already become as political in its nature as America's first three constitutional crises were in theirs.

Let us acknowledge, then, the importance of Hegel's dialectical form and the impact of that dialectical form on American history. Let us acknowledge, specifically, the notion that the dialectical form is the form of the contradiction and that the dialectic, in its second stage, is the form of a choice between a resolution of America's historical crisis that utilizes the analytic cognition and a resolution that utilizes the synethetic cognition. For those who are content with what the American government has become, and there are many such people, the resolution of an issue like the seemingly irresolvable budget deficit typically involves granting more power to one of the branches of the government.

Those who argue this position support a constitutional revision like President Bush's advocacy of a line-item veto, wherein the president is given a significant new measure of power at the expense of the Congress. This solution, cognitively, is analytic. It encourages no change, indeed it ensures the perpetuation of, the same dyadic, transactional form of intergovernmental and citizen-to-government interaction that relies on the analytic cognition. It attempts to resolve a difficulty like the budget deficit only by permitting the balance between objective groups, the executive and the legislative branches of the government, to be altered.

In contrast, the solutions put forward by CCS, although never discussed in this context, are almost entirely synthetic in their cognitive form. They fit well into the historical, dialectical mode that Hegel de-scribed. As important as the federal budget deficit is, or as important as any substantive issue is that may currently confront the American gov-ernment, these issues alone do not approach the form of constitutional crisis that either fits the Hegelian prescription for historical progress or fits the cognitive form of the debates of America's first three constititu-tional crises. Substantive political issues, by themselves, never beget the dialectical form. No new, qualitatively dissimilar political variable, no political consideration that requires the synthetic cognition in order to create the contradiciton that a traditional understanding cannot compre-hend, is presented by an issue like the budget deficit. Rather, it is what the government either chooses to do or not do in dealing with an issue like the budget deficit that either generates the synthetic cognition within its decisional structures, or stifles it.

One other thing is certain about America's fourth constitutional crisis. It is that the crisis of the American government, and the argument over possible changes in the government's structure, will increasingly reveal the dialectical form in the argument over the issue as the issue works its way through America's contemporary history. Like the three previous constitutional crises, and like the crises of civilizations that Hegel de-scribed from a philosophical perspective and Toynbee and others de-scribed from a historical perspective, the most important single fact concerning America's constitutional difficulty is that the dialectical na-ture of the crisis will pit one form of understanding of the crisis against another form of understanding. One form of that understanding, of course, will be analytic, the other synthetic. As surely as the cognitive differentiation that Hegel described is the key to the dialectic, so too an understanding of that dialectic in the political context that Hegel would have us place it today is the key to understanding America's current constitutional crisis. It is also the key to the solution.

If Hegel taught us one thing, it is that the structure of understanding of any current historical crisis is not the structure of understanding of the last historical crisis. Hegel also taught us that the improvement of human understanding begins internally, not externally, the human mind's gathering *wisdom about itself* being the true path of history. Similarly, if Freud taught us one thing, it is that the reasons why people prefer to do the things that they do are deeply psychological and that we must be introspective about our psychologies in order to understand what we are doing. If Jung taught us one thing, it is that human psychologies, normal human psychologies, are different and that people's attitudes and behaviors reflect that difference. Whoever would stand on the shoulders of these three giants, I think, will need to find that a differentiated, relativistic view of human natures must lie at the core of an epistemologically as well as a substantively postmaterial, that is, idealistic, political philosophy. The issue of political efficiency is as inextricably linked to the issue of political equity, or justice, as it has always been. If alternative preferences for the written and unwritten constitutional structures of the American government, like the structures of the human mind, reflect the marvelous variety of human minds and human psychologies, then the most central issues of American politics can never be considered again as mere considerations of governmental inefficiency or "gridlock."

CONCLUSION

At the conclusion of what is still but a bare outline of an original philosophy of politics, there are but a few things about which I feel confident. About these few things, however, I do not feel there is much room for compromise.

The first, of course, is the reality of human psychological relativism. To reverse its most serious error, which has dogged Western political thought with but marginal exception since the time of the Greeks, political philosophy must never again assume that there is a single human nature. Accordingly, the quality of reason, an outgrowth of the human mind or, better, minds, must never again be considered as singular either. Reason is an aggregate, and if political reality is given meaning by different human minds, then a balance of different human psychologies, as well as a balance of the psychologically driven beliefs and actions of different political actors, must be included within any depiction of political equity. If psychological differences exist among normal human natures, then an understanding of those differences, at least as they exist along the single most significant psychological spectrum and among other psychological proclivities as we learn more about them over time, can underpin a relativisitic philosophy of politics.

I am confident as well that an increased understanding of the relativity of human natures bespeaks the ascendance in the twenty-first century of an epistemologically idealist, as opposed to an epistemologically materialist, political philosophy. Psychological relativity is a relativity of the mind and spirit and my theory originates in the skeptically based relativity of those differences in the forms or, to use Kant's phrase, the *categories* of idealistic meaning that different minds impose on the world. Though the philosophical and real-world political contributions of both liberalism and Marxism will never be lost, a psychologically relativistic theory represents a higher and more complex standard for political equity than either of its predecessors.

Those who will be most comfortable with a return to the idealist vision, those who reject the essentially materialistic vision of the current philosophies, are probably themselves of one psychology or mind, incidentally. In what I predict will be a growing debate between the idealistic and the materialistic vision, I think that the advocates of the idealistic position will more frequently be found to be made up of the affectively introspective and cognitively synthetic mind. The materialistic position, already to some extent but even more certainly in the future, will be advocated by the affectively extrospective and cognitively analytic mind. The epistemological argument itself, in other words, will soon reflect the psychological relativity.

Also, just as there will continue to be conflict among the different meanings that are imposed on political reality and those who place them there, so too there will continue to be conflict among different standards for political equity. But only an equitable resolution of the primary conflict among different political meanings in the first instance can bring about a relativistic standard of political equity. This standard defines equity, in its simplest portrayal, as a fair balance of judgments on both substantive equity and the political arrangements that bring equity to any polity. Accordingly, political institutions that impose meaning on political reality must reflect balance in order both to know political reality equitably and provide for the institutional and procedural arrangements that best generate equitable public policy.

Another consideration: though the battle between the materialistic theories, the liberal and the Marxist theories, may occasionally appear to present a winner between them, let me caution two things. First, the defeat of Marxism in Eastern and Central Europe will not diminish the importance of that still rapidly growing portion of the global population that lives in a condition that continues to propel a materialistically based radical perspective. Whether it is called Marxism or not makes little difference. Aristotle spoke of equity far better than Marx but material deprivation will foster objectively-based political discord regardless of which political philosopher is cited.

Also, let us not forget that much as with Weber's prediction that both modern capitalism and modern socialism would become bureaucratic states, the differences between the materially based theories of those nations that adopted either of the two materialistic perspectives, though considerable, are still slightly less than the noisy proponents of both positions have tried to have us believe since World War II. The victory of one materialistic philosophy over the other in the real world will have no bearing on the psychological inequities that all modern, institutionally bureaucratic governments now visit on their citizenries.

Only one more thing seems certain to me now. It is that just as an understanding of psychological differentiation is imperative for a new theory of politics, so too it is imperative for an understanding of history and where it is that any nation stands in the grand flow of history. Relativity should put an end to Hegel's notion that history moves as a "single, ordered whole." History's cycles, when Hegel's omission is corrected, will fairly depict the alternating dominance and subordination of different kinds of minds as each mind seeks to define and move the realities of the day in their direction. These cycles will also depict the alternation, however uneven, of the three cognitively separate stages of the dialectic, each stage contributing what it naturally does to the path of human history. Just as an idealistically based political theory will facilitate the recalculation and readjustment of equitable balances among political knowings of reality, so too an idealistically based theory, as with what Keynes believed in economics, will require the conscious moderating of history's often painful cycles. Consciousness of the differences among human psychologies is the key to the amelioration of the most severe costs of psychologically driven cycles.

For all of its own omissions, and there are many, the psychologically relativistic philosophy of politics that I have outlined is an original theory. It was born out of an attempt to understand why it is that people of somewhat similar circumstances believe what they believe and do what they do about politics at the end of the twentieth century in the developed world. Without diminishing the importance of the existential circumstances of any citizen, this theory explains the differences among the political beliefs and actions of postmaterial citizens in a way that clearly places essence before existence, mind before matter. Its insistence that the political well-being of the members of any class or group can no longer be objectified and singularized, and its insistence that the political position of the members of any class or group must now be fairly portrayed in terms of the subjective differentiations that exist among the members of that class or group, is long overdue in political philosophy.

NOTES

1. Human Differentiation

1. Oswald Spengler, *The Decline of the West* (New York: Alfred A. Knopf, 1922), 60.
2. See, e.g., Arthur R. Jensen, "How Much Can We Boost IQ and Scholastic Achievement?" *Harvard Educational Review* 39, no. 1 (1969); William Shockley, "Negro IQ Deficit: Failure of a 'Malicious Allocation' Model Warrants New Research Proposals," *Review of Education Research* 41 (1971); Stephen Jay Gould, *The Mismeasure of Man* (New York: W. W. Norton, 1981); Leon Kemin, *The Science and Politics of I.Q.* (New York: Halstead Press, 1974).
3. Walter Kaufmann, *Discovering the Mind,* (New York: McGraw-Hill, 1980), vol. 3, *Freud versus Adler and Jung.*
4. Richard J. Bernstein, *Beyond Objectivism and Relativism: Science, Hermeneutics and Praxis* (Philadelphia: University of Pennsylvania Press, 1983), 14.
5. Ibid., 60–62.
6. Ibid., 61.
7. Plato, *The Republic,* 2d ed., trans. Desmond Lee (New York: Penguin Books, 1944), 209.
8. Ibid., 207.
9. Ibid.
10. Abraham Maslow, *Motivation and Personality,* 2d ed. (New York: Harper and Row), 35–47.
11. Mahmoud A. Wahba and Lawrence G. Bridwell, "Maslow Reconsidered: A Review of Research on the Need Hierarchy Theory," *Organizational Behavior Human Performance* 15 (1976).
12. Ross Fitzgerald, "Human Ideas and Politics: The Ideas of Christian Bay and Herbert Marcuse," *Poltical Psychology* 6, no. 1 (1985): 87.
13. Herbert Marcuse, *One Dimensional Man* (Boston: Beacon Press, 1964), 6.
14. Fitzgerald, "Human Ideas and Politics," 105.
15. Ibid., 103.

16. Sigmund Freud, *Civilization and Its Discontents*, ed. James Strachey (New York: W. W. Norton, 1961), 86.
17. Kaufmann, *Discovering the Mind*, vol. 3.
18. Jean Piaget, *The Origins of Intelligence in Children*, trans. Margaret Cook (New York: International Universities Press, 1952).
19. Lawrence Kohlberg, *The Psychology of Moral Development: The Nature and Validity of Moral States* (San Francisco: Harper and Row, 1984), 7–169.
20. Herbert Simon, "Human Nature in Politics: The Dialogue of Psychology with Political Science," *American Political Science Review* 79 (1984): 294, 295.
21. Ibid., 295.
22. Ibid., 297.
23. Ibid., 301.
24. Ronald Inglehart, *The Silent Revolution: Changing Values and Political Styles among Western Publics* (Princeton: Princeton University Press, 1977).
25. James Savage, "Post Materialism of the Left and Right: Political Conflict in the Post-Industrial Society," *Comparative Political Studies* 17, no. 4 (1985).

2. Relativism and Political Theory

1. Carl J. Friedrich, ed., *The Philosophy of Kant* (New York: Modern Library, 1949), xiii.
2. Ibid., xxii.
3. Ibid., xxix.
4. Karl R. Popper, *The Open Society and Its Enemies* (Princeton: Princeton University Press, 1950).
5. Judith Shklar, *Freedom and Independence: A Study of the Political Ideas of Hegel's Phenomenology of Mind* (Cambridge: Cambridge University Press, 1976), 36.
6. J. N. Findlay, *Hegel: A Reexamination* (New York: New York University Press, 1958), 20.
7. Ibid., 108.
8. G. W. F. Hegel, *The Science of Logic*, vol. 2, trans. W. H. Johnston and L. G. Struthers (London: George Allen and Unwin, 1961). Hegel's discussion of cognition is contained in the chapter entitled "The Idea of Cognition."
9. Ibid., 788.
10. Ibid.
11. Ibid., 788–89.
12. Ibid., 789–90.
13. Ibid., 790–91.
14. Ibid., 791, 796.
15. Ibid., 791.
16. Ibid., 793.

17. Ibid., 793–94.
18. G. W. F. Hegel, *Encyclopedia of Philosophy*, trans. Gustav Eric Mueller (New York: Philosophic Library, 1959).
19. G. W. F. Hegel, *The Phenomenology of Mind*, trans. J. B. Baillie (London: George Allen and Unwin, 1966), 108.
20. Steven B. Smith, "Hegel's Critique of Liberalism," *American Political Science Review* 80, no. 1 (March 1986): 125.
21. Jean Hyppolite, *Studies on Marx and Hegel*, trans. John O'Neil (New York: Harper and Row, 1969), 9.
22. Ibid., 9–13.
23. Yirmiahu Yovel, *Kant and the Philosophy of History* (Princeton: Princeton University Press, 1980), 4.
24. Ibid., 6.
25. Ibid., 8.
26. Ibid., 8, 154.
27. Ibid., 239.
28. Findlay, *Hegel*, 116–48.
29. Ibid., xiv.
30. Ibid., xv.
31. Ibid., xvi–xvii.
32. Ibid., xviii.
33. Ibid., xx.
34. Ibid., xx–xxii.
35. Ibid., xxiv.
36. Ibid., xxvi–xxvii.
37. Ibid., xxix.
38. Smith, "Hegel's Critique of Liberalism," 112.
39. Shklar, *Freedom and Independence*, 145.

3. The Psychological Differentiation

1. Spengler, *Decline of the West*.
2. Carl Jung, *Types Psychological*, trans. H. Godwin Baynes (London: Routledge and Kegan Paul, 1923).
3. Graham Wallas, *Human Nature in Politics* (London: Constable, 1908), and idem, *The Great Society* (New York: McGraw-Hill, 1914); Emory Borgardus, *Leaders and Leadership* (New York: Atheneum, 1968); Harold Lasswell, *Psychopathology and Politics* (Chicago: University of Chicago Press, 1930).
4. Harold Lasswell, *Power and Personality* (New York: Viking Press, 1948), 39–60.
5. T. W. Adorno, Else Frenkel-Brunswick, Daniel J. Levinson, R. Nevitt Sanford, *The Authoritarian Personality* (New York: Harper and Row, 1950).
6. Richard Christie and Maria Takoda, eds., *Studies in the Scope and Method of the Authoritarian Personality* (New York: Free Press, 1965).

7. Hans Eysenck, *The Psychology of Politics* (London: Routledge and Kegan Paul, 1954).
8. Milton Rokeach, *The Open and Closed Mind* (New York: Basic Books, 1965), 55–56.
9. Eysenck, *Psychology of Politics*, 111.
10. Christian Bay, *The Structure of Freedom* (New York: Atheneum, 1968), 206.
11. William P. Kreml, *The Anti-Authoritarian Personality* (London: Pergamon Press, 1977).
12. Herman Witkin, *Personality through Perception* (New York: Harper and Brothers, 1954).
13. Ibid., 4–9, 118–19.
14. Ibid., 86, 467–68.
15. Ibid., 474.
16. Ibid., 468.
17. Joseph R. Royce, "Cognition and Knowledge: Psychological Epistemology," in *Handbook of Perception* ed. Edward Canterelle and Morton P. Friedman (New York: Academic Press, 1974) 1:150.
18. Ibid., 150.
19. Joseph R. Royce, "Pebble Picking vs. Boulder Building," *Psychological Reports* 16 (1965): 447–50.
20. Royce, "Cognition and Knowledge," 150–51.
21. Pitirim Sorokin, *The Crisis of Our Age* (New York: Dutton, 1941); Carl H. Pribram, *Languages of the Brain* (Englewood Cliffs, N.J.: Prenctice-Hall, 1971); idem, "Neurological Notes on Knowing" in *The Psychology of Knowing*, ed. Joseph R. Royce and W. W. Rosenbloom (New York: Gordon and Breach, 1972).
22. Royce, "Cognition and Knowledge," 159.
23. Howard Gardner, *Frames of Mind: The Theory of Multiple Intelligences* (New York: Basic Books, 1983), 267.
24. Ibid., 325–26.
25. Ibid., 326.
26. Ibid., 325.
27. William P. Kreml, *Relativism and the Natural Left* (New York: New York Unversity Press, 1984).
28. Ibid.
29. Ibid.
30. Lon Fuller, *The Law in Quest of Itself* (Boston: Beacon Press, 1940), 118.
31. Kreml, *Relativism and the Natural Left*, chap. 1.
32. Kreml, *Relativism and the Natural Left*, chap. 3; G. L. S. Shackle, *Epistemics and Economics* (Cambridge: Cambridge University Press, 1972).
33. Sherman R. Krupp, "Types of Controversy in Economics," in *The Structure of Economics*, ed. Sherman R. Krupp (Englewood Cliffs, N.J.: Prentice-Hall, 1966), 47; Schackle, *Epistemics and Economics*, 5.
34. Georg Simmel in *The Encyclopedia of Philosophy*, ed. Paul Edwards (New

York: Macmillan, 1977), vol. 7; Rolf Dahrendorf, ed., *Essays in the Theory of Society* (Stanford: Stanford University Press, 1958).
35. Kreml, *Relativism and the Natural Left.*
36. Franz Boas, quoted in Murray J. Leaf, *Man, Mind, and Science: A History of Anthropology* (New York: Columbia University Press, 1979), 199.
37. Michael A. Arbib, *In Search of the Person: Philosophical Explorations in Cognitive Science* (Amherst: University of Massachusetts Press, 1985), 89.

4. Hegel and the Decline of the Ideal

1. Walter Kaufmann, *Hegel* (New York: Doubleday, 1965).
2. G. W. F. Hegel, *Philosophy of Right*, trans. T. M. Knox (London: Oxford University Press, 1967), 11.
3. Hyppolite, *Studies in Marx and Hegel*, 3.
4. Ibid., 11–15.
5. Hegel, *Philosophy of Right*, 2.
6. Ibid., 20–21.
7. Ibid.
8. Ibid., 4.
9. Ibid.
10. Ibid., 12.
11. Ibid., 16.
12. Ibid.
13. Shklar, *Freedom and Independence*, 145.
14. Hegel, *Philosophy of Right*, 16.
15. Ibid., 23.
16. Ibid., 24.
17. Ibid., 25.
18. Ibid., 29.
19. Ibid., 33.
20. Ibid., 31.
21. Ibid., 37.
22. Ibid., 37–38.
23. Ibid., 38.
24. Ibid., 40.
25. Ibid., 41.
26. Ibid., 57.
27. Ibid., 109.
28. Ibid., 110.
29. Ibid., 111.
30. Ibid., 112.
31. Ibid., 115.
32. Ibid., 122–23.
33. Ibid., 124.
34. Ibid., 125.

35. Ibid., 126.
36. Ibid., 155.
37. Ibid., 155–56.
38. Ibid., 156.
39. Ibid., 167.
40. Ibid., 179.
41. Ibid., 181.
42. Ibid., 176.
43. Ibid.
44. Ibid., 189.
45. Ibid., 176.
46. Ibid., 197.
47. Ibid., 196–97.
48. Ibid., 196.
49. Karl Löwith, *From Hegel to Nietzsche* (New York: Garland, 1984), 6.
50. Ibid., 8.
51. Ibid., 14.
52. Ibid., 45.
53. Ibid., 46.
54. Ibid., 137.
55. Ibid., 76.
56. Ibid., 71.
57. Ibid., 75.
58. Ibid., 82.
59. Ibid., 45.
60. Ibid., 46.
61. Ibid., 70–71.
62. Lucio Colletti, *Karl Marx: Early Writings* (New York: Vintage Books, 1975), 19.
63. Ibid.
64. Ibid., 22.
65. Ibid., 40.
66. Ibid., 91.
67. Ibid., 98.
68. Ibid., 121.
69. Ibid., 127.
70. Ibid., 145.
71. Ibid., 146–47.
72. Milovan Djilas, *The New Class: An Analysis of the Communist System* (New York: Praeger, 1957).
73. Karl Korsch, *Marxism and Philosophy*, trans. Fred Halliday (New York: Modern Review Press, 1971).
74. Wilhelm Reich, *Character Analysis*, 3d ed., trans. Vincent Carfango (New York: Simon and Schuster, 1972).
75. Erich Fromm quoted in John Rickert, "The Fromm-Marcuse Debate Revisited," *Theory and Society* 15, no. 3 (1986): 353.

76. Rickert, "The Fromm-Marcuse Debate Revisited," 353.
77. Ibid., 356.
78. Ibid., 376.
79. Marcuse, *One Dimensional Man*, 6; Adorno et al., *Authoritarian Pesonality;* James Ogilvy, *Many Dimensional Man* (New York: Harper and Row Publishers, 1977).
80. Kaufman, *Discovering the Mind*, vol. 3.

5. Liberal Democracy

1. John Locke, *Two Treatises on Civil Government* (New York: Cambridge University Press, 1960).
2. John Locke, *An Essay Concerning Human Understanding*, ed. Aelxander Campbell Fraser (New York: Dover, 1959).
3. Ibid. 1:41.
4. Ibid. 1:1vi.
5. Ibid. 1:48.
6. Ibid. 1:37.
7. Ibid. 1:121.
8. T. C. Tipton, ed., *Locke on Human Understanding Selected Essays* (Oxford: Oxford University Press, 1977), 1–18.
9. Locke, *Essay Concerning Human Understanding* 1: 215.
10. Ibid. 1:215–16.
11. Ibid. 1:218.
12. Ibid. 1:221.
13. Ibid. 1:381.
14. Ibid. 1:382.
15. Ibid. 1:1vi.
16. Ibid. 1:403.
17. Ibid. 1:397.
18. Ibid. 1:413.
19. Jeremy Bentham, *The Theory of Legislation* (London: Routledge and Paul, 1950).
20. James Mill, *Elements of Political Economy* (London: Henry G. Bohn, 1844).
21. John Stuart Mill, *Principles of Political Economy* (London: Parker and Son, 1852).
22. John Stuart Mill, *A System of Logic*, ed. J. M. Robson (Toronto: University of Toronto Press, 1973).
23. Ibid., 306–7.
24. Ibid., 497.
25. Ibid., 506.
26. Ibid.
27. Ibid., 509.
28. Ibid., 507.
29. Ibid., 509.
30. Ibid., 585.

31. Ibid., 605.
32. Ibid., 606–7.
33. Ibid., 607.
34. Ibid., 608.
35. Ibid., 587.
36. Ibid., 585.
37. Ibid., 590.
38. Ibid.
39. Ibid., 608.
40. Ibid., 598.
41. Ibid., 587.
42. Ibid., 509.
43. Max Weber, *Economy and Society*, ed. S. Roth and O. Wittick (New York: Bedminster Press, 1968), 224.

6. The Equity of the Theory

1. Werner Feld, Alan T. Leonard, and Walter W. Toxey, Jr., eds., *The Enduring Questions of Politics* (Englewood Cliffs, N.J.: Prentice-Hall, 1969), 148–49.
2. *The Works of Aristotle* (London: Oxford University Press, 1949), vol. 9.
3. Ibid., 1133b, 34–36.
4. Ibid., 1131b, 10–13.
5. John Rawls, *A Theory of Justice* (Cambridge: Harvard University Press, Belknap Press, 1971), 3.
6. Ibid., 12.
7. Robert Nozick, *Anarchy, State, and Utopia* (New York: Basic Books, 1974).
8. Ibid., 9.
9. Ibid., 18.
10. Fred Greenstein, "The Impact of Personality on Politics: An Attempt to Clear Away the Underbrush," *American Political Science Review* 61 (1967).
11. Ibid., 629.
12. Ibid., 631.
13. Ibid., 637.
14. Ibid.
15. Ibid., 630–31.
16. Weber, *Economy and Society*, 223.
17. Ibid., 220–23.
18. Ibid., 272.
19. Ibid.
20. Ibid., 273.
21. Anthony Downs, *Inside Bureaucracy* (Boston: Little, Brown, 1967), 159.
22. Ibid., 88.
23. Ibid.
24. Ibid., 89–90.

25. Ibid., 105.
26. Howard B. Aldrich, *Organization and Environments* (Englewood Cliffs, N.J.: Prentice-Hall, 1979), 109.
27. Ibid., 259–60.
28. Downs, *Inside Bureaucracy;* Nozick, *Anarchy, State, and Utopia;* Weber, *Economy and Society.*
29. Margaret G. Hermann and Nathan Kogan, "Effects of Negotiators' Personalities on Negotiating Behavior," in *Negotiations,* ed. Daniel Druckman (London: Sage, 1977), 253, 268.
30. Harold H. Kelley and John W. Thiabaut, *Interpersonal Relations* (New York: John Wiley, 1978).
31. Ibid., 302.
32. Ibid., 308.

7. *Structures and Cycles*

1. Weber, *Economy and Society,* 246.
2. Ibid., 253.
3. Downs, *Inside Bureaucracy,* 159.
4. Ibid., 164.
5. Aldrich, *Organization and Environment,* 206.
6. Ibid., 259.
7. Ibid., 260.
8. Ibid., 66–67.
9. Pitirim Sorokin, *Social and Cultural Dynamics* (Boston: Porter and Savert, 1957), 57.
10. Ibid., 28.
11. Ibid., 47.
12. Ibid., 648.
13. Arnold Toynbee, *A Study of History* (London: Oxford University Press, 1934), 321.
14. Ibid., 276.
15. Ibid.
16. Ibid., 321.
17. Ibid., 276.
18. Edward Gibbon, *Decline and Fall of the Roman Empire* (New York: P. F. Collier and Son, 1899).
19. Mancur Olson, *The Rise and Decline of Nations* (New Haven: Yale University Press, 1982), 2, 18.
20. Ibid., 20–23, 34–35.
21. Spengler, *Decline of the West,* 79.
22. Ibid., 94.
23. Ibid.
24. Ibid., 98.
25. Ibid., 99.

26. Joseph A. Schumpeter, *Business Cycles* (New York: McGraw-Hill, 1939), vol. 1.
27. Ibid., vi.
28. Ibid.
29. Ibid., vii.
30. Ibid., vi–vii.
31. John Maynard Keynes, *The General Theory of Employment, Interest, and Money* (New York: Harcourt, Brace, and World, 1935), 250.
32. Frank Klingberg, *Cyclical Trends in American Policy Moods* (Lanham, Md.: University Press of America, 1983); idem, "The Historical Alternation of Moods in American Foreign Policy," *World Politics* 4 (1952).
33. Robert Elder, Jr., and Jack E. Holmes, "International Economic Long Cycles and American Foreign Policy Moods," in *Rhythms in Politics and Economics*, ed. Paul M. Johnson and William K. Thompson (New York: Praeger, 1985), 240.
34. Ibid., 239.
35. Keynes, *General Theory of Employment, Interest, and Money*, 252.

Part 2. The American Political System

1. Charles A. Beard, *An Economic Interpretation of the Constitution of the United States of America* (New York: Free Press, 1935).
2. Ibid., xii–xiii.
3. Ibid., xiii.
4. Ibid., 12.
5. Ibid., 14–15.

8. Theory and Structure

1. Hegel, *Philosphy of Right*, 219–20.
2. Ibid., 220.
3. Ibid., 221.
4. Ibid.
5. Ibid., 221–22.
6. Ibid., 222.
7. Ibid.
8. Seymour Martin Lipset, *The First New Nation* (New York: Doubleday, 1967), 2.
9. Louis Hartz, *The Liberal Tradition in America* (New York: Harcourt, Brace and Jovanovich, 1955), 11.
10. Ibid., 6.
11. Daniel Boorstin, *America and the Image of Europe* (New York: Meridian Books, 1960).
12. Ibid., 99–117.
13. Ibid., 21.

14. Ibid., 140.
15. Ibid., 121.
16. Daniel Boorstin, *The Genius of American Politics* (Chicago: University of Chicago Press, 1953), 8.
17. Ibid., 2.
18. Ibid., 16.
19. Ibid., 16, 26.
20. Henry Steele Commager, *Jefferson, Nationalism, and the Enlightenment* (New York: G. Braziller, 1975), 137.
21. Ibid., 160.
22. Ibid., 161–62.
23. Ibid., 163.
24. Alexander Hamilton, quoted in ibid., 183.
25. Daniel Boorstin, *The Americans: The National Experience* (New York: Random House, 1965), 391.
26. Ibid., 393.
27. Ibid., 401.
28. Ibid., 404–5.
29. Commager, *Jefferson, Nationalism, and the Enlightenment,* xvii.
30. Daniel Boorstin, *The Lost World of Thomas Jefferson* (Chicago: University of Chicago Press, 1981), 170.
31. Ibid., 172.
32. Ibid., 162.
33. Ibid., 241.
34. Ibid., 205.
35. Dumas Malone, *Thomas Jefferson as Political Leader* (Berkeley and Los Angeles: University of California Press, 1963), 33.
36. Ibid., 65.
37. Alexander Hamilton, James Madison, and John Jay, *The Federalist Papers,* (Toronto: Bantam Books, 1982), 42–49.
38. Ibid., 224.
39. Ibid., 246.
40. Ibid., 263.
41. Ibid., 261.
42. Ibid., 261–65.
43. Ibid., 263.
44. Ibid., 264–65.
45. Maurice Duverger, *Political Parites,* trans. Barbara North and Robert North (New York: John Wiley, 1963), xxiv.
46. Ibid.
47. Ibid., xxv.
48. Ibid., xxiv.
49. Hamilton, Madison, and Jay, *Federalist Papers,* 42–43.
50. Boorstin, *Americans,* 427.
51. Ibid., 100–101.

52. J. D. Meyer, *Alexis de Tocqueville* (New York: Harper and Bros., 1960), 90.
53. Marvin Zetterbaum, *De Tocqueville and the Problem of Democracy* (Stanford: Stanford University Press, 1967), 2.
54. Ibid., 6
55. Seymour Drescher, *Dilemmas of Democracy: Tocqueville and Modernization* (Pittsburgh: University of Pittsburgh Press, 1968), 46.
56. Zetterbaum, *De Tocqueville and the Problem of Democracy*, 134.
57. Ibid., 29–30.
58. Ibid., 93.
59. Theodore J. Lowi, *The End of Liberalism* (New York: W. W. Norton, 1969); Grant McConnell, *Private Power and American Democracy* (New York: Alfred A. Knopf, 1966).
60. C. Wright Mills, *The Power Elite* (Oxford: Oxford University Press, 1956).
61. Lowi, *End of Liberalism*.

9. The American Legal System

1. Hamilton, Madison, and Jay, *Federalist Papers*, 394.
2. Charles S. Hynneman and George C. Carey, *A Second Federalist* (Columbia: University of South Carolina Press, 1967).
3. Hamilton, Madison, and Jay, *Federalist Papers*, 395.
4. Ibid., 396.
5. Ibid., 405.
6. Ibid., 406–8.
7. Ibid., 407.
8. Ibid., 396.
9. Karl Llewellyn, "A Realistic Jurisprudence—The Next Step," in *Readings in Jurisprudence*, ed. Jerome Hall (Indianapolis: Bobbs-Merril, 1938).
10. Ibid., 1095.
11. Ibid., 1096.
12. Ibid., 1098.
13. Ibid., 1099.
14. Lon Fuller, "American Legal Realism," in Hall, *Readings in Jurisprudence*, 996.
15. Karl Llewellyn, "The Constitution as an Institution," in Hall, *Readings in Jurisprudence*, 970.
16. Ibid., 976.
17. Ibid.
18. Ibid., 976–77.
19. Ibid., 976.
20. Ibid., 977.
21. Lief H. Carter, *Reason in Law*, 2d ed. (Boston: Little, Brown, 1984).
22. Oliver Wendell Holmes, Jr., cited in ibid., 150.
23. Benjamin Cardozo, cited in ibid., 150.

24. Ibid., 78.
25. Ibid., 173.
26. Edwin Meese III, Speech before the American Bar Association, reprinted in *The Great Debate: Interpreting Our Written Constitution* (The Federatist Society: Washington, D.C., 1986), 9.
27. William J. Brennan, Jr., "Speech of the Text and Teaching Symposium" Georgetown University, 1985, reprinted in *Great Debate*, 19–20.
28. Alexander M. Bickel, *The Least Dangerous Branch* (Indianapolis: Bobbs-Merril, 1962), 48.
29. Ibid., 200.
30. *Brown v. Board of Education of Topeka*, in *Cases in Constitutional Law*, ed. Robert F. Cushman, 5th ed. (Englewood Cliffs, N.J.: Prentice-Hall, 1979) 563–67; *Baker v. Carr*, in ibid., 18–23; see also *Muller v. Oregon* 208 U.S. 412 (1908).
31. *Griswold v. Connecticut*, in Cushman, *Cases in Constitutional Law*, 301–4.
32. Henry J. Abraham, *The Judicial Process*, 3d ed. (New York: Oxford University Press, 1977), 315–53.

10. *Three Constitutional Crises*

1. Louis M. Hacker, *Alexander Hamilton in the American Tradition* (New York: McGraw-Hill, 1957).
2. Ibid., 249.
3. Ibid., 248.
4. George Rogers Taylor, ed., *Hamilton and the National Debt* (Boston: D. C. Heath, 1950), 9.
5. Ibid., 10.
6. Ibid., 13.
7. Ibid.
8. Ibid.
9. Hacker, *Alexander Hamilton*, 147–54.
10. Samuel McKee, Jr., ed., *Alexander Hamilton's Papers on Public Credit, Commerce, and Finance* (New York: Liberal Arts Press, 1957), 99.
11. Ibid., 102–3.
12. Ibid., 106.
13. Ibid., 121.
14. Ibid., 122.
15. Saul K. Podover, *The Complete Jefferson* (Freeport, Conn.: Books for Libraries Press, 1943), 342.
16. Ibid., 344.
17. Hacker, *Alexander Hamilton*.
18. Ibid., 165–66.
19. Ibid., 187–88.
20. McKee, *Hamilton's Papers*, 223.

21. Ibid., 200.
22. Ibid., 201.
23. Ibid., 220.
24. *McCulloch v. Maryland,* in Cushman, *Cases in Constitutional Law,* 122–29; *Gibbons v. Ogden,* in ibid., 171–76.
25. *Gibbons v. Ogden,* in Cushman, *Cases in Constitutional Law,* 172.
26. Ibid., 125, 172.
27. Gordon Post, ed., *John C. Calhoun: A Disquisition on Government* (New York: Liberal Arts Free Press, 1953), viii–ix.
28. Ibid., xiv–xviii.
29. Ibid., xxii.
30. Ibid., 37.
31. Ibid., 28.
32. Hamilton, Madison, and Jay, *Federalist Papers,* 43.
33. Ibid., 37.
34. Ibid., 14.
35. Ibid., 15.
36. Ibid., 7.
37. Robert W. Johannsen, ed., *The Lincoln-Douglas Debate* (New York: Oxford University Press, 1965), 4.
38. Ibid., 14.
39. Ibid.
40. Arthur Bestor, "The American Civil War as a Constitutional Crisis" in *Essays on the Civil War and Reconstruction,* ed. Irwin Unger (New York: Holt, Rinehart and Winston, 1970), 4.
41. Ibid., 6.
42. Ibid., 15–16.
43. Richard Allen Hackman, *Lincoln v. Douglas: The Great Debates Campaign* (Washington, D.C.: Public Affairs Press, 1967), 13.
44. Ralph A. Ross and G. Alan Tarr, eds., *American Constitutional Law* (New York: St. Martin's Press, 1983), 220.
45. Ibid., 224.
46. Ibid., 223.
47. Arthur S. Link, *American Epoch* (New York: Alfred A. Knopf, 1959), 365.
48. Ibid., 368–69.
49. Ibid., 372–73.
50. Ibid., 383.
51. Arthur Schlesinger, Jr., *The Politics of Upheaval* (Boston: Houghton Mifflin, 1960).
52. Ibid., 15–68.
53. Ibid., 196.
54. Ibid., 385, 392.
55. Ibid., 392.
56. Ibid., 411.
57. Ibid., 412–13.

58. Ibid., 410
59. Ibid., 413.
60. Ibid., 443.
61. *Schecter Poultry Corporation v. The United States,* in Cushman, *Cases in Constitutional Law,* 65–69, 197–200.
62. Ibid., 69.
63. Ibid., 68.
64. Ibid., 199.
65. *Carter v. Carter Coal Company,* in *Constitutional Law and Judicial Policymaking,* ed. Joel B. Grossman and Richard Wells (New York: John Wiley, 1972), 271–76.
66. Ibid., 273.
67. Ibid., 274.
68. Ibid., 273.
69. Ibid., 275.
70. *West Coast Hotel Co. v. Parrish,* in Cushman, *Cases in Constitutional Law,* 269–73.
71. Ibid., 271.
72. Ibid.
73. Ibid.
74. Ibid., 272.
75. *NLRB v. Jones and Laughlin Steel Corp.,* in Cushman, *Cases in Constitutional Law,* 200–205.
76. Ibid., 202.
77. Ibid., 204.

11. America's Fourth Constitutional Crisis

1. Robert Reich, *The Next American Frontier* (New York: Penguin Books, 1983); idem, *Tales of A New America* (New York: Random House, Times Books, 1987); Lester Thurow, *The Zero-Sum Solution* (New York: Simon and Schuster, 1985); idem, *The Zero-Sum Society* (New York: Simon and Schuster, 1980).
2. Paul Kennedy, *The Rise and Fall of Great Powers* (New York: Random House, 1987).
3. James MacGregor Burns, *The Power to Lead* (New York: Simon and Schuster, 1984); James L. Sundquist, *Constitutional Reform and Effective Government* (Washington, D.C.: Brookings Institution, 1986); Charles M. Hardin, *Presidential Power and Accountability,* (Chicago: University of Chicago Press, 1974).
4. Hardin, *Presidential Power,* 3.
5. Llewellyn, "The Constitution as an Institution," 976.
6. Ibid., 977.
7. Ibid., 978.
8. Inglehart, *Silent Revolution.*

9. Alexis de Tocqueville, *Democracy in America,* ed. Phillips Bradley (New York: Alfred A. Knopf, 1956), 179.
10. Ibid., 70.
11. Ibid., 237.
12. Ibid., 238.
13. Ibid., 249.
14. Ibid., 191.
15. Ibid., 197.
16. Howard Lee McBain, *The Living Constitution* (New York: Macmillan, 1937), 11.
17. Ibid., 16.
18. Ibid., 19, 25.
19. Ibid., 28.
20. Ibid., 30.
21. Ibid., 33.
22. Edward S. Corwin, *The Constitution and What It Means Today* (Princeton: Princeton University Press, 1958), xx.
23. C. H. Pritchett, *The American Constitution* (New York: McGraw-Hill, 1977).
24. Ibid., 44.
25. Ibid., 50.
26. McBain, *Living Constitution,* 33.
27. Sundquist, *Constitutional Reform,* 69.
28. Ibid.
29. Committee on the Constitutional System, *A Bicentennial Analysis of the American Political Structure* (Washington, D.C.: 1987), 6.
30. John A. Ferejohn, "On the Decline of the Competition in Congressional Elections," in *Studies of Congress,* ed. R. Parker (Washington, D.C.: CQ Press, 1986), 44–63.
31. Ibid., 54.
32. Ibid., 58.
33. Sundquist, *Constitutional Reform,* 163.
34. Burns, *Power to Lead,* 103.
35. Ibid., 102–3.
36. Ibid., 103.
37. Ibid., 16, 103.
38. Roger H. Davidson, *Congress in Crisis: Politics and Congressional Reform* (Belmont, Calif.: Wadsworth, 1966), 129–42.
39. Ibid., 125–44.
40. Leroy N. Rieselbach, *Congressional Reform in the Seventies* (Morristown, N.J.: General Learning Press, 1977), 9.
41. Ibid., 16.
42. Ibid., 24.
43. Ibid., 45.
44. Ibid., 45–48.

45. Walter J. Oleszek, *Congressional Procedure and the Policy Process*, 2d ed., (Washington, D.C.: CQ Press, 1984), 12.
46. Ibid., 39.
47. Ibid., 36.
48. Peter Osterlund, "Congressmen Unhappy with Life on Hill, Survey Shows," *Christian Science Monitor*, 19 January 1988, 7.
49. Stephen S. E. Frantzich, "Opting Out," *American Politics Quarterly* 6, no. 3 (July 1979): 254.
50. Ibid., 263.
51. "In the Senate of the 80's, Team Spirit has Given Way to Individualism," *Congressional Quarterly*, 4 September 1982.
52. Ibid., 2175–76.
53. Ibid., 2176.
54. Ibid., 2177.
55. Ibid., 2178.
56. Ibid., 2179.
57. Ibid., 2180.
58. Oleszek, *Congressional Procedure*, 39.
59. William Crotty, *Party Reform* (New York: Longman, 1983), 8–9.
60. Ibid., 9–11.
61. Nelson Polsby, *Consequences of Party Reform* (Oxford: Oxford University Press, 1983), 16–36.
62. Ibid., 34–35.
63. Ibid., 65.
64. Ibid.
65. Crotty, *Party Reform*, 42–43.
66. E. E. Schattschneider, *The Semi-Sovereign People* (New York: Holt, Rinehart and Winston, 1960), 20.
67. Ibid., 34.
68. Ibid., 56.
69. William Crotty and John S. Jackson III, *Presidential Primaries and Nominations* (Washington, D.C.: CQ Press, 1985), 160.
70. Federal Election Commission, Washington, D.C., Press Release, Oct. 9, 1989.
71. Ibid.
72. *Common Cause News*, 7 April 1987.

12. Equities and Remedies

1. Peter Bachrach and Morton Baratz, "Two Faces of Power," *American Political Science Review* 56 (December 1962): 947–52.
2. Ibid., 948.
3. Ibid., 949.
4. Rexford Tugwell, *The Enlargement of the Presidency* (New York: Doubleday, 1960).

5. Ibid.
6. Hardin, *Presidential Power.*
7. Ibid.
8. Ibid.
9. Committee on the Constitution System, *Bicentennial Analysis.*
10. Ibid., 9.

INDEX

ABOUT THE AUTHOR

WILLIAM P. KREML holds a J.D. from Northwestern University Law School and a Ph.D. in political science from Indiana University. He has been a candidate for the United States Senate from South Carolina and in 1988 entered selected Democratic primaries for president of the United States. An activist, therefore, as well as an intellectual, this is his third work on psychological relativism. He is currently Professor of Political Science at the University of South Carolina.